· Writing,
· Illustrating and
· Editing
Children's Books

· *Jean Poindexter Colby*

HASTINGS HOUSE · New York

Copyright © 1967 by Jean Poindexter Colby

All rights reserved. No part of this book may be reproduced without written permission of the publisher.

Published simultaneously in Canada by Saunders, of Toronto, Ltd., Don Mills, Ontario.

Library of Congress Catalog Card Number: 66-10796
ISBN 8038-8038-3

Printed in the United States of America

Second Printing, May 1970

Third Printing, November 1974

PERMISSIONS

Permission has been granted by the American Library Association *Bulletin*, the Arrow Book Club, *the Atlantic Monthly,* the Authors Guild Inc., *the Bookmark, Book Production,* Carnival of Books, the Children's Book Council, *Elementary English,* Enoch Pratt Public Library, Famous Artists School, *The Horn Book, Junior Libraries, Library Journal, Life Magazine,* Little Brown and Co., Inc., *the New York Herald Tribune Book Week,* the New York Public Library, *the New York Times Book Review, Publishers Weekly, Quill & Quire,* Random House, Scholastic Book Services, *Top of the News,* Frederick Warne and Co., Weston Woods Studio, *the Wilson Library Bulletin,* and *Young Children* to reprint the quotations used in this book.

TO MY UNCLE
Joseph Hawley Chapin

JOE CHAPIN was my friend and inspiration through childhood, college days and the early years of my marriage until his death in 1939. He was the dean of art directors and served in that capacity at Charles Scribner's Sons for thirty-nine years. I spent many a vacation perched on a stool in his office on the fourth floor of the Scribner building, watching and wondering and trying to absorb as much as I could. Famous people wandered in and out or stayed to chat, because everyone liked Joe.

A special booklet was brought out about him after his death in 1939, stating that he had designed practically all the volumes of the Scribner Illustrated Classics, the Vierge *Don Quixote*, the Pulitzer Prize edition of *The Yearling* by Marjorie Kinnan Rawlings, and Fairfax Downey's *Portrait of an Era — As Drawn by Charles Dana Gibson.* He was an active member of the Art Directors' Club and prominent in the Society of Illustrators, besides being one of the founders of the American Institute of Graphic Arts and a member of the Century, the Players, The Coffee House and the Dutch Treat Club.

In the booklet published by Scribners in his memory were articles by N. C. Wyeth, Charles Scribner, Charles Dana Gibson, Reginald Birch, Charles Baskerville, Jr., Fairfax Downey, and other famous authors and artists. Many attributed their start to him.

FOREWORD

IT HAS BEEN genuinely difficult to arrange the material in this book. There are many different facets of children's book publishing, and the people involved in it have many diverse jobs, problems and points of view. Because of this situation, it has been impossible for me to dwell exhaustively on any one subject or phase. Instead, I have tried to give an idea of the field of children's books as a whole and to show the interrelation of its parts, hoping to lead my readers into further investigation on their own in the work that interests them the most.

I have tried to avoid the technical, although there is much in publishing that is technical. I have in several instances duplicated my material, sometimes because I thought it could stand reemphasis and sometimes because I anticipated certain readers limiting their attention to a specific section of the book.

It is a book for beginners in the field and for those who may know some branch well but not the others.

The information in it may vary greatly from that which other authors, illustrators and editors have found to be true. The reason for this is simple — my experience has been different from anyone else's. Also it probably has been more varied, which is the only valid reason for writing the book at all. I am hoping that having covered so much ground, what I have learned in so doing may be helpful.

ACKNOWLEDGMENTS

I am deeply grateful to the following people who have taken the time to read the book in manuscript form and have helped me a great deal with their interest and discerning comments:

Eloise Rue, associate professor of the School Library and Information Science at the University of Wisconsin in Milwaukee, Wisconsin.

Katherine Jeffery, librarian in charge of work with young adults, the Milton Public Library, Milton, Massachusetts.

Helen B. Crawshaw, assistant editor of *The Horn Book*, Boston, Massachusetts.

Alan Frese, sales manager of Hastings House, New York, N. Y.

I appreciate the help given me by the librarians of the Brookline Public Library, Brookline, Massachusetts, who assisted me with my research, especially Louise Rowley, children's librarian at the main library.

I also appreciate the suggestions given me by Phyllis Cohen, editor of the *Young Readers' Review*, Greenfield Park, N. Y.

I am especially indebted to:

Margareta Franzen Lyons, art director of Charles Scribner's Sons, for designing and illustrating this book. She was also designer and illustrator of its predecessor, *The Children's Book Field*.

Al Lichtenberg, art director of Hastings House, for his helpful comments on the illustration, design and production chapters.

I am also indebted to my husband, Fletcher Colby, and to my children, Peter, Toni and Jean, for their patience with and enthusiasm for this time and room consuming project.

CONTENTS

CONTENTS

PART I

WRITING

1 · What Makes a Good Book Good

It is my belief that the fundamental requirements for children's books are much the same as those for adult books. A few age-group limitations exist, and there is a certain need for simplicity and directness, but who would claim that most of the qualities listed below are not also found in the best adult books?

1. A GOOD CENTRAL IDEA. An accomplished author will not start a book until he is sure that he has a basic thought worthy of developing into book form. Then when he plans his work, this central theme holds from the first paragraph to the last with everything else subordinate to it.

As to what constitutes an idea worthy of book form, Dorothy Broderick said in *Junior Libraries,* December, 1960: ". . . it seems to me that any study of the world's literature shows that the great writers are concerned with the fundamentals of life, and the merely good or mediocre writers are concerned with factual descriptions of existing situations." This is as true of children's literature as it is of adult literature. A classic instance of a book with a strong central idea is *Big Susan,* by Elizabeth Orton Jones (Macmillan).

2. DEFINITE APPEAL for the audience at which it is directed. This is especially important in children's books, because no piece of work, no matter how estimable, will be enjoyed or absorbed by youngsters unless it is interesting to children, and written for them in an attractive manner.

Eleanor Cameron, in the October 1962 issue of *Wilson Library Bulletin,* enlarges on this requirement: "Any good children's book should possess drama, vitality, warmth, vividness, possibly wit and humor, and its own dignity. . . ."

Excellent examples of appeal in picture books are *The Little House* by Virginia Lee Burton (Houghton, 1942) and *Make Way For Ducklings* by Robert McCloskey (Viking, 1941). Note the publication dates. These books are still great reading.

3. ORIGINALITY OF IDEA OR INDIVIDUALITY OF PRESENTATION. A truly original idea delights a child and makes an editor's eyes sparkle if it is convincingly presented. Some of the most outstanding books in this respect have been *Twenty-One Balloons* and others by William Pène du Bois (Viking), and the picture books by Dr. Seuss (Random). These are distinctive and individual in style as well as in central idea. I like *A Wrinkle in Time* by Madeleine L'Engle (Farrar, Straus) and Joan Balfour Payne's *The Piebald Princess* (Farrar, Straus). They both write so freshly one immediately settles into the flow of the story; and in each case, even though they are very different, there is strength and conviction from start to finish.

4. GOOD WRITING. The old standards of unity, coherence and emphasis still hold. Ramshackle organization of mate-

rial, poor paragraphing or a halting flow of ideas and words can smother the most charming material.

Edward Weeks, former editor of *The Atlantic Monthly,* said something pertinent to this subject in his column, *The Peripatetic Reviewer.* While discussing the teaching of English to the modern generation, he states:

> They [nine-tenths of English students] need to be *shown* how to read, and they need to be *shown* that there is a syntax, a bone structure of each sentence, without which clarity cannot be achieved. They need to know the agreement between subject and predicate, the difference between "will" and "shall" and that to use the word "massive" three times in a single paragraph has less than massive effect.

That applies to the majority of authors whose manuscripts I have to read. They have no respect for that all-powerful tool — the English language — which is theirs to use.* If they have learned to use it carefully and effectively, their craftsmanship is obvious from the first paragraph, sometimes the first sentence. Take, for instance, the first sentence of *Chitty Chitty Bang Bang* by Ian Fleming (Random):

> "Most motorcars are conglomerations (this is a long word for bundles) of steel and wire and rubber and plaster and electricity and oil and gasoline and water, and the toffee papers you pushed down the crack in the back seat last Sunday." Lovely!

Probably the difference between the amateur and the professional writer shows up most here. The ability to have a "literary style" is usually born with the author, but this does

---

* See Alfred Knopf's remarks on this subject on page 15.

not grow and flower into effectiveness except with long experience and definite effort. A feeling for words comes in here, too, and the advantage of a large vocabulary even in children's books. Words do not have to be long and special to be right. For example, read *The Tale of the Flopsy Bunnies* by Beatrix Potter (Warne), or *Bears* by Ruth Krauss (Harper).

5. EVEN, SURE PLOT DEVELOPMENT, if it is a story. *Careful, well-organized handling of material,* if it is nonfiction. Good fiction embarks upon the plot immediately. One of my *Junior Reviewers** long ago said of a Shannon Garst book, "She starts the story with the first word." After that the professional author keeps it in mind continually and includes little that does not advance or round it out in some way. Present-day adventure stories exemplify this point, such as the books by Leonard Wibberley (Farrar, Straus), or those by Margaret Bell (Morrow).

Historical fiction, too, can be just as absorbing as modern mysteries. See, for instance, Walter Edmonds' *The Matchlock Gun* (Dodd), and Esther Forbes' *Johnny Tremaine* (Houghton). These books make profitable study for any author who would like to see how historical research can be used to good advantage in children's literature. It is so smoothly woven into the narrative that it colors and enhances the plot rather than loads it with information.

* *Junior Reviewers* was a monthly reviewing magazine which I ran for years from my home in Newton. In 1952 I sold it to R. Maxwell-Willeson and William Dennen. The name of the Junior Reviewers *Catalog of The Best Books for Children* was taken over by the Bowker Company, and the New England Mobile Book Fair by Louis Strymish. I kept only the Junior Reviewers Manuscript Testing Service. This was renamed The Manuscript Service and is still going. Mrs. Florence Buck is the manager.

Historical nonfiction can be just as engrossing as fiction if the author has a firm hold on his era, writes with verve, cleaves to the line of steady development of events or facts and allows no irrelevant digression. Velma Varner, children's book editor of the Viking Press, states the case well in the November 1962 issue of *Quill And Quire,* a Canadian magazine published in Toronto for the book trade: "The elements that make good nonfiction for children are the same as those that make good nonfiction for adults. There must be clarity of writing, accuracy and authority in the special field the author is presenting, and the material must be written in an interesting manner."

For good examples I suggest *The Wildlife of Africa* by Jocelyn Arundel (Hastings), or the classic adult book *The Sea Around Us* by Rachel Carson (Oxford).

6. ADEQUATE CHARACTERIZATION. The lack of this is especially evident in fiction for younger children. Many authors are so concerned with story development and vocabulary that they don't "waste" time building up their characters as people. This is very wrong because — as in adult books — convincing action often stems from personality itself rather than from outside forces. Read Eleanor Estes' *The Moffats* (Harcourt), and her other books to see expert characterization. The Elizabeth Enright *Melendy* books (Holt) are also excellent in this regard.

7. MOTIVATION BY THE CENTRAL CHARACTERS. In children's books this means that the children not only do the majority of the planning of action, but they *carry it through.* There is no place for coincidence in juveniles any more than in adult books, and there should be no entry of clever adults who "show the route" to help the boys and girls to success.

7

The triumph of the young characters must be of their own doing or the self-identification of the reader and his final satisfaction in the book will be destroyed. See how effective and essential this motivation is in Anne Molloy's *Three Part Island* (Hastings).

8. AN EFFECTIVE AND APPEALING SENSE OF HUMOR. It is amazing how comparatively few people have humor in their writing. Many authors try to be funny, particularly in juvenile manuscripts, but few succeed. I can remember telling an author once that her story was adequate but lacked humor. She sent it back with all the "saids" changed to "laughs"!

Authors with a true sense of humor — which is nothing more or less than the capacity to understand and enjoy life, and the equal ability to put this understanding and enjoyment on paper — are rare jewels. They are not made by courses in literature or by discourses such as this; they are born. We Americans have more than our fair share of this precious quality, and we should cherish it. That we do recognize and revere a sense of humor is proved by the continued popularity of the books by Mark Twain — *The Adventures of Tom Sawyer* among others. More modern examples are *Homer Price* and many more by Robert McCloskey (Viking), the *Babar* stories by Jean de Brunhoff (Random House), *Ellen Tebbits* and others by Beverly Cleary (Morrow), and the *Curious George* books by H. A. Rey (Houghton). Incidentally, please do not confuse sarcasm with humor. Sarcasm and other adult forms of wit have no place in children's books.

As Ruth Hill Viguers put it in the February 1965 issue of *The Horn Book:* "Many adult readers who appreciate the sophistication of the book [*Harriet the Spy* by Louise Fitzhugh, Harper] will find it funny and penetrating. Children, however, do not enjoy cynicism. I doubt its appeal to many of them. This is a very jaded view on which to open children's windows." Whatever your opinion is of *Harriet the Spy* — I personally think most children *would* enjoy it — Mrs. Viguers is right about cynicism. If you are a thoroughgoing cynic, write for adults.

Some sophistication, however — if that is the right word — *is* appreciated by the young. *Madeline* by Ludwig Bemelmans (Simon and Schuster) is a good example of a book for quite small boys and girls and yet one that the most worldly-wise parent would enjoy reading aloud to them. No one can say that the tiny listeners come away with a vivid idea of Paris or anything else educational, but the inevitable howls of laughter are heartwarming that greet: "But the biggest surprise by far — on her stomach was a scar," and almost every other sentence in the book.

It is a close line to draw — this sophistication business — but the young will draw it for you neatly. You can read some of the present-day picture books with their weirdly modern illustrations that may rate them AIGA acclaim — to utter silence and eventually empty chairs.

These eight attributes probably would hold for any kind of literature for any age, but in juvenile writing there are further requirements that are exigencies of the trade. These will be amplified in the chapter on children themselves and so will only be mentioned briefly here.

a. THE RIGHT SUBJECT MATTER, with its development slanted correctly, for each age group. For instance, some of

9

the *First Book* series (Watts) show how nonfiction material once considered suitable only for adults can be successfully presented for children. George Frederick Mason has created a nature series (Morrow) for children in the elementary grades in which he has used quite technical nature information in a manner that youngsters find absorbing.

The Landmark Books (Random) and the *North Star Books* (Houghton) contain good examples of biography and/or historical events brought into sharp focus for the middle age group, the 9 to 12's. Some volumes are better than others in this respect.

For junior high boys and girls two outstanding authors of nonfiction are Genevieve Foster and Olivia Coolidge. Would-be writers for this age could not do better than to study their capable organization of complicated material and their robust writing style.* They might also note with profit their historical accuracy. This is one of the MUSTS that should be taken for granted by editors but unfortunately cannot be . . . until you have confidence in that particular author.

My very first act as a children's book editor was the correction of an error so blatant it seemed impossible that it had slipped by the editor, the copy editor, everyone. I had hardly taken off my coat that first day when the proofs of a geography kind of book were laid on the desk. My assistant said, "I just thought you would like to see these endpapers. It is an example of what you will have to check after you know your way around. They have been okayed by everyone and actually are printing now." I sat down and glanced at them, admiring the color and the way the author-

* See Chapter 5 for a description of how Mrs. Foster works.

artist had managed to incorporate so much interesting information on a map, when my eyes lit on this sentence, prominently displayed: "Africa is the largest continent in the world." The presses had to stop.

I wish I could say I caught all other errors from then to now or did not make any of my own, but I cannot. I've made a lot. However, the incident made me a persistent questioner, and I have sent many an author to the library *to be sure* he was right — or have gone myself. Remember, as an author it is *your job to be right* about every single thing you say in nonfiction. Historical and foreign backgrounds in fiction also must be exact. Scholarship comes in handy in this regard; so does professional integrity and intelligence in the preparation of notes before writing the book, and the index and bibliography after it *is* written.

In the sports field, John Durant, an author trained in the exacting area of newspaper writing — where you lose your job if you make too many errors — has turned overused subjects like the Olympics or heavyweight boxing into literary achievements. *The Highlights of the Olympics* and *Heavyweight Champions* (Hastings) are excellent reading as well as precise reporting.

b. The art of letting the illustrations tell at least half the story, if the manuscript is intended for little children. Beni Montresor, in his Caldecott Award acceptance speech* in Detroit, 1965, said: "For me a picture book is a book whose content is expressed through its images. . . . The story told with pictures has a language all its own: the visual language, and therefore it is with this

* *The Horn Book*, August, 1965.

language that a picture book must express itself." Thus, a true artist must absorb the essential impact of the book with his mind and soul and then let it flow out through his fingers and his brush. He adds to the book another dimension: the visual, and with it he can also add wit, color, light, life itself at the same time. The author has to let him do this — give him an opportunity to do it.

You cannot think of Claire Bishop's *Five Chinese Brothers* (Coward-McCann) without seeing Kurt Wiese's pictures. The simple colors and effective flat areas of Marcia Brown's *Stone Soup* (Scribners) are part and parcel of this old tale. Wanda Gag's *Millions of Cats* (Coward-McCann) makes you see how words and pictures emerge in a book as one integrated whole. *Where the Wild Things Are* by Maurice Sendak (Harper) is a modern example of the same thing.

c. SOME AUTHORS NEED HELP on several features of their work, while they are proficient and masterful at others. Writing ability varies just as people do. But one thing is certain: in order to write well for children *you must like them, know their interests and respect them.* Then you will say what you have to say directly and sincerely. Children will enjoy your books because you know what they like and what they understand. You have not forgotten the joys and sorrows of childhood, nor do you now laugh at them or underrate them. You write your best because you know from your own close experience that children are appreciative, sensitive and wise in their own way. You know that they learn easily, that they can be led from one truth to another, and that there is no greater pleasure or reward than in widening their enjoyment and knowledge.

OTHER PEOPLE'S OPINIONS

You have read the qualifications I think a book should have. Now let us hear from some of the high ranking authorities in the various areas of juvenile writing.

FICTION

Rumer Godden, in her address at the national convention of the American Library Association in Cleveland, Ohio in July 1961 said:

> The story must progress in a straight line, with no sidetracks, no soliloquies, no flashbacks. The entire background of the characters must be explained in their actions and dialogue. . . . Writing is self-expression, but when you start to write you learn something is trying to express itself through you. . . . You are a sieve — a reed through which the wind blows. It is a very humbling process.

FANTASY

Eleanor Cameron in "The Unforgettable Glimpse" in the *Wilson Library Bulletin of October 1962* speaks of the requirements of fantasy:

> Fantasy differs from the stories of reality, first of all in the originality of its conception and its imaginative virtuosity — the tossing up of ideas like fantastic, brilliant balls of the most dazzling color and variety, changing before the eye. There are delicious surprises, breath-taking events, the introduction of unheard of beings. . . . Where is the limit to these enchanting beings? No limit — that is the delight of it, as long as the fantasists continue to swing in great arcs by the

13

tough and shining filaments of their imaginations. . . . In fantasy, a premise must be established, a certain logic laid down, boundary lines drawn. The author works within a frame of reference. He gives himself, perhaps unconsciously, a certain discipline. For instance, the frame of reference in *The Borrowers* is quite different from that in *Alice in Wonderland.* . . . And now, concerning style. In the writings of the great fantasists, particularly Walter de la Mare, Eleanor Farjeon, Selma Lagerlof, Kenneth Grahame, George MacDonald, Hans Andersen and Rudyard Kipling, there is evident a quality which can only be called poetic overtone. I do not mean that their prose attempts to be poetry. I mean that in the use of words, in the very structure of the sentences, there is an evocation of far more than is actually said on the printed page.

HISTORICAL FICTION

Carolyn Horovitz, in an article called "Dimensions in Time" in *The Horn Book*, June, 1962, says:

In viewing the field of historical fiction critically, the concept of time must be faced as a central issue. Why time? Why has the author delved into another period, and what relationship has the story with that period? Does the story grow out of the time, or is it a case of a plot artificially imposed upon another period for the sake of color?

Hilaire Belloc in "The Character of an Historical Novel" (*One Thing and Another.* London: Hollis & Carter, 1955) says that the prime test of success in historical fiction is not only in how well the past is made to live but how well its 'inconceivable oddities' are made conceivable, its 'incomprehensibles' illuminated so that the reader perceives the past as if it were the present. Such a fusion of scholarship and imagination means that time, as an element, slips from the self-conscious 'historical' to a simple matter of living reality.

WHAT MAKES A GOOD BOOK GOOD

GENERAL NONFICTION

Alfred Knopf, in his article "Publishing Then and Now" in *Publishers Weekly,* November 23, 1964, states:

> . . . What about writers of nonfiction? Here the literate publisher soon becomes bored stiff by men and women (and there are so many of them) who have good material but can't organize it or write decently. . . . How can this be so? Absence of training — rhetoric and composition it used to be called — the consequent lack of an ear, and laziness, sheer laziness. And above all, that ever-present editor who makes it so easy to get a book accepted for publication. The writer who can't do his job looks to his editor to do it for him, though he wouldn't dream of offering to share his royalties with that editor. . . .

Mr. Knopf refers to writers of adult nonfiction but this statement can well be applied to juvenile writers.

BIOGRAPHY

Houston L. Maples, in the fall children's issue of the *New York Herald Tribune Book Week,* November 1, 1964, claims:

> The writer of biography for the young is faced with a multitude of thorny problems, for the adult activities of great men and women are not always entirely within the scope of the young reader's sympathies, interests or even comprehension. Yet omission or simplification of historical fact in an effort to increase story appeal, or spurious dramatization calculated to heighten interest may lead to a shallow, overly-glamorous picture of the hero.

MODERN POETRY

The articles on poetry for children are many, but, like the subject itself, they seemed written in a world apart, and not something that could be used to help would-be poets for children. Instead I choose to recommend an article, "The Transformation of a Poet: John Ciardi," by Patrick J. Groff in the April, 1964 issue of *The Horn Book*. It deals with only one poet, John Ciardi, and is not especially flattering to him, but it brings up most of the issues that concern modern poetry for children. For instance, he says,

> [that Ciardi believes] . . . poems should have an attractive playfulness, and an immediate appeal, an ease of apparent meaning, and an evident understatement. But they should also have a profundity, a purpose not immediately discoverable, which is often seen as ambivalence or a refusal to be specific. These qualities should lead to a poem's enduring appeal, reading by reading, year after year.
>
> . . . the second prerequisite of good children's poetry [is] that it intensify the child's sense of life. This is sometimes done with inventive metaphors . . .
>
> Words are the remaining details critical to a poem's distinctiveness. As we have seen, Ciardi not only believes but demonstrates that while feeling, suggestions and images arise from words they should run free of them. Words, he explains, are only surfacing materials that cover a poem's inner life . . . (Ed. note: the book from which Mr. Groff obtained Mr. Ciardi's beliefs is: *How Does A Poem Mean* by John Ciardi. Houghton)

SCIENCE

There are a few simple truths in this paragraph taken from *The Bookmark*, June, 1965:

> When children's literature was in its infancy, many authors tried to disguise facts as fiction. Inanimate objects were personified as 'Mother West Wind' or 'Little Sara Seedling.'

Anthropomorphism is now deplored and has largely disappeared from good science writing. . . . Though concepts may be difficult, if they are worth presenting, they should be presented without condescension or patronization.

Irving Adler and his wife Ruth have published many science books with John Day Co. Mr. Adler had an informative article, "On Writing Science Books for Children" in the October 1965 issue of *The Horn Book,* in which he says:

Our primary goal is to present scientific ideas so simply that they can be followed and understood by an unsophisticated reader. . . . The science writer, too, must decide what to leave out and what to put in. He must select and organize his material so that the essential idea is developed logically and clearly and is not obscured by unnecessary detail. Of course he must be careful not to distort an idea when he simplifies it. The key to presenting a complex idea simply and accurately is to break it up into its constituent parts and then to present the parts one at a time in the proper sequence.

Rose Wyler made some good points on science writing in the *New York Times Book Review* of November 1, 1964:

The season's new elementary science books will appeal to teachers and librarians as useful adjuncts to primary grade curriculums. Parents seeking scientific adventures with their children may not respond to them, nor will children without prior interest in the given subject. Most of the books assume the reader is seeking more information, thus do not even try to engage young readers through problems that concern them; the leads or hooks, so to speak are lacking.

The main virtue of the books is their simplicity. . . . They thus teach children something important, the satisfaction of finding out. Yet one cannot but wish for more than this — for books that are not only readable but communicate the thrill of discovery and the excitement of science."

William Carey Parker II has something to say about biographies of scientists in his article, "Glamorizing Science" in the November 1, 1964 issue of the *New York Herald Tribune Book Week Fall Children's Issue:*

[there are] . . . two unfortunate tendencies in the purveyors of science to the secondary schools, especially in the area of scientific biography. The first is the ease with which the great episodes of science become romanticized . . . and the coy exchange of adventure for artifice. Competition in the biographical market seems to spawn an over-dramatization of scientific research and its discoveries with the result that the reader occasionally experiences a *deja vu* sensation — the stories seem the same, and only the name of the scientist and his discoveries are changed. The second not-so-laudable tendency [is] presenting science as a series of dramatic, only casually related vignettes. . . . The underlying idea is that the shorter and more dynamic the message, the more likely its reception. In a more insidious form, it is the feeling that the average reader won't take a solid column of newsprint.

TEENAGE FICTION

Fortunately, there is a trend away from the saccharine "girl's novel." There is and always will be a need for the "happy" girl's books — escape literature for the young — but it is being felt at the upper elementary-junior high level and the offerings are apt to be better written, more purposeful, more close to life than the *Sue Barton* and other series which have flourished for so long. Ursula Nordstrom, children's editor at Harper & Row, stated the need for change in her article "Honesty in Teenage Novels" published in the November 1964 issue of *Top Of The News.*

With honesty in picture books and middle-aged books, why suddenly at the teenage level, the time of life's most intense problems, turn to whipped cream? We cannot believe that young people really need books which never even suggest the possible frustrations and difficulties that life can hold. . . . So often it seems to an adolescent that almost everyone else has all the answers, is sublimely self-confident, has fine family relationships, knows how to talk to the opposite sex. Except him. Seldom can a Negro boy or girl, or indeed a girl or boy of any color who is lonely and different in any way, find a book which has a reality for him. He needs some books in which mothers and daughters do not always get along well, in which boys do not always know what to say, in which boys do not always mature at the 'normal' time. A teenager, as he lives his own life, is not protected from reality. If books try to protect him from harm, they will supply him only with escape literature, and so deny him a true outlook on the world.

TEENAGE NONFICTION

Most junior and senior high school boys and girls read adult books. That is as it should be. There are many, many books of all kinds and on all subjects that can be appreciated and understood by this age. One of the best lists for this group is put out by the New York Public Library and can be obtained from them for 50¢ each. Authors who wish to write for this age can get an excellent idea of the wide range of material from this list, but they should bear in mind, as Margaret Scoggin, Chairman, The Committee on Books for Young Adults at this huge library serving so many thousands of people, states — 80 percent of the 1500 titles recommended are adult publications. In other words, if you write for adults you may find an unexpectedly large audience in the high schools, and, vice-versa, if you write a really top-notch, thorough, interesting nonfiction book for this group, you may find it selling to young adults and adults. The field is wide in age range and huge in scope. This one list has an index of over sixty different subjects! Buy a new typewriter ribbon now.

YOUNG ADULT FICTION AND NONFICTION

This is a relatively new category of human life found only in libraries, I believe, but set aside as a group by librarians because it needed to be. It is another name for teenager or senior high school student, and covers ages 13 to 18 or from grade 8 through high school. The previous quotations and remarks about teenage fiction and nonfiction cover this group.

The Bookmark of January 1965 states:

> The purpose of having a special service to this age group is to introduce adolescents to the world of adult reading and to effect a smooth transition from juvenile books to adult books. A young adult collection should be designed to meet the needs unique to this age group: to broaden understanding of themselves as individuals; to extend this understanding to encompass the family, the community, and the world; to develop lifetime habits of reading and library use.

The Enoch Pratt Free Library, Office of Work with Children in a directive written in May 1956 and reprinted in 1962 entitled *Selection Policies for Young Adult Books* advises:

That the young adult collection should be composed of books that widen the boundaries of the adolescent's thinking, that enrich his life and help him fulfill his recreational and emotional needs. . . . All types of readers must be considered in setting up a collection [for this group]: simple teen-age stories of boy-girl relationships teach young and reluctant readers a love of reading — the first step in the development of any reader. At the other end of the scale is the older, better reader who is forming his own philosophy and wishes to read adult titles that throw a clear light on the process of living. As the young adult collection serves primarily as an introduction to adult reading, in this library the majority of titles purchased are duplicates of adult books.

So it is a wide area, this teen age book group. It covers almost every kind of book. I do not think it is one that parents consciously buy for — the youngsters are old enough to do their selecting — but teachers and librarians *do* buy for it, and their standards for it are very high.*

---

* *Author's note:* there has been some discussion as to whether this section should not go into the next chapter since this concerns age group requirements, but to my mind it belongs here because this chapter outlines my standards and also those of other people for certain kinds of juvenile literature.

2 · Meeting Your Market: The Children

I do not know any more about children than a great many other people and not nearly as much as child psychologists and educators who have made a study of them. My own knowledge comes from being with children, working with them, playing with them, teaching them and trying to raise three of them.

In a sense this chapter is looking at children's books hindside first. Instead of "Here are the books: How shall we evaluate them as juvenile literature?" we are regarding the situation this way: "Here are the children. How do the books meet their requirements?"

We must recognize at the start that a child is constantly developing in reading interest and ability as well as in physical growth. *Age groups are arbitrary and actually are never the same for any two children.* We generalize for the sake of convenience and base our grouping for the most part on the fact that (according to educators) almost every child is ready and eager to learn to read by six years of age, often earlier.*†

Before and after the ready-to-read age, the grouping is based on physical, mental and emotional development as found to be average by educators and psychologists. This average concerns itself with fairly normal children — not those extremely bright or those markedly subnormal.

The primary thing for a writer to do is to think of a child as being a person from the start, achieving more and more personality, confidence, and mental scope until he becomes a mature individual. How do books fit in with this person's world? What does he need in books? What can he enjoy? What is he capable of understanding?

THE BABY AGE, 1 and 2

A child's first interest in a book is probably limited to

---

* Hartup, William. "Early Pressures in Child Development." *Young Children.* May, 1965. p. 274.

". . . Virtually all students of development processes have acknowledged that the timing of developmental events is, to some extent, unique for each individual child. The time schedule or stages formulated for various aspects of behavioral development are not rigid but apply within fairly broad limits. Nevertheless, the critical-periods notion is the reason why eight out of ten textbooks in child psychology are organized in terms of chronological age and why children are not taught to read until they are six."

† Newman, Robert E. "The Kindergarten Reading Controversy." *Elementary English.* March, 1966. p. 237.

". . . There simply is too much evidence that children can take the first steps toward reading when they are five years old to take our time debating this here. . . . My point is that we should teach a child to read well enough before he reaches age seven, eight, or at the most nine, so that for a few years at least, he can read and enjoy the books that answer the questions he is asking, and tell the kinds of tales he enjoys reading. If we don't, too many children won't experience for an extended period during their childhood the deep involvement with books and reading which is basic to building the desire and motivation for a lifetime of avid, thoughtful reading. . . ."

23

pictures: identifying familiar objects like a ball, spoon, dog or cat. My youngest child began to drag books around the house crying, "Read, Mumma! Read, Mumma!" at the age of a year and a half. But the other two Colbys waited until they were two or three years old. Probably two years of age is average for the start of book interest.

Since a very small child's environment is limited and his greatest needs are security and protection, the requirements for such books are:

1. FAMILIAR AND APPEALING SUBJECT MATTER. No strange worlds, please. He is interested in his family, himself, the daily routine of existence, common objects and the well-known animals, especially pets. He likes to hear the human voice, but not for long periods of time. He wants to look at and feel everything.

2. REASSURING PRESENTATION. Nothing scary.

3. SIMPLICITY OF BOTH TEXT AND PICTURES. One thing or thought at a time.

4. BREVITY, since the young child's attention span is short: one-half to five minutes — twenty-four pages at the most.

5. COLORED PICTURES with objects fairly realistically portrayed. He knows very little, so that if you present him with a picture of a purple cow, he will carry a misconception in his mind until he is forced to correct it, and there are few cows available to look at nowadays — at least in many areas.

6. A GREAT PREPONDERANCE OF PICTURES over text, as most of the message is conveyed through the eye rather than the ear. Authors are slow and somewhat unwilling to admit this, probably because the facts show that in nursery-age

books the artist is the more important — although first he must have something to illustrate! Perhaps the best solution of this age-old argument is for the good artist to learn to write, or to use a well-loved classic like *Mother Goose* or a fairy tale like *Snow White* to show off his talents.

7. DURABILITY, as the child will probably try to taste, throw and tear the book. Also, if he likes it, he will want to have the story read to him scores of times, which means a lot of handling. My children, who are now grown up, still cherish some of their simplest picture books. They are battered in a dignified manner but still intact.

Because most mothers of young children are too busy to read and often too burdened with other necessary purchases and expenses to buy costly picture books and because "baby books" are soon outgrown, the market and the field of writing here are limited to the low-priced field. There is a great deal of nonroyalty material available also, but the demand for new, good material for this youngest reader is great.

Good examples of "baby books" are those made completely of cloth — *Play With Us* (Hampton) and *I See* (a Peggy Cloth Book, Platt & Munk). The simpler editions of Mother Goose may also be used, such as *The Real Mother Goose* (Rand-McNally) and *Mother Goose or Old Nursery Rhymes,* illustrated by Kate Greenaway (Warne). An exciting modern *Mother Goose* is illustrated by Brian Wildsmith (Watts). His *1, 2, 3's* (Watts) is a brilliant colored counting book. A beautiful book, although heavy to hold if you already have a child in your lap, is Marguerite de Angeli's *Book of Nursery And Mother Goose Rhymes* (Doubleday). It is a handsome volume worth keeping for a second generation.

Books that have music for the Mother Goose or other nursery verses are fun, too. Babies love to be sung to, and this is a good way for them to start acquaintanceship with books. It is excellent for the reader's vocal cords and sense of equanimity, and may be a laughable but always a treasured experience. The Colby family all but wore out Berta and Elmer Hader's *Picture Book of Mother Goose* (Coward-McCann) in this process.

THE FIRST REAL BOOK AGE, 3 to 5

This age group varies widely. There are children who can follow a line or two of text like *Davy's Day* by Lois Lenski (Walck), and there are those who can understand and enjoy quite an involved picture book like *The Country Bunny* by DuBose Heyward and Marjorie Flack (Houghton). Let us suppose, however, that you have in mind those tiny listeners who can sit still for ten to twenty minutes, if amused, and who are able to follow a slight story as well as look at the illustrations.

The illustrator is still 60 per cent important, though, as the book stands or falls on his work. Again, it is much better for an author to be able to illustrate his own text, but before attempting this he must have both talent and art training. Needless to say (see Chapter 1), he must also have a very good idea to start with.

Books for this age are deceptive. They look absurdly easy to write and not too difficult to illustrate — look at *The Bundle Book* by Ruth Krauss, illustrated by Helen Stone (Harper): wonderful. Publishers' mail pouches are full of the most inadequate offerings from would-be authors because of this misconception. Such manuscripts are apt to have a weak central theme, dull "proper" writing and often are accompanied by really poor art work. Don't think that because these books are short they are easy to do. They are not.

Requirements for this age are:

1. AN APPEALING, EFFECTIVE IDEA.

2. SIMPLE, REASSURING PRESENTATION.

3. MATERIAL BASED ON A CHILD'S SMALL WORLD. Main interests are family, other boys and girls, animals, nature, weather, mechanical objects — in fact anything in the world around him. Unless he is very well oriented, fairy stories should be used carefully. Some of them are quite frightening.

4. BREVITY — forty-eight pages, general limit.

5. ILLUSTRATIONS on every other page at least, with some color.

6. STURDY FORMAT. Large type.

7. OTHER IMPORTANT QUALITIES ARE:
   a. Beauty of language.
   b. Humor.
   c. Distinguished use of line and color in illustrations.

The 3-to-5-year-old needs books for wholesome entertainment, reassurance, the widening of his world and the increase of his knowledge.*

While the speech of a child of this age is limited, he can often understand quite adult conversation and is open to many subtle impressions. For instance, the attitude of the

---

* Hartup, W. H. *Ibid.*, p. 275. "Independence, for the young child, involves taking initiative, overcoming obstacles, persistence in activity, just wanting to do things, and wanting to do things by oneself."

reader is very important. Sometimes a relatively low-grade book will pass muster because Daddy reads it with gusto. A topnotch book to try is *Noodle* by Munro Leaf, illustrated by Ludwig Bemelmans (Lippincott). If you do, you will have a dog fairy in your life forever.

This is the age to introduce poetry, especially when it is read with obvious pleasure. Fortunately, there are many good poetry collections for this age. Two are: *Inheritance of Poetry,* collected by Nora Unwin and Annis Duff (Houghton) and *Silver Pennies* by Blanche Thompson (Macmillan).

Humorous books are very welcome. Supposedly, a sense of humor cannot be acquired, but it certainly can be cultivated. And this is the time to start. Authors and illustrations endowed with humor should try at least one book for this age. Children value a sense of the ridiculous, particularly when applied to things they know or situations they can appreciate.

Some wonderful books to laugh with are: *Caps For Sale* written and illustrated by Esphyr Slobodkina (Scott), *Mister Penny* by Marie Hall Ets (Viking) and the *Babar* books by Jean de Brunhoff (Random House). Dr. Seuss is another favorite author with his *McElligot's Pool* (Random House) and many other constant laugh-provokers. I personally prefer his older (in publication date) to his newer limited-vocabulary books although I know the latter are very successful with beginning readers. The simpler Beatrix Potter books like *The Tale of Tom Kitten* (Warne) are musts for this age. Authors would do well to read them aloud to a young audience and watch their charm take hold. Although constantly imitated in both text and pictures they have never been equaled.

THE BEGINNING-TO-READ-THEMSELVES GROUP, 6 to 8

The children of this age group are not only beginning to read but also to reason quite deeply. Unfortunately, their knowledge of worldly matters and their capacity to understand the spoken word exceeds their reading ability. Therefore, their books should be divided into two types: those that are to be read to them and those they can read themselves.

In writing for either group, the author should realize that the average child is now alert, appreciative and capable of reasoning, but that physically and emotionally he still needs protection. He has made a major adjustment in that he now recognizes that he is one of many and can no longer be the center of attention at all times. His first school experiences have taught him this. It is important to further such objectivity in books and to treat the child carefully as "not a baby," and to show him respect and consideration.

Requirements for this age are:

1. APPEAL IN BOTH TEXT AND ILLUSTRATIONS.

2. CONVINCING AND UNDERSTANDABLE SITUATIONS.

3. SUSPENSE AND ACTION IN A STORY. Some characterization but no emotional problems. Clarity and brevity in nonfiction. The length depends on whether the child has gone beyond the story-a-night stage. Most of them can now be read to in installments so that a fiction book can contain fifty to sixty printed pages, but nonfiction should be kept well under that number.

4. GRAPHIC, WELL-DRAWN ILLUSTRATIONS. They can be quite free and modern, if well done, and not necessarily in color, although this is always attractive to the young.

A book designed and written for a beginning reader should have:

    a. SIMPLE VOCABULARY (not necessarily limited to a word list). No long, colorless words, although a few rich "teasers" can be included, like the oft-quoted "soporific" from Beatrix Potter.

    b. SHORT SENTENCES. Not choppy ones, but dependent clauses should be avoided.

    c. LARGE-SIZED TYPE — 14 point or better. Plenty of space, or leading, between lines and fairly wide margins.

    d. DURABLE BINDING.

Because of the limitations of style in books designed for children to read by themselves this is a hard group to write for, and not many people want to do it.* However, it is worthwhile, both financially and esthetically, for children welcome with great gusto the stories they can master. The best way to go about writing such a book is to tell the tale as well as you can. Then if the vocabulary and sentence structure are too advanced, according to your editor, simplify

---

* Martha Condit, an elementary school librarian in Montclair, New Jersey, put the situation quite well in an article, "Trade Books For Beginning Readers," *Wilson Library Bulletin*, November, 1959.

"In books for this age, the narration should move smoothly with careful attention to clarity and detail. Plots, while simple, must develop logically. Direct and clear conversation that helps the story along, aids the young reader. Repetition has a place at this grade level. The elements of surprise, good humor and liveliness give the child great satisfaction. The young reader wants his books to have an inherent but not blatant moral quality, and there should be a sense of completeness. Most of the vocabulary should be composed of words the child has previously met in reading. Sentences should be short and simple." In 1959 Miss Condit found a "dearth of material" for the late first grade or early second grade reader. At this writing, there is much more such material.

them afterward. Don't pedagogically prepare manuscripts of short words and expect them to be published because the vocabulary is right. More than correct form is needed to make a good book for any age group.

I personally have a profound dislike for vocabularized books. I feel that this de-juiced form of literature should occur only in what educators call "basal readers," and should be left to educational publishers. On the other hand, Dr. Seuss and other authors have proved you can write acceptable stories with a given number of words, and there certainly is a market for them at the present time. Whether the use of the Initial Teaching Alphabet (known familiarly as i.t.a.) or other new reading aids will do away with or lessen the need for these books, no one can say at present. (See Part III, Editing, Chapter 4, for more about i.t.a.)

So-called "easy reading" books interest me much more. Every child at some stage in his reading career (whether it be for two months or two years or more) needs these books in order to get into the stride of reading. For bright boys and girls, the acquaintance is short; for slower minds, the meeting is prolonged and may decide whether the child in question is to read from then on or not. As an inspired public library trustee puts it in an article, "Nuts To Excelsior" (*Library Journal,* December 15, 1964), "If the easy-reading, pure-recreation books stay, the children will stay. Give them straight uplift, and it's the end of the literary line for some of those who need civilizing most. That's one of the sad things about our society: the younger generation is so much like the older one."

Lilian Moore of the Arrow Book Club in an address given at the International Reading Association Conference May 1, 1959, in Toronto, Canada, said,

For the poor reader and the uninterested reader, we especially need to break through the vicious circle of non-reading. The poor reader needs the most practice in reading — and gets the least. He reads words where others read sentences. He reads sentences where others read paragraphs. He reads paragraphs where others read pages.

No one should intentionally write for the poor reader, but if he writes a simple but rousing or amusing tale that avant-garde readers of seven and eight years old will tear through, it can be used nicely for their more slowly moving cousins of nine, ten, or even twelve years of age. It probably will not be classed as literature, but it may lead many a boy or girl on to reading literature. I would be proud to have written it and, as editor, I would be proud to publish it. An example is *Billy Jo and the Rangers* by Harry Harris (Hastings). A friend of mine wrote me about this book: "I gave it to a *very* reluctant reader of eleven. His mother said he approached it like a live bomb but the first page got him and he started ahead instead of putting it down, and he kept going. She said it was the first time he had done this."*

Now let us get back to less utilitarian books, like fantasy, that add so much to this age group.

Examples of successful (nonvocabularized) tales for this age are: *Many Moons* by James Thurber, with Louis Slobodkin's wonderful pictures (Harcourt), *Charlotte's Web* by E. B. White (Harper), and *The Hundred Dresses* by Eleanor Estes (Harcourt). An excellent book for a changeover from

---

* Phyllis Cohen, editor of *Young Readers Review,* says she had the identical reaction with Guernsey Van Riper's *Babe Ruth: Baseball Boy* (Bobbs Merrill). This is a title in the *Childhood of Famous Americans* series, one which is not high in the favor of some critics but which has started many an active youngster on the road to loving books.

this age to the next is *The Courage of Sarah Noble* by Alice Dalgliesh (Scribners). I consider it one of the best books ever written for children. Leonard Weisgard's pictures contribute to its perfection.

Examples of schoolbook type and easy-to-read texts are: *Two Is a Team* by Jerrold Beim (Harcourt), the *Martin and Judy* series by Verna Hills Bayley (Beacon), and *Tiny Toosey's Birthday* by Mabel G. La Rue (Houghton).

THE MAJOR READING AGE, 9 to 12

This is commonly known as the "middle age" of reading. Heretofore the child has not had the ability to read all he wants to, and hereafter — at twelve or so — he does not have the time because of homework and other activities. But in this glorious period he can and does drink deeply and often of the wonders of books.

The average ten, eleven, and twelve-year-old is rebellious, for he wants to get as far away from babyhood as possible, and he cannot seem to do this fast enough. Grown-ups exert too much and too many kinds of restraint on him. His mind and his body dart around like streaks of lightning, ever alert and seeking knowledge, adventure or mischief — sometimes all three. He wants these elements in daily life, and he needs them in books.

His mind mops up ideas like a sponge. There is no limit to his interests. He does not like things kept from him. Illness and death are part of life's experiences and should not be excluded from his life or his reading. Practically speaking, the only taboos for this age are emotional, intellectual or political situations to which he may respond but which he cannot understand.

Children of this age make wonderful companions. A writer would do well to find a pal of nine, ten, or eleven if he wishes to write for this group. He will be fully repaid for his time, and no other experience or study will be so informative or convincing. He will soon see that this is the age of frankness, discernment and rapidly growing intelligence. It is also the age of curiosity and unbounded enthusiasms. It is *the* reading age.

Books for this group should have:

1. SOLID WORTH AND APPEAL in both text and illustrations, or be really high-flying fantasy.

2. CLARITY. The length of sentence should be watched somewhat as well as the extent of reasoning. The possible subject matter is boundless.

3. CONTINUED INTEREST. If a story, it should have plenty of action, characterization and atmosphere. If nonfiction, it should be presented in an interesting, lucid manner.

4. CORRECT MOTIVATION. If possible, the children in the story should carry out the plot and figure things out for themselves, not be pushed around like puppets for plot purposes.

5. LITERARY AND MORAL DEPTH. The book should — to use the vernacular — "have something to it." This age wants meat and should be allowed access to the best ideas and concepts.

6. A POSITIVE ATTITUDE. There should not be the slightest hint of "writing down."

7. THE RIGHT SLANT FOR THE SEX the writer is aiming at. This is the beginning of "boys'" and "girls'" books. Actually an author would do well to write so as to interest both sexes whenever that is possible. Often it is not.

8. DISTINGUISHED, WELL-DRAWN ILLUSTRATIONS. They can be quite modern and free if not too sophisticated.

9. ATTRACTIVE DECORATION, TYPOGRAPHY, PAGE SIZE AND GENERAL FORMAT. These attributes are important for this age. Color is not necessary, but a nice open appearance and lively drawings increase the appeal and worth of a book tremendously. Many good stories have sunk into oblivion because not enough time, thought — and perhaps money — were spent on their makeup. Crowded, solid-looking pages of small type are enough in themselves to make children turn away. Good writing can so easily be spoiled in this way.

The extras that pay dividends to author and publisher are again: literary value, such as the expert creation of atmosphere or characterization, humor and a general insight into children's feelings and problems.

There are hundreds of good books for this age. Certain skilled authors come to mind, though, such as: Eleanor Estes, Lois Lenski, Anne Molloy, Elizabeth Coatsworth, Lillie V. Albrecht, Laura Ingalls Wilder, Kate Seredy, Holling Clancy Holling and countless others. The list is constantly being expanded, thank goodness, and there is always room for more.

OLDER CHILDREN

This age group can be termed "teen-age," although that is often a misnomer, for children of eleven or twelve are sometimes found here. To my mind the teen-age book grouping is for the child who has mastered the techniques of reading and is on the threshold of being adult. He has matured physically and is juvenile only in scope and kind of emotion. He lacks worldly experience, but his judgment is often instinctively good. Mentally, he is keen and extremely able. He can think and reason quickly and enjoys those mental processes. His emotional stability is precarious, but books can strengthen this by widening his outlook, experience and understanding.

He is anxious to take his share of responsibility, and his dearest wish is to be treated with the respect accorded an adult. He still gangs together with other youngsters because he feels insecure and a little scared of the adult vistas suddenly close to him. He rebels against restrictions, although he wants and needs daily association and friendship with an older person. That older person must be sure to meet him on the same level as his own.

In the last century a boy of fourteen was supposed to be grown up. At least he was considered old enough to earn his living and make his way in society.

Today, our modern children are not as ready to go out into the world, for we do not give them responsibilities early enough. They do not have the same opportunities to exercise their own judgment, because their lives have become regimented and because the new fields of business and trade now require many more years of schooling and preparation. For example, few boys, if any, can now ship on oceangoing vessels and learn at first hand, as they used to, about navigation and the far corners of the earth. On modern ships there is little or no need for them, and furthermore, laws and unions and other obstacles stand in their course. They have to find their own way of becoming men while continuing their schooling. Working in supermarkets, drugstores and gas stations is not conducive to attaining maturity or even stability except perhaps in money matters. One sixteen-year-old youngster told me the reason many teen-agers drive so fast and explore sex so early is that those were the only two really adult things they could do!

Books can help the growing-up process in the right way. They can help to bridge the present-day gap between adolescence and adulthood. Their requirements are about the same as those of good adult reading except in length, in mental complexity and in emotional depth.

These books for older children should have:

1. FORCEFULNESS.

2. DEPTH OF PROBLEM AND POINT. For a story, the material should be extensive in plot, situation and characterization. In nonfiction, it should be clear, concise and fairly thorough.

3. ADULT AS WELL AS JUVENILE PROBLEMS should be included.

4. THE MOTIVATION should come (in a story) from the girls or boys involved. The attitude toward them should be of equality with adults.

A good many authors have tried to corner the teen-age market by writing light, colloquial fiction — sometimes about careers or obvious problems set up by the author for the young people to overcome. There is a market for these but, as with light novels for adults, it is a limited one. Such books become dated very quickly, and are not as popular now as they were ten or twenty years ago.

Older boys and girls want material worthy of their mettle. They want books written interestingly, to be sure — who doesn't — but the author who writes for them should study their situations for subject matter. Family is still important, because the high-schooler has to contend more than ever for what he considers his rightful position. Competition for college is a predominant subject right now. The discovery of the presence of the other sex in society is eternally intriguing.

World affairs, if brought close to the reader by some connection with his own life, make good reading. And the exciting events and personalities of history offer a limitless field. Science and its ramifications have come to life in a great rash of nonfiction and will be increasingly important. In short, there is nothing you cannot write about if you have good taste and good sense in selecting your subject and if you then use the material so that it lives for the reader.

The fact remains, though, concerning any age you choose to write for — and I say this again and again at the risk of overemphasizing it — you will save yourself a lot of trouble and you will write better, and more humanly, if you mix with and try to know the children for whom you are writing.

Among the authors who present food for thought and inspiration to this age, I have great respect for Olivia Coolidge, who has contributed excellent nonfiction on a multitude of subjects, and Leonard Wibberly, who can write either fiction or nonfiction masterfully. Katherine Shippen has an adroit hand with science as does Genevieve Vaughan-Jackson, who illustrates her own books with vigor.

But the great mass of junior high and high school girls and boys read adult fiction and nonfiction. That is as it ought to be, and they should be able to pick and choose at will, guided to the high spots, we hope, by discerning librarians, teachers and parents.

In summarizing this chapter I would like to quote from an article in the December 11, 1964, issue of *Life,* where there is a statement on page 116 that backs me up:

What is a good children's book and what are the ingredients that go into the making of one? Recently this question was put to three of the foremost editors in the profession — Annis Duff of Viking [now retired], Margaret McElderry of

Harcourt Brace, and Ursula Nordstrom of Harper & Row. They replied with such unanimity of thought, even of language, that one quote may stand for all: "A good children's book is as much a work of art as a good book for adults, and frequently more difficult to write. It must be inspired, not manufactured to order, and the author must have as much respect for his readers as he has for himself."

3 · How Not to Write

The policy of reading the "cold" or unsolicited manuscripts that are sent in at random undoubtedly varies in different publishing houses. Therefore, I am speaking only of what has happened to those that have been under my jurisdiction.

I receive an average of eighty or more manuscripts a month. This adds up to a thousand a year, plus the fifty or so that come in from regular authors already on my team. Out of this number only about twenty are published, or less than 3 per cent of the total manuscripts received in a year. A larger publishing house will publish more books spring and fall than I do, but they receive many more scripts so in most cases it averages out.

This percentage would seem very small — except that the great majority of the scripts show no reason for having been written. Some authors admit that — I know, because I've asked them! They say they just thought they would "try it because it looks easy" or they say writing was something they did "to amuse themselves" or "to pass the time." They fail to take their writing seriously and so move on, perhaps, to other fields of endeavor.

Those who do take their writing seriously, however, will be interested in the fact that we do read every manuscript received, and I believe that is true of almost all juvenile departments. First of all, each incoming script is catalogued, then given a number, and a form is filled out with name, address, title, instructions on how to return it to the author (if stamps are enclosed, which is very important), and space for the reviewer's comments. Any correspondence accompanying or pertaining to the manuscript is also attached to this form. And here may I say again, if any explanatory letter is necessary, make it *short*. These forms are kept for permanent record, and it is often interesting to note that some of our present bestselling authors made their start years ago sending in "rejects." Naturally, what every writer wants is a letter from the editor telling him what is the matter with his script and how to correct it. Anyone can see, though, that with a large number of manuscripts arriving daily, such a procedure would be impossible.

Yet — each manuscript is read. This may take up to a month or six weeks or even more, depending on the pile of work that is looming over the department. But each piece of writing does get a reading, either by the editor or a trained assistant.

After a manuscript is read, the reader enters on the form a brief synopsis of the story to identify it, followed by his opinion of the work. This should tell its virtues, its faults and its sales possibilities and should justify his final comment, which is either "To consider" or "To decline."

A previous chapter outlined the virtues that my readers

and I look for in my department. The presence of one or more of these lands the manuscript in the "To consider" pile. I read all these and after a good deal of thought and consultation, decide (a) whether the company should publish them, (b) whether they show enough promise to encourage the author or (c) whether, in my opinion, they are not for us. Those in the last category and those that have already been turned down by my assistants receive a letter of declination, and the manuscripts are returned to their authors or agents.

That sounds as if all the manuscripts were sieved before they reached an editor. In many publishing houses this is not true, nor is it with me, for I personally find time to read most of them. And, naturally, I read all work coming from one of our already published authors, and any manuscripts that I have encouraged from the start or that have been revised under my directions. Believe me, that is plenty of reading!

Some authors have been told that when an editor suggests revision, it does not mean she wants to see the manuscript again. Frankly, I cannot imagine an editor taking that much trouble unless she did want to, and my advice to authors would be to send it back when revised. However, the author's attitude should not be: "I have made the revisions you have suggested. Now you've got to take it."

This question of revision and time wasted by authors and editors on poor manuscripts has always worried me. What is really the matter with the tons of material received? How can I tell — sometimes on the basis of a quick reading — that the manuscript in hand is worthless as a publication possibility?

To answer these questions I took at random one hundred

manuscripts* and studied them and their blanks listing the reasons for declination. The manuscripts were of all kinds and lengths, slanted at all the different juvenile age groups. But, in spite of that, it was easy to see they suffered from some universal faults.

Here are these faults, listed in order of their importance. The numbers in parenthesis indicate the total number declined for that particular fault out of the one hundred manuscripts under examination.

POOR WRITING. (12). This means that the authors expressed themselves so badly that no one would consider their material, no matter what they wrote about. Nothing can be done for these people except perhaps to give them a course in composition or grammar.

DULL MATERIAL. (13). Many writers think that children will like anything, and, of course, some people can make the most exciting tale sound dull. I receive a lot of historical manuscripts that are dull; also childhood reminiscences, or lessons in goodness. Most of these cannot be salvaged, because the writer himself is not inspired. Some can be saved by having the author read good books that are similar but have the spark that glows and leads the reader on. A fine example of heavy, factual material fascinatingly presented is *Augustus Caesar's World,* as well as others by Genevieve Foster (Scribners).

LACK OF POINT. (12). Often a writer has interesting ma-

---

* The original one hundred manuscripts discussed in *The Children's Book Field* were submitted to Houghton Mifflin when I was editor there. The new lot of one hundred were sent to Hastings House. Even though fourteen years had gone by the results were very much the same except for a slight difference in ages and a need for two new points to cover the change in *direction* of children's books during this era.

terial but it does not make a complete story, a nonfiction book or anything. Recently we received a travel manuscript filled with intriguing details, but they were poured out in a disjointed manner. The author was urged to read *Vast Horizons* by Mary S. Lucas (Viking) and to try to arrange his material in a more effective way.

IDEA TOO SLIGHT FOR A BOOK. (13). Many picture-book scripts come in with lovely pictures but too little story and a weak ending. Sometimes the author's idea is good, but it doesn't have enough substance for a story or even a picture book. In several such cases the authors have submitted their stories to magazines at my suggestion, but mostly they write back asking for advice on how to strengthen their ideas into books. Occasionally it is possible to help them along, but usually the padding of slight material does not work successfully.

In other words, you usually cannot build up a slim idea into one worthy of book form. You see it tried occasionally — a tiny little situation stretched out with dialogue, set in big type with lines far apart, and expanded with lots of impressive, modern pictures. But it still does not add up to a book. Some examples of stories that have tiny ideas, but are valid books for all that, are many by Margaret Wise Brown — for instance, *Where Have You Been?* illustrated by Barbara Cooney (Hastings). What a wonderfully light but firm touch that author had. And how well Barbara Cooney has interpreted it.

PLOT OR CENTRAL IDEA NOT CLEAR AND WELL ORGANIZED. (8). This may sound like a repetition of a previous item, but it really is not. In such stories the idea is good and there is a point, but the hero goes galloping around doing things that have no relation to the plot. In nonfiction of this kind there are bunches of material that are irrelevant and yet cannot readily be subtracted because not enough substance will be left. In other instances the actual arrangement of sections of the book, or pages, or paragraphs, is not good even though the material and background are excellent.

To help correct this fault, I sometimes suggest diagraming the plot, or, in nonfiction, the main body of the material. Even so simple a thing as reading aloud may help. One author who skillfully organizes difficult material is Leonard Wibberley. Read his *Thomas Jefferson* series (Farrar, Straus). Jean Lee Latham also did a wonderful job of organization in *Carry On, Mr. Bowditch* (Houghton), as did Elizabeth Baity in *Americans Before Columbus* (Viking).

LACK OF JUVENILE APPEAL OR TOO ADULT AN APPROACH. (8). This results when an author chooses a central idea that is not interesting to children or when the central idea is developed or expressed in a boring way. It is usually the latter, since children are interested in practically everything; although common sense would rule out such subjects as nuclear fission, the minor French painters, the theories of Kant, and so on. Books (usually modern picture books) laden with adult wit or sarcasm belong in this category, too.

POINT OF VIEW, ORGANIZATION AND PRESENTATION OF MATERIAL, SENTENCE STRUCTURE, VOCABULARY and many other things have a bearing on this very tenuous point. Writers who do not slant their work correctly for children usually do not know them very well. Others "write down" because they feel superior to their audience and show this by their patronizing phrasing or motivation.

Two authors whose love and understanding of children

45

are revealed in their books are Louis Slobodkin (*Magic Michael, Clear The Track, The Seaweed Hat* — all published by Macmillan) and Marguerite de Angeli's *Up The Hill, Bright April, Door In The Wall* (Doubleday).

INCORRECT MOTIVATION. (7). This often means that an adult predominates in the story, perhaps in planning the action or carrying it out. To be sure, few children in real life direct their own fate; but they can have a hand in it, or they can help in solving a family or adult problem. Certainly wise parents and teachers often withdraw their presence purposely so that the child can "work it out himself." For instance, in *Three Part Island* by Anne Molloy (Hastings) the three children work out the division of a Maine island in a way that no adult could foresee. What fun!

LACK OF ORIGINALITY, OR TOO MUCH. (12). Since Virginia Lee Burton wrote *Choo Choo* in 1937 and *Mike Mulligan* in 1939 (Houghton), there has been an endless stream of personalized mechanical objects in books. Tractors that are homesick, trains that are shy, fire engines that are lonesome — too many have been published. It is a worn-out theme, but manuscripts featuring it come in almost every day.

This holds to some extent for fantasy, too. Lewis Carroll and Eugene Field successfully bewitched children with their make-believe (and still do), but they have also led countless numbers of would-be authors to put down on paper the most extraordinary flights of fancy in prose and verse. Good fantasy is published now, but it takes a very gifted person to write it successfully. A few authors like Mary Norton, whose *The Borrowers* (Harcourt) is so delightful, and Joan Balfour Payne, who wrote *The Leprechaun of Bayou Luce* and

46

Charlie From Yonder (Hastings) started with fantasy and have successfully kept it up. Most beginning authors do not have that light, magic touch that marks the creator of true fantasy.

Perhaps the best advice for aspiring authors who try fantasy unsuccessfully is to say, "Wait awhile. Write about the world you know. Write about the things that children are interested in that really exist. Start on something easy, and then when you have a book or two going, write all the fantasy you want." But by that time these authors probably will have realized the difficulties and limitations of fantasy, or perhaps will have learned that the best fantasy is tied down to earth. In other words, when fantasy is successful, it is often an amusing treatment of ordinary situations or objects or problems that a child knows as part of daily life. *Stuart Little** and *Charlotte's Web* by E. B. White (Harper) are eloquent examples of this fact.

AGE-RANGE DIFFICULTIES. (4). Some beginning authors do not know children and children's books well enough to gauge ideas, vocabulary, and so on, accurately. Most of the time this can easily be fixed, but it helps tremendously for would-be authors to read books that are slanted correctly at a certain age. Many children's book catalogues are arranged by ages, and any author can get a fairly good idea of the requirements and the limitations of the age groups by reading four or five from each group or consulting the children's librarian in the nearest school or public library.

* The cinema version of this book showed how unsuccessful the realistic recreation of a fantasy can be. In book form, with Garth Williams' illustrations, it took off. In the movies with real people and a toy mouse, it was terrible.

This subject was dealt with at length in Chapter II, but here are a few perfect examples for each age group: *Copy-Kitten* by Helen and Alf Evers (Rand McNally) — nursery school age. *Blueberries for Sal* by Robert McCloskey (Viking) — the 4 to 7's. *Joey and Patches* by Margaret and Helen Lossing Johnson (Morrow) — beginning readers, 6 to 8. *Betsy Tacy* and many of the other books by Maud Hart Lovelace (Crowell), or the *Little House* series by Laura Ingalls Wilder (Harper) — the 9 to 12's. *David Livingstone* by Jeanette Eaton (Morrow) and *Champlain: Northeast Voyager* by Louise Hall Tharp (Little, Brown) — junior high school age.

May I say here, though, that really good authors usually need no coaching in age-group requirements. Their work fits naturally into one of the groups. And really, really good authors can be read and enjoyed by several or all the age groups, including adults. For example, *Winnie The Pooh* by A. A. Milne (Dutton), or *Mary Poppins* by P. L. Travers (Morrow).

OUT-OF-DATE MATERIAL. (9). Many writers, perhaps born early in the century, write stories that are supposedly modern but are really a recreation of their own childhood. This is fine if the era is defined as such but — to take two recent examples — modern boys and girls cannot quote glibly from Shakespeare (unfortunately) nor are they used to coping with a household of many servants. In other words, if your material is dated, be sure it is obviously and thoroughly of an era. Then it can be delightful.

MATERIAL THAT WILL GO OUT-OF-DATE FAST. (3) Books on space, tractors or motor cars are good examples of perilous publishing, because they might be out-of-date before they are bound. Certain publishers do specialize in them, however, and if your script is of this sort, these are the ones to whom to send it.

Keeping previously published books up-to-date is a problem that an editor has to face anyway. Hence new books with that problem built in are not too salable unless they are exceedingly timely and well done, thus guaranteeing a quick sale.

In 1962 Hastings House contracted for a book on the United States Presidents who were interested in sports: *Sports of the Presidents* by John Durant. It was written, set in type and about to be paged when President Kennedy was assassinated.

We stopped production. The author was far (in miles) from a reliable source of information on President Johnson as a sportsman, so as editor, I was elected to find out if LBJ played golf, tennis or what. Trips to the public library disclosed that there was remarkably little information on the man and nothing on the sports he played except the fact that he rode a horse to school as a youngster and he did not indulge in sports in the teachers' college he attended. Mr. Durant made what he could of this and other like bits that had come his way. We set the new information in type, fitted it in some way, and the book was published — late. Other books on the Presidents had to be similarly and expensively revised. It is not a task an editor plans for himself unless the subject really warrants it.

OVERDONE SUBJECTS. (9). Because of the tremendous number of children's books being published today, there is a necessary amount of duplication of subject. Every editor keeps an eye on the general field and tries to avoid bringing out new books on subjects or people that have already been well covered. Of course, if the author has a new point of view or different material or is approaching a younger or older age group than has been done before, that is different. But on the whole, there have been too many biographies of such American heroes as Lincoln, Franklin and Kennedy and too many presentations of shells, seeds, birds, trees, pond life and so on to risk another . . . at least for a while. Probably there will be four more published next season.

This effort to be different has led to the publication of some rather odd books but some of them have been good. Others have stayed in their storehouse bins because of lack of interest.

So these points cover two "don'ts." 1) Don't select a common subject unless you have a new slant on it. To find out, consult your public library and subject indices. 2) Don't pick an idea that is so limited in appeal and scope that a publisher cannot possibly find enough customers to buy it. Plantigrade animals, for instance (man is one of them), make up a scientific group because they walk on the whole soles of their feet. But who cares? I doubt if you could sell a publisher a book about them, although he walks on the soles of his feet every day. I will admit, though, that such a book might come out tomorrow.

Other common faults, which are relatively unimportant but occur fairly often, are:

Manuscripts in doggerel or monotonous rhyming verse.

Texts on foreign travel with flat, factual daily life scenes and poor photographs. A typical title is *Mary and Ben Visit Vienna.*

Meaningless picture-book texts accompanied by terrible

art work. And by "terrible" I mean pictures that most third graders would recognize as poor art.

The presentation of some group or race through caricature, or by excessive use of dialect.

Most retellings of the classics.

Attempts at vocabulary-controlled stories or verse, so studied in their use of words that all spontaneity is lost if it was ever there.

Stunt writing or reliance on a trick. For instance, books that whistle, dance or sing.

It is obvious that many of the reasons for declining a manuscript are overlapping. Some concern the material, and some concern the presentation of material. It is obvious, also, that a sound, original idea enables the author to avoid the worst faults and that writing ability plus respect for and knowledge of children will get him by most of the others. Once over these hurdles, all he has to do is write! And rewrite!

4 · Practical Advice For Authors

Here are the mechanical details of how to present a manuscript to a publisher:

1. Manuscripts should be typewritten, double-spaced, on good white paper of standard 8½" by 11" size, leaving at least 1½" margin on all *four* sides. Number the pages consecutively from first page to last, not by chapters. Do not send carbon copies, but always have one or two made. If your book is accepted you will need two: the original is used for editing, layout and typesetting. The first carbon goes to the artist. The second carbon you keep *yourself,* although the editor may ask for it to submit to a book club. Be sure all carbons are complete, have all corrections on them and are readable.

2. Your manuscript should include title page, table of contents, introduction or preface — if desired — a list of your previous books, bibliography, etc. An index is usually made later, after the book has been set in galleys and these divided up into page proofs.

3. Manuscripts should be mailed or expressed to a publisher with a short note giving the author's name and address and any absolutely necessary details.

4. Don't expect your opus back before two weeks to two months. After that you may telephone or write and inquire about it.

5. Do not submit the manuscript in person. The book must stand and fall on its own merits. Always enclose stamps and a mailing envelope for its return, or request that it be returned express collect.

6. Make an appointment to see an editor in a publishing house only if an interview seems *absolutely imperative*.

7. Do not claim that the manuscript has been read and enjoyed by dozens of children. The editor will not be favorably impressed with this kind of statement. Too many authors of inferior material have made it.

8. Do not think that because you know someone in the firm or a friend of the editor, you stand a better chance of getting your book published.

9. Don't send a manuscript to more than one publisher at a time. That is illegal and even if it were not, it might get you into an embarrassing situation.

10. Don't expect an editor to tell you what is wrong when he or she returns it. He just does not have time.*

* Often if a manuscript shows promise but not enough to definitely encourage the author, I suggest taking a writing course. There are too many to list here and they change from year to year, but ask your local librarian or someone at the nearest big university. Several are given in the winter in New York, and there are many all over the country in the summer, even on Cape Cod! The Bread Loaf Writers' Conference at Middlebury College in Vermont is one of the best. Eunice Blake, for years the renowned editor at J. B. Lippincott, is in charge of the juvenile division. A course is only as good as its instructor, which is one reason Bread Loaf is so popular.

11. Once your manuscript is accepted, remember that it is part of a production schedule, and it is up to you to keep it there. By that I mean you should do what you are asked to do promptly, or you will be holding up the schedule and may lose your book's place on it. The result: postponement to the next season's list. For instance, if revision is required, do it and return it to the editor by the deadline. If biographical information is asked for, supply it along with a glossy proof of a clear photograph, not a cloudy snapshot taken ten years before. *Especially,* return your galleys immediately. In other words, sit right down the morning after you receive them and read them word for word, using the correct proofreader's marks to correct any mistakes. (See opposite page.) Authors who complain about typographical errors in their books are at least partly responsible for not having caught them.

The same thing holds for okaying illustration proofs, flap copy, supplying indexes and other elements of a book. Fortunately, most authors are professional in their attitude toward this sort of thing and are a pleasure to work with.

A DISCUSSION OF MONEY IN GENERAL, CONTRACTS, COPYRIGHTS AND AGENTS

It is generally conceded that being an author is fun, although the pleasures are mixed; and often an author has wished he were something else. Still, it is nice to have one's thoughts and efforts appear in the form of a printed, bound book, and the profession of writing is normally considered a dignified one.

Dignity, however, butters no bread, sends no children

PROOF MARKS

MARGINAL MARK	CORRESPONDING MARK IN PROOF	MEANING
the ∧	Every man has in him possibility	*insert*
ꝰ	Every man has in him the possibility	*invert*
ⱹ	Every man has in him the∕ possibility	*take out*
⊂	Every man has in him the possi bility	*close up*
l.c.	Every Man has in him the possibility	*lower case letter*
w.f.	Every man has in him the possibility	*wrong font letter*
tr	Every man has in him possibility the	*transpose*
stet	Every man has in him the possibility	*let stand*
☐	∧Every man has in him the possibility	*indent em quad*
#	Every man has in him thepossibility	*space*
ʏ∧	Every man has in him the possibility	*even spacing*
⊥	Every man has in him the possibility	*push down space*
¶	purpose. Every man has in him the	*make paragraph*
[	[Every man has in him the possibility	*move over*
(y?)	Every man has in him the possibilities	*query to author*
X	Every man has in him the possibility	*broken letter*
⊙	Every man has in him the possibility	*period*
⌄	Every mans possibility lies within him	*apostrophe*
⌄⌄	Every man has in him the possibility	*quotation marks*
–∕	Some men sidetrack possibility	*hyphen*
caps	Every man has in him the possibility	*capitals*
sm. c.	Every man has in him the possibility	*small capitals*
rom.	Every man has in him the possibility	*put in roman*
ital	Every man has in him the possibility	*put in italic*
b.f.	Every man has in him the possibility	*bold-face*

N O T E : Reader's Queries on margins of proofs should be answered by author. Failure to do so will delay the progress of book.

through college and pays no taxes. What, therefore, are the material benefits attendant on the printed word?

These are varied. They range from practically nothing to funds sufficient to support a family nicely. The exact monetary figure depends on a multitude of items, such as the amount of talent in the book, its degree of popularity, the number of copies published, whether it has hit any of the literary jackpots, whether it is kept in print, and so on.

Speaking very generally, money from books comes in various ways:

Outright sale
Royalties on the hardbound edition
Paperback rights and royalties
Book clubs
One-shot magazine sale and magazine or newspaper
 serialization
Foreign sale
Movie, radio, television, video tape and recording rights

These items differ widely, depending on whether the book is for the juvenile or the adult market. I shall concern myself with juveniles.

OUTRIGHT SALE

Authors can receive an outright payment (a lump sum) on the acceptance of the manuscript. In this case the publisher pays no royalties. The manuscript then becomes the publisher's property to use as he wishes. This kind of deal is common in the inexpensive book series — i.e., those that sell from 25 cents to $2 and also in some other series or publishing programs. The price paid varies from $100 up, but usually, I believe, is from $300 to $500. As this is a relatively small sum for a book that may sell for years, it is better for the author to try for royalties, even though a year or more may pass before they amount to anything.

On the other hand, many authors make a good living turning out short stories or short nonfiction pieces for the inexpensive series or for magazines. You can — if you write enough and can find a market for them.

ROYALTIES ON HARDBOUND BOOKS

These differ according to the book under consideration, the author's previous sales record, the publisher's general practices, the market for that kind of book and the possibility of the author's supplying more good books.

Some authors think that some publishers have a questionable moral code — that they steal ideas or pirate material. If writers select established publishers, they need have no fears. Obviously, firms could not stay in business very long if their dealings with authors, artists and the book trade in general were not honorable.

Authors also feel sometimes that they receive too small a part of the publisher's dollar — this is especially true of those new to the field. They have visions of the publisher making at least $1.50 out of a $3 book. This is not so. Sylvia Porter, a well-known financial analyst, gave the costing of a $4 book in detail in *Book Production* magazine, August, 1961. When manufacturing, promotion, advertising and overhead (salaries, rent, telephone, heat and supplies) were added up, the company came out with an approximate 10 per cent profit. Today it would be closer to 6 per cent because of the drop in the dollar and increased expense all along the line. However, the figures on individual books differ greatly; hence it is impossible to be exact on this point. It is safe to say, though, that the publisher's take is somewhere between 3 per cent and 8 per cent, depending on the volume itself and the over-all project, and taking for granted that the first edition sells out in a reasonable period of time so the company does not have to pay interest on the investment that is tied up and the advance that has been given on signing the contract.

With all this in mind, let us look at the general royalty scheme.

Royalties in the children's book world are different from those in the adult world. They are smaller but often more lasting. A juvenile of reasonable virtue can sell for ten or twenty years or longer if there is nothing in it that dates it. (A book may be dated by time references, slang, illustrations or in a dozen ways.) For example, as a juvenile editor I have sent out sizeable royalty checks of $2,000 or more twice a year to authors who have not written anything for a decade.

Royalty rates for "beginning"* authors of children's books are different in many contracts. And it might be well to say right here that my information in this chapter is based on a study of contracts from eight publishers, on facts given me by several agents and on data provided by five authors who have worked for several different publishers. Many firms offer a sliding scale: 5 per cent of the retail price on sales up to 5000, 7½ per cent up to 10,000 and 10 per cent after that. This scale can start higher and go higher, but do not be

---

* This term or "first authors" is used to indicate those who have not previously had a book published.

distracted by an offer of "15 per cent after a sale of 15,000" or so. Your first book will probably never get there.

Other firms offer 7½ per cent of the retail price on all sales of the first book and a promise of a straight 10 per cent on further books. The latter is a fair deal on a first book, and a straight 10 per cent of the retail price is good for the books that follow. A few companies offer beginners 7½ per cent or 10 per cent of the *net* price, which is the retail price minus the trade discount. For example, most firms give 40 per cent or more trade discount to wholesalers or jobbers. Thus the author would receive 10 per cent of $2.50 (if that is the retail price) minus 40 per cent or $1.50, which equals 15 cents a book, or about 6 per cent of the retail price. That is not a very big royalty. But if you have to choose between this arrangement and not having your book published at all, you had better give the matter serious thought. Getting your first book accepted and out in the world is a big hurdle to be over. Acceptable contracts usually come more easily after that.

The libraries' insistence on reinforced bindings has resulted in another "net" price. This may include a goodly proportion of your sales if your books sell well to institutions, such as schools and public libraries. Ask your editor for an explanation of this when your first royalty accounting comes in or better still before you sign the contract. In some cases this net price on library bindings means the author gets *more* rather than less, because the net price is often more than the trade or retail price and usually he receives the same royalty as on the retail price.

In the case of a picture book, where the artist is just as important as the author, the royalties are generally split, with one-half going to each one. Sometimes it may even go the other way — with the artist receiving more than the author. For example, in my first book, *Peter Paints the U.S.A.* (Houghton), the artist, Arnold Bare, already well known for his excellent work in two other picture books, received 7½ per cent while I, the unknown author, got 2½ per cent. That was not a very good deal for me; but the pictures *were* more important than the text, and it was his idea in the first place. I developed and wrote it. Well, it was a start.

On most picture books the author gets 5 per cent and the artist 5 per cent on royalties and all other sales. This is true (unless otherwise specified in the contract) even if the text alone is used in a collection, the reason being that without the pictures, the book would not have attracted the attention of the editors of the collection.

One exception to the above — and there are many — is a volume in an inexpensive or low-priced series. Half-royalty may be offered in this case, because big editions are printed and the author more than makes up the money from increased sales by being part of the series. On such a series the total royalty might be 5 per cent to the author or 2½ per cent each to author and artist.

A sliding scale offering high royalties after a sale like fifteen or twenty thousand copies is both a virtue and an evil. As a reward for a top sales record, it is a justified bonus. Occasionally, however, such a scale or other promises are used by new companies to pry authors away from the firms who have recognized their talents and already established them. Most wise authors are content to stay where they have been well edited and well treated, where their wishes on format receive consideration and where their books are kept in print as long as possible. The last factor is particularly important.

The Authors League in New York has a suggested scale of royalties and other contractual terms that will help to give its members adequate protection, but up to now there have been so many variants, it has not succeeded in devising a contract that all publishers can use as a whole. It is an excellent organization, however, and well worth joining. It is concerned with the professional interests of published writers — the business and contractual relationship they have with trade and reprint publishers, with film and television producers, foreign markets, and so on. They suggest fair tax treatment for their members, and work for universal copyright treaties and for freedom of expression in publishing and the theater. At the present writing their dues are $30 a year. Their address is 6 East 39th Street, New York, N.Y.

Here are their views on the changing field of copyrights and contracts. This is an excerpt from a letter written to me on the subject by Peter Heggie of the Authors League:

Take just the one concern of the future storage of copyrighted material on tape or film, of the communication of words over distances, and their reproduction on various print-out devices for readers. How will authors fare in this complex, automated "publishing" of the future — that may replace publishing as we know it? How will they be compensated, so that they can continue to support themselves in the writing of new works for the new technology of publishing? There are decisions being made now, specifically in connection with the revision of the copyright law, which will affect the way these things go for years to come, and before we are fully aware of what the technological changes will mean to us. The authors and playwrights, by working through The Authors League of

America, can speak effectively on the question of copyright revision.

There is truth in the above statement, and the Authors League does a lot of good; but most publishers cannot go along with their request for a sliding scale of royalties based on the amount of discount on each sale. It is not so much that the idea is bad, but that it is impractical. Think of the paper work and man-time involved in reporting the royalties on just one title! Every sale, whether for one copy or one thousand, would have to be figured separately. If the authors want their publishers to have enough time, energy and money to produce their books nicely, sell them widely and promote them properly, it would be wise not to tie them up in knots at the home office every time an order is sent in.

There is some talk that royalties generally may have to be reduced because of high production costs. It seems unfair to me for authors to take a cut when increases in the cost of printing, binding and labor are the real causes of the trouble. On the other hand, high prices have forced some companies to give up publishing so-called "deluxe" juveniles. They are expensive to produce with their colorful illustrations and irregular format, and there seems no end to the cost spiral.

At present most publishers are not cutting royalties but are raising prices. Of course, this automatically raises royalties, but it also has resulted in putting hard-bound picture books — and, in fact, most children's books — beyond the reach of parents, thereby eliminating almost all bookstore sales. This is most unfortunate. Perhaps the new surge toward juvenile paperbacks will help the situation, but it is difficult to print picture books on paperback stock and bind them so they will last. However, with the use of a harder surface paper, a great deal could be done. In fact, as I write this, there is a growing new market for juvenile paperbacks. This delights me, because I want children to be able to own lots of books as I did when a child.

Several publishers are looking for paperback material for the middle (9 - 12) and teen-age market, and other companies are bringing out their old favorites in paperback.* One of the exciting things about juvenile paperbacks is that experiments have shown that they can be successfully sold in schools as well as stores.† Thus the school makes a small profit, children are exposed to good books and, best of all, they can actually afford to choose and buy them for themselves.

Paperback royalties for adult books and juveniles heretofore have usually been shared more or less equally by publishers and authors because the hard-cover version has come out first. That situation is changing in the adult field now that some new books are appearing first in paperback form. This is not true yet to any extent in juveniles, but it may happen. If it does, these royalties should be negotiated.

BOOK CLUBS

The children's book clubs are smaller in membership than those in the adult field, partly because they are subdivided

---

* The paperback publishers have about exhausted the classics — at least one would think so. The October 1965 Cumulative issue of *Paperbound Books in Print* (Bowker) lists 15 *Adventures of Huckleberry Finn,* 10 *Adventures of Tom Sawyer,* 12 *Moby Dick,* 12 *Silas Marner,* and so on!

† Newman, Robert E. *Elementary School Paperback Project.* A report by the Assistant Professor of Education, Principal of the Lower School, The Laboratory Schools, University of Chicago. Chicago: January 5, 1965.

into age groups, but they are still nice for an author to attain. Some of the clubs are the Junior Literary Guild, the Weekly Reader Children's Book Club and the Scholastic Book Clubs.

In a sale to a book club or a reading circle (these exist in the West and Middle West — in Colorado, Illinois, Iowa, Kansas, Ohio, and a few other states) the author and the publisher receive a smaller percentage than on single-copy sales, but the number sold usually more than makes for this. One or two of the book clubs have a large library membership that cuts into the publisher's sale to library suppliers. Sometimes it is difficult to decide whether to allow a club to take a title because of this cut. On the whole, though, I believe the clubs serve a worthy purpose of providing good books to the public and to libraries at a reduced cost, and I try to cooperate with them in every way possible.

MAGAZINES AND MAGAZINE SERIALIZATION

Again the adult field has the advantage, because there are innumerable magazines and newspaper periodicals looking for adult material; whereas in the juvenile field, magazine publishing for children is limited at the present time. There are several monthlies that have an abundance of photographs and illustration, but the real contents boil down to a very brief story, a serial, a short nature-study article, a few games, crossword puzzles and some special departments. Most of these have been chosen a year or more in advance.

Exceptions are the church magazines. I especially recommend the Methodist publications produced in Nashville, Tennessee. The editors of these publications take pains to select material from good authors, for which they are willing to pay well. Their periodicals are not slicked up with expensive formats, but they contain material that is high grade and enjoyable, too.

Many authors have started to write for magazines and have gone on to books. I often suggest that certain scripts submitted to me would be more suitable for magazines than books, especially when they are rather thin in content. Several authors have written that they sold them to magazines and got their professional writing start in this way.

Other sources of income are the many local papers. They often run a story or two on their children's page on Saturday. And while an author will not get rich on the remuneration, being published does help to get his name before the public, even if only in a small way, and it gives him a lift psychologically, which everybody needs, especially authors.

MOVIE, RADIO, TELEVISION AND RECORDING RIGHTS

MOVIE RIGHTS. Few juveniles are taken by the movies. Probably one reason is that there are so many classics available on which the movie companies do not have to buy the rights or pay a royalty. These books are out of copyright and hence in "the public domain." (The length of copyright is explained later on in this chapter.) Many authors feel that their stories have cinema possibilities. Occasionally, I have agreed that this is true and have tried to draw movie scouts' attention to them. Nothing ever came of my efforts, however, and up to the present I have been convinced that selling a juvenile to a Hollywood studio is almost an impossibility. However, there have been a few exceptions to this lately, especially with novels for the older age group that are almost adult fare and with such classic titles as *Stuart Little* by E. B. White (Harper), and perhaps the time will come when Hollywood agents will consider a good juvenile with plenty of character, action and a colorful background. Until there is a real change, however, an author need not worry about the movie-rights clause in his contract. A publisher may fill the clause out with the percentage greatly in the author's favor, but that is probably the first and last action ever to be taken in that direction.

RADIO AND TELEVISION RIGHTS. Everyone believes that children's books have a future on television. At the moment there is some concrete progress to report, especially on educational TV, and interschool TV, but this is to be regarded as promotion (and very good promotion), not as a program in itself, bought and paid for. On the regular channels the television powers-that-be are reluctant to pay for the use of copyrighted material when there is so much standard fare — *Jack and the Beanstalk,* etc. — available for nothing. There are quite a few programs where readers hold up picture books and read or tell the story as they turn the pages. This method is better than nothing, but it is not very good and often sends the majority of the young audience scuttling for stronger fare.

The same situation of inferior and too few programs holds true in radio. On Saturday morning there are several programs on which stories are told or dramatized for children. Some of the broadcasters have taken the trouble to write the publishers for permission to read the books aloud, but many of them go gaily ahead with the idea that both authors and publishers will be glad of the publicity.

So far there are only a dozen or so exceptions to this poverty in worthwhile programs, although more have been announced.* One is Ruth Harshaw's "Carnival of Books,"

* See the *Literary Market Place* (Bowker).

which is produced by Station WMAG-NBC in Chicago in cooperation with the American Library Association. It is also broadcast in Pittsburgh, on WJAS, in Philadelphia on WRCV, San Francisco on KNBR, and on WSPA in the following South Carolina cities: Spartanburg, Columbia, Charleston and Florence. It is rebroadcast on the National Association of Educational Broadcasters' Network. Check your local educational station.

This fine program, which has been broadcast on NBC radio for twenty years, is devoted to one author at a time, who is usually present. There are juvenile critics who take part in the program, and there is always a spirited dramatization of one of the author's latest works. Mrs. Harshaw records in several big cities in the United States and in England, where she uses panels of British young people. In 1956 she recorded authors all over Europe. Her recent British series is presented in cooperation with BBC and the public libraries of the London boroughs. *

Another unusually good program that now appears on both radio and TV is the "Teen Age Book Talks" with Margaret Scoggin, coordinator of Young Adult Services in the New York Public Library, as permanent moderator. This unrehearsed program gives high school boys and girls a chance to speak their minds on books of interest to them and to question guest authors. Membership in this program is open to anyone over twelve living in greater New York. Fifteen to twenty youngsters are used on radio; five on TV. The only membership requirement is a pledge to read in advance the books to be reviewed and join in the programs

---

* I have just learned as I read proof that this outstanding program will be discontinued. How sad! However, Lavinia Russ of *Publishers Weekly,* has started a somewhat similar one in New York City.

for which the books are read. Listeners may send in suggestions for books to be discussed, although the final decision lies with the moderator.

This program appears in New York City Saturday morning on WNYC AM and FM, and on TV on Channel 31 WMYCT. It is live on Tuesday at 3 P.M., is repeated the same night at 7:30 on video tape and is rebroadcast on FM on WNYE in seven hundred junior and senior high schools. It is a fine example of up-to-date, forward-looking educational coverage and a splendid job done.

As I write this, more and more notices are arriving at my office, announcing TV or taped book programs sponsored by state or city educational services.These are used widely in schools and are excellent promotion but are not paid for. The benefits are obviously mutual.

Because of the situations described above, the money that authors of juveniles derive from radio, TV and video tape is small at the moment, but the promotion value is high. Sometime in the future publishers as well as authors are hoping for a change.

RECORDING RIGHTS. There have been some advances in this direction in the past years. For quite a while the Weston Woods Studio has been making excellent recordings, motion pictures, film strips and tapes for use in schools and libraries. A small percentage is paid to the publisher for use of the books featured and, of course, it is excellent publicity. A first-rate example of their work is the much admired *The Lively Art of Picture Books,* featuring Robert McCloskey, Maurice Sendak and Barbara Cooney. Maurice Sendak also has a film of his own in which he traces the development of *Where the Wild Things Are* (Harper), a Caldecott Medal Winner, and shows the work of other artists whom he admires. Morton Schindel, the creative owner and manager of Weston Woods, has also just released a film of the gay Lisl Weil and her performance in *The Sorcerer's Apprentice* (Little, Brown). There are fifty or so other sound film-strip sets to be bought or rented on such fine books as *Crow Boy* by Taro Yashima (Viking), *Petunia* by Roger Duvoisin (Knopf) and *The Fox Went Out On a Chilly Night* by Peter Spier (Doubleday). A brochure is available from this company, which is located in Weston, Connecticut.

Some of the Golden Books and the Landmark Books now appear in record form and can be bought in the bookstores and local markets. Other series and some individual titles are also going to be or have been recorded. For instance, Robert Brooks in Volumes I and III and Jessica Tandy and Hume Cronyn in Volumes II and IV give readings from Kenneth Grahame's *The Wind in the Willows* (Scribners) on an LP record from "Pathways of Sound, Inc.," a company in Cambridge, Massachusetts, specializing in recordings for children. Maurice Evans reads from *Winnie-the-Pooh* by A. A. Milne (Dutton) on another release by this company. They have quite a wide choice of famous children's books read by equally famous actors — but to be included your books practically have to be classics.

There is a great future here for children's books, because more and more schools are putting in equipment of the most advanced kind. Of course, parents, too, can obtain these records or films for home use, and there are many more than those I have mentioned. Ask at your local bookstore 'or library, and play them before you buy them.

Now, what part the author has in these recordings, either financially or as the originator of the book, is hard to say exactly. Each case is different so far, with each company making its own agreement. My advice would be to have recording rights included in the television and radio clause of the contract under the same terms or to have it specified that individual sales to different companies are to be agreed on as they come up.

FOREIGN SALE

The majority of contracts call for a 50-50 split on any monies obtained by sale in foreign countries — Canada is the exception to this. Ordinarily this country is included in the United States sale, since U.S. publishers have regular Canadian representatives or salesmen.

Foreign sale is becoming quite important.* Many foreign countries are feeling the educational impetus toward more and better children's books, and there is a definite market for titles that are not too American in content, attitude and spelling. (Of course, the latter is immaterial except to English or African publishers, but they make rather a point of it. I have gotten around this difficulty in some instances by agreeing on a text with a foreign publisher before it is set in type, often using the English spelling of such words as *colour,* etc., and having an explanatory note about it stripped into our edition. I believe most children are interested in the fact that the English language can vary so much.)

There are several foreign book fairs annually, of which two are quite important: Frankfurt, Germany, and Bologna, Italy, the latter being entirely devoted to books for children and youth. The flyer on this year's Bologna fair said that: "About 170 publishers from sixteen countries in Europe,

* See *International Publishing,* Part III, Chapter 4, C.

70

Asia and North America are expected to attend." I spoke about the fairs to several London editors on a recent trip to England, and they were most enthusiastic. If a publisher wishes to have a booth but cannot send representatives, a staff that speaks three or four languages will be supplied, or several publishers can combine on a booth. Translation and illustration rights are the center of discussion, and it is interesting to note that these fairs are open only to booksellers, agents and publishers. The result is that many handsome foreign picture books and high-type books for older boys and girls are appearing in this country. It is also true that an equal number of fine American books are being translated and sold abroad.

These foreign deals are tricky, both for the United States publisher who is buying foreign books and possibly importing sheets or for a United States publisher who is selling one of his books to a foreign concern. Obviously it is important to the author to have a publisher with active foreign contacts. These rights can mean real money to him — not in large amounts, because overseas they do not get the prices for books that we do — but it can mount up.

Editorially speaking, it is important that an American firm have a man or men who know foreign *and* American import regulations. These are many and complex, and they change from year to year. At Hastings House I have been most fortunate in having the help of Russell Neale, who has made a study of foreign contracts and printing abroad, as well as the regulations of the U.S. Customs Department.* I have learned a great deal from him and from my own dealings with foreign publishers and printers.

* As of February 1, 1967, under the Florence Agreement, books, sheets and other parts of books may be imported into the U.S.A. free of duty. This does not change copyright rulings.

ADVANCES

An advance is a sum of money paid by the publisher when the contract is signed, either in one sum or in agreed-upon installments while the manuscript is in preparation. This is supposed to bind the deal and tide the author over until the book is published and begins to earn an income. This money is an advance payment of royalties; in other words, *an advance is money that comes out of the author's earnings* eventually. Hence, common sense decrees that one should not give or accept large advances, since a book could take a long time to earn them.

You may say that here I am speaking from the publisher's point of view only, but that is not true. If an author is in need, I believe an advance anywhere up to $1000 should be given. But payment of more than that — except in an unusual instance — means that the author will go without royalties for a year, perhaps, because royalties often are not paid on publication date but are "accrued" until such a date as is named in the contract.

If an author can afford it, I recommend a smaller advance of about $250 to $500. Such figures fluctuate, however, and should not be taken too rigidly. Most publishers have their own practices as far as advances go, and some are quite liberal. However, if you are an author of adult books who wishes to sell one in the juvenile field, do not expect an advance of thousands of dollars or so, even though you received one of that amount for your last novel or biography.

There are many other clauses in a contract besides those I have discussed. I shall not take them all up, because most of them are included to meet contingencies that seldom arise, especially in the publication of juveniles. A few, however, can bear some explanation and emphasis.

First of all, you as author are responsible for what is in the book. If the work is a piece of nonfiction, you are supposed to be sure of your facts, your dates and so on. If the opus is fiction, you are responsible for its being really "made up," and not a semiconcealed description of a family you know, or some event taken from real life that you might be sued for revealing.

You are also responsible for any plagiarism, either conscious or unconscious. In other words, your publisher takes for granted that you are not using other people's material or plots or pictures or what-will-you and putting these out as your own. If you use excerpts from other people's writings, *you* (not your publisher) have to get permission from the publisher of those writings and put this information in a list of permissions in your book. Sometimes such material must be paid for.

The book is *copyrighted,* usually in your name. The publisher does this for you, but *you* have to renew the copyright (again through him) if you are lucky enough to have written a book that is still selling after twenty-eight years, the term of copyright. A book's copyright may be renewed once for another twenty-eight years (fifty-six in all),* but after that it becomes public property or is in "public domain." You and your publisher still control the set of plates or film, however, and many a book sells on merrily after fifty-six years in its original edition even though cheap editions of

---

*As previously mentioned, because of the practices of photocopying there there may soon be changes in the U.S. copyright law. Watch for such a notice, as it will concern you and your books.

the same are available. Nowadays plates are not used as much as they were, but the original book can continue to be published by photocopying the pages.

A few authors think it is necessary to copyright their manuscripts before sending them to a publisher. That is not so. Occasionally, a manuscript may be lost in transit or by a publisher, but if you have a carbon — and, of course, you have — that is not an irreparable loss. The main point to realize is that publishers do not steal ideas or manuscripts, as I have said previously. So, rest easy. When you send your precious words to a publisher, they are safe. Ordinarily the trouble will not be that he wants to pirate your work, but that he will not appreciate it enough! You will generally get the manuscript back in extra good condition. In my experience the only theft of ideas has been by other authors. This is most uncommon, but when you have an inspiration, tell your publisher, not your author-acquaintance.

Another clause that is important to authors is the one stating that *"Expense of Author's proof corrections* (other than corrections of printer's errors) *exceeding 10 per cent of the cost of composition shall be charged against the author's royalties."* This means that, when you get the galley proofs of your book, you should make as few changes as possible, since, for instance, the substitution of a long word for a short one, or the addition of a phrase, may make it necessary for the printer to reset a whole long paragraph. Any extensive rewriting of a book in proofs would run the author's alterations well over the 10 per cent of the total first composition cost. That is why that proviso is put there: to prevent authors from wholesale rewriting, as many want to do when they see their words in print. So, remember, make your corrections *before* the manuscript goes to the typesetter. Keep your hands off after that even though you may think you see many obvious improvements you could make. Consult your editor before making any major changes. Rewriting at this stage seldom helps a bit and frequently delays publication.

Author additions (or "A-A's," as they are known in the trade) are almost impossible to make when the script is set by the new computerized setting, so make up your mind that your doom is sealed when you hand in your script for the last time.

In *Publisher's Weekly* of April 5, 1965, in their section on "Bookmaking" there was an interesting report of a conference in Washington, D.C., March 2 - 3, 1965, on computer application to typesetting. A speaker, Professor C. J. Duncan of the University of Newcastle-on-Tyne, one of England's computer typesetting authorities, said, "We should train our young generation of authors not to 'fiddle about' with the text. We must get them to write accurately. The author is then responsible for the text; the publisher for deciding what format it is to take, and the printer for the manufacture of it."

Burton L. Stratton of Harvard University Press, in a recent management session of the American Book Publishers Council, reported in the same issue of *Publishers Weekly,*

Aside from the Churchillian notion that a composing machine was invented to help an author make up his mind, there is no surer way to encourage laxity and break down craftsmanship than (1) to deliver a slovenly manuscript to the printer, and (2) literally rewrite the book at the galley stage. . . . As things stand, it is uneconomic for us to consider the use of computers tied in with photocomposing machines if galleys must be shown to the author and additional changes made in both galleys and pages. In other words, *unless we control the manuscript* to that extent, *we are prevented from benefitting from modern technology.*

Hence, it means that authors who make a lot of corrections are keeping us from using the new methods and thereby are helping to raise the price of books, thus preventing them from reaching people who could otherwise afford to buy them.

A clause often misinterpreted is the one stating there will be a reduction in royalty on small printings of 2,000 copies or less, after the book has been out three or more years and has sold less than 200 copies during the last royalty period. Usually one-half of the regular royalty is given in this case. Such a readjustment often enables a publisher to keep a book in print where he otherwise might not be able to. Small printings are expensive, and it is sometimes better for the author to take this reduction after his book has been out several years than to have the book go out of print.

There are many other clauses of a similar nature — for instance, the one that covers the sale of books in unbound press sheets to binderies that sell reinforced bindings to libraries. All these special contingencies have been worked out, and if you, as author, are interested in them, your editor will explain them. If your editor and his company are intelligent and honest, their contract will also be workable and honest. You must have faith in them and in their ability to publish books. If you do not, go elsewhere. But remember the old saying about the bird in hand! This holds true in regard to book contracts.

AGENTS

Literary agents are an important part of any publishing picture, especially in adult books, because they represent many authors who do not know the varied literary markets or are too busy to look after the details of their business or who feel they are not experienced enough in business to do so. In this capacity of business manager and business-obtainer, agents render valuable service. In addition, some of them guide their clients with editorial suggestions and criticisms. However, many writers have the misconception that agents are necessary in order to get a book considered by a publishing house. By the time you have read this far, you realize that this is not so. Another common misbelief is that an agent is necessary to insure an author's being fairly treated. Again, you know this is not so. Others believe that an agent takes the cream of a book's profit for himself. That also is untrue. His commission is usually 10 per cent of the author's royalties and of other receipts from sales of subsidiary rights.

The actual facts are that an agent is not necessary for the placement of either juvenile or adult books. Many more adult writers than juvenile employ them because of their usefulness in finding the right publisher and in obtaining extra sales for the manuscript in the magazine, TV or cinema world. Agents have a broader knowledge of contract details and markets than most authors and often are valuable in securing more money for authors. They may also be more businesslike in collecting it, although most publishers pay twice a year at a certain date, and no agent is needed just for that. Agents help in reminding authors and artists of deadlines and often nurse their charges along like foster parents.

The agents can and do perform for juvenile authors all the tasks mentioned above. The juvenile market, however, has become so tight, with publishing lists filled years in advance, (yes, actually) that the best agent in the world cannot guarantee to place a book. However, the good ones know the editors and their specialties and provide valued contacts.

The facts are, though, that agents are selective in the material they handle and take on few beginning juvenile authors. Therefore, it is usually necessary to start on one's own. After an author has sold one or two books, he may want to turn his affairs over to an agent, at which point he can probably do so. There is a list of literary agents in the *Literary Market Place* (Bowker), should an author wish to contact one. Less than 5 per cent of the authors I have dealt with in the last twenty years have agents.

DO'S AND DON'TS FOR

1. *UNPUBLISHED AUTHORS*

REMEMBER THAT AUTHORSHIP IS A PROFESSION. You must take it seriously and give it the time and dedication it requires. As Margot Benary-Isbert said in the *Horn Book* of April 1964,

> It does not matter whether you do a short essay about the eye of a spider . . . or the great novel of the twentieth century . . . or simply . . . and not so very simply, either — a children's book. In each case you have to be dedicated to your work, to recognize it as what the saint would call a vocation, which necessarily excludes many other things you would like to do. It means renouncement of comforts, of hobbies, of

joys; it can mean at times renouncement of your nearest and dearest.

At the present time, because of high costs, an editor hesitates to launch a new author, even though he shows great promise. It takes too long for his worth to be recognized and for the publisher to get the initial investment back. Large editions are imperative now, since there is no profit until the book in question has "turned the corner" or paid for itself. This magic figure used to start at 2000 or 3000 copies depending on the book. Now it is often 7000 to 10,000 copies, or more if the book is a color job with costly camera and press work. Often an editor would like to take a book but finds it impossible to plan on enough market for it to justify the expense of production. Remember that, you authors and artists, when you start visualizing a book. Keep it practical in production details. For instance, scripts of four hundred or more pages have a strike against them because of length, as do picture books of five or six colors unless the artist can show he knows how to achieve these by separations with three or four.

Don't be discouraged too easily. I have published manuscripts that have obviously been the rounds of many publishers and yet have succeeded on my list. Two such books were on controversial subjects that necessitated a certain amount of editorial courage. Their history was given with the authors' consent in an article by me published in *Top Of The News* April 1965 and one by Helen Kay in the same magazine in November 1965.

If you have sent out a manuscript five or six times and have received nothing but form rejection letters, it might be well to try to persuade your local children's librarian or a teacher of your acquaintance to read it. Before doing so, *be sure they will give you an impartial judgment.* Enthusiastic praise by friends who do not know children's books is worthless and misleading.

THINK TWICE BEFORE GIVING YOUR BOOK TO A "VANITY" PUBLISHER. These are companies that charge you to publish it. They make promises they sometimes do not fulfill; their products rarely are bought by stores or libraries, and an unwary author may find himself paying some thousands of dollars for a few bound copies of a book with his name on it.

The practices of such houses have been investigated by the government on several occasions, and it is interesting to note that the Federal Trade Commission decided in 1960 that so-called "vanity" or "cooperating" publishers could use the word "royalty" only to describe those payments to authors that exceed the amount of the subsidy paid by authors for the publication of their book.

Any author wanting to know more about this kind of publishing should read "A Grim Price For Flattery" on page 40, *Publishers Weekly* of August 24, 1959.

DO'S AND DON'TS FOR

2. *PUBLISHED AUTHORS*

DON'T REGARD EVERY WORD YOU WRITE AS A HOLY THING. And, on the other hand, don't change or subtract anything that you think is vital to your piece of work. I never insist that my suggestions be followed. Most of my authors seem to think that a fair proportion of them make sense, but if they object to any, we talk it over. I try to show why I think a certain change is an improvement; they tell me why they want to keep the original wording. If they insist, it stays

. . . that is, unless I feel that to publish the book with that wording would jeopardize its success, the name of my company or the name of the author. That practically never happens.

Sometimes I have to ask for cutting so that the book will fall within a feasible production length or to give room for illustrations. You cannot have a few pages hanging off a form (books are printed in "forms" of thirty-two pages), so that you are left with twenty or so blank pages that have to be thrown away. But that sort of thing is obvious. Revision is usually no problem with an intelligent author, but as Ursula Nordstrom, the great editor of Harper, said in the November 1964 *Top Of The News:* "Revision, the willingness to consider it, and the ability to do it, are important."

I am taking the liberty of quoting with the authors' permission from two letters that have just come in:

May Justus writes,

> "I feel so grateful to you for encouraging me to develop this book beyond the slight picture book I had in mind at first. After I got the enlarged conception of it, it was really fun to do it — all the different details and characterizations."

Ruth Langland Holberg said,

> "I think you made my book turn out better than I was able to — that seems to be an editor's work to make the writer better than he or she is."

I have also received my share of "squawks." Here are a couple.

> "I don't see how you think those cuts would help it. Why, to take Cynthia out of the book completely would be like killing her." Cynthia deserved to die — at least, in my opinion.

"I don't understand why you want to change words like 'temerity' and 'trepidation.' If children don't know the meaning of those words, they ought to learn them."

WATCH YOUR DEADLINE DATE. Plan your work day by day to meet it. If you find you simply cannot, report this to your editor immediately and work out a later one.

DON'T TRY TO WORK WHEN YOU ARE TIRED. Sometimes when my children have embroiled me in time-consuming projects or problems, I have tried to do my writing at night. With me it just does not work. I only have to tear it up later on. You may be different, lucky you.

READ YOUR CONTRACT AND YOUR ROYALTY STATEMENTS CAREFULLY. If there is anything you do not understand, ask about it. Once, years ago as editor, I discovered that foreign royalties on authors from A to C were being deducted (one girl had charge of this segment of the alphabet) instead of added to the royalty total. This practice had gone on for two royalty periods, and no official or author had caught it. Now, with computers, such errors are not apt to happen, although I have heard of amusing mistakes under the new system.

IF YOU HAVE HAD ONE OR TWO (OR MANY) BOOKS PUBLISHED, continue to be modest and gracious, especially with others less fortunate than yourself. I was a professional actress for a few years, and even during this brief period, I found that the really talented people were the kindest, the least self-satisfied, vain or condescending and the most courteous. Their behavior offstage was almost a test of greatness. Go you and do likewise.

5 · A Few Case Histories

ONE. TWO. THREE. GO.

Every would-be author asks, "How do you get started?"
I always answer, "There is no magic formula. You work
and work. You keep sending your stories or books to publishers. If you get a chance, take a course in writing at a
good summer school or college. If you have a spark, some
one will see it . . . eventually."

I do think that is true. The capacity to write or the lack
of capacity to write is quite obvious. Any editor worth his
salt will encourage the first and discourage the second. However, editorial tastes differ, as do circumstance and environment. So, perhaps the most helpful thing I can do is to give
two different examples of, "How do you get started?" The
first instance shows how a fine author started on a long
career. The second shows the start and finish of an author
who shot her first and last bolt at the same time and it was
a good one. The gamut of what can happen runs anywhere
between these two extremes.

One late afternoon I stopped at a school in Boston to pick up my first-born. The headmistress, on seeing me, came brandishing what was obviously a manuscript, a long one. This often happens. Just as my husband and I never took a trip without his being called on unexpectedly to see a patient, so do I find almost every one has a manuscript of a children's book. It may be the gas station owner, the nurse who tends you in the hospital, or the man in the next room (at the hospital!).

In this case it was a teacher, who had written such a wonderful version of the Greek myths that the school had had it mimeographed each year for the class studying Greek and Roman society. If it was that good, might it not possibly make a real book? I said yes it might, because one does not argue with one's daughter's headmistress; but the prospect of reading another version of the Greek myths did not fill me with joy at the moment. However, read it I did, and every tale made me like it better. The next day I found out in the library that there were seven other versions of Greek myths, but, on investigation, none was any better or even as good as the mimeographed manuscript I had in my hand. In such a way did I meet Olivia Coolidge. I am sure that she would inevitably have become the great interpreter of history of whom we are so proud, but anyway that is an example of one author's start.

The case of May Heath is quite different. Her book, *Iowa Hannah* — the story of the pioneer trek by her grandfather and grandmother from southern Illinois to Iowa in 1853 — came in to the Junior Reviewers Manuscript Testing Service in 1955.* It lacked organization and had a "story" frame-

* See page 6 for an explanation of this service.

work (the grandmother telling the events) which made it sound awkward and old-fashioned. In spite of all this, though, there was a light shining through it, dimly at this time because of the above mentioned difficulties, but a light just the same. . . . A note accompanying the manuscript stated that four or five publishers had turned it down, which was not surprising. Could the Manuscript Service help?

A report was sent back to Mrs. Heath with advice on revision, and in about six months the manuscript came back again. It was improved to the point where it was thought an editor might want to have further revision done according to his own wishes, so it was sent to one publisher after another for four years. Five companies turned it down without the slightest sign of interest.

At this point I recommended that it be read by some of the Junior Reviewers — a staff of children of assorted ages who were kept for this purpose. Maybe they could point out what was wrong. At least they could tell if the book had appeal for children.

A report was received from the Ridington family in Westminster, Maryland, saying in part:

> The thing that seemed to impress the children was the simplicity of the story, the fact that it was not made exciting by Indian massacres and the usual pioneer stuff, but rather by everyday details of a sort of life that interested them because it was so different from ours. It has a flavor of its own. Obviously it is not polished and perfect; perhaps that is what makes it ring so true.

Ah, the light was still there — strong enough for others to see, at least some others.

At that point I had joined Hastings House as editor and

decided I would find out what I could do about making the manuscript publishable. So I wrote Mrs. Heath my thoughts and a wonderful correspondence began. It turned out my author was 80; the episodes in the book had really happened. It was actually the story of the founding of Waterloo, Iowa — and May Heath. Through her writing and her letters came the light that I have mentioned, that of a fine, almost noble woman.

The book was published in March, 1961 and Mrs. Heath died a month later. Her son, Judge George C. Heath of the District Court of Iowa, wrote, "I regret that Mother never had the opportunity of meeting you as she appreciated so much your very valuable assistance." I was the one to be grateful; not Mrs. Heath. It was a great source of satisfaction to me to have known her and to have published her book.

TO CUT OR NOT TO CUT

I was the editor for a series on important historical figures that involved in each case a famous writer and a famous illustrator. The format for the book was set: a certain page size, a certain text area, so many pages of text, so many pages of pictures.

The authors were drawn from the adult field because of their fame or erudition on a given subject and the one in this case was particularly renowned both for his scholarship and his writing ability. He was an internationally known figure and lectured all over the world so it was hard to pin him down on revision. At least that is what I found out when his text came in and turned out to be a third too long and another third too complicated for our format and age-group plans. I wrote him a diplomatic letter, which was returned for a better address. I telephoned, cabled and wired. Nothing happened. Finally I saw his name on the passenger list of an Atlantic liner and sent one of our representatives to meet him. They missed. After a year, one of my letters finally entered his orbit, and he answered that he would not rewrite, he would not cut, he was satisfied with the text as it was.

That made him a committee of one. I was told to persuade him to do as we wanted, but it is hard to persuade someone you cannot get hold of by any means known to man. Finally, I suggested to the president of our company that we proceed no matter what happened. I would cut the text a third; in places I would rewrite the text; I would probably ruin it, but at least we would be fulfilling our obligations (the orders were mounting to the twenty-thousand mark) and if the author objected, the officers could truthfully blame me. So we did. Or I did. The book came out. Authors' copies were sent to the original address, and to my utter amazement I received a letter from the author thanking me for a handsome book and commenting that he was so glad it had not been necessary to cut or alter his text.

AN EXAMPLE OF STRENUOUS HISTORICAL RESEARCH

Genevieve Foster has been mentioned as one of the greatest historians for children. I had the opportunity to hear her describe something of her method in this regard.

One of the unique qualities of her series: *George Washington's World, Abraham Lincoln's World,* and others, is that the reader is able to see not only what is happening in the country of the main character but all over the world.

Furthermore, this cross-section is revealed for all aspects of culture such as sculpture, drama, painting and literature as well as wars and explorations.

To accomplish this, Mrs. Foster has to do research on practically every facet of life on every continent in the century with which she is dealing. This could result in a colossal jumble of facts, but instead this wise and clever author has devised a series of world charts, each of which is devoted to what is going on in that certain subject in, say, London, Philadelphia, Paris, Rome, Athens, Peking, Calcutta, and so on — if those cities were in existence in the century in which she was working.

This is a remarkable achievement for any century, but when you consider that Mrs. Foster's research — beginning with Julius Caesar and continuing with Christopher Columbus, John Smith, George Washington, Benjamin Franklin, Thomas Jefferson and Abraham Lincoln — spans two thousand years of world history, it is a stupendous one. Realizing this, her publisher, Scribners, is proudly bringing out her charts as a separate volume (her editor, Janet Loranger, calls it a "guide to horizontal history") so that they may help the reader. They will indeed be a welcome aid to children and teachers, and also an inspiration for other authors in the field of history.

PART II

ILLUSTRATION
AND
PRODUCTION

1 · Illustration, a General View

Many volumes have been written on this subject, and three especially good ones deal solely with the juvenile field — namely, *Illustrators of Children's Books,* 1744-1945, compiled by Bertha E. Mahoney, Louise Latimer and Beulah Folmsbee; a supplement to this, *Illustrators of Children's Books,* 1946-1956, compiled by Ruth Viguers, Marcia Dalphin and Bertha Mahoney Miller (*Horn Book*);* and *The Illustration of Children's Books* by Henry Pitz (Watson-Guptill). The first two books deal with the history and trends of juvenile illustration plus biographies of the artists mentioned, and the volume by Mr. Pitz (I also recommend his *The Practice of Illustration*) gives the background, growth and technical methods of the artist who occupies himself with this branch of publishing. Other books on this subject are listed in the bibliography. There is also a series of articles in *The Horn Book* by artists well known in children's books

* A third book in this *Horn Book* series is in preparation.

that tells about various techniques used in illustration. I have cited some of these later on in this section. And there are quantities of separate articles in other magazines by men and women well known in this field.

In fact, so much has been written in magazines and books and said in speeches that this segment of my book will not attempt to deal with the history or theory of past or present illustration but will concern itself with the changes that have taken place in this type of art and will try to show what is in demand now and, in a small way, how to execute and sell it.

Almost ever since books have been written, they have been illustrated. Some of the old decorations — for instance, the illuminations of the medieval parchment scrolls — are very beautiful. But not until books were printed from movable type and plates did artists become known as illustrators per se. And it has only been in the last sixty years that the illustration of children's books in America has been recognized as an art in itself.

The growth of this art parallels the growth of children's books. In 1893 the first room devoted entirely to children was opened in a public library. Pioneer work of all kinds to promote children's reading was done in different parts of the country, but a leading figure responsible for much progress, both practically and esthetically, was Anne Carroll Moore, at one time children's librarian in the Pratt Free Library in Brooklyn and later superintendent of children's work in the New York Public Library. Her impact on children's books as a whole and the illustration of them was considerable.

Many of the first books for children were written in England by authors who are still beloved: Lewis Carroll, Robert Louis Stevenson, Rudyard Kipling, Kenneth Grahame and

Beatrix Potter, to name a few. But America soon started its own juvenile hall of fame with Joel Chandler Harris, Frances Hodgson Burnett, Kate Douglas Wiggin, Mark Twain, Thomas Bailey Aldrich and Louisa May Alcott.

The excellence of the volumes by these authors did much to interest artists in illustrating children's books. The great artists in both England and the United States realized that this was an outlet worthy of their talent, and so we have the beautiful work of Randolph Caldecott, Kate Greenaway and Walter Crane, followed in the twentieth century by Reginald Birch, Edwin Abbey, Arthur Rackham, Beatrix Potter, Ernest Shepard, A. B. Frost, Frederic Remington, Jessie Wilcox Smith, Howard Pyle and his pupil, N. C. Wyeth.

In those days, an artist was much more limited in his use of color than present-day artists are. Illustrations in color could not appear on a text page. They had to be printed separately on heavier, coated stock, and were usually "tipped in" by hand or wrapped around one or more signatures when the book was being prepared for binding. It was not until after World War I that color in offset lithography was developed to the point of practical, general use in books.

This step in manufacturing was a significant one in the history of children's book illustration, since both text and colored illustrations could appear on the same page without having to be printed on coated stock. Also, other techniques besides line drawing could be used. Furthermore, it made the illustrations much more an intrinsic part of the volumes, and for that reason there began to be more interest in the appearance of the book as a whole. Design and typography came into prominence, and the interrelation of drawings and type has been considered important ever since.

There also came a change in the kind of illustration in

children's books. Our ties with England and with English illustration and bookmaking were not broken, but they became only one part of the art picture.

Fascinating new names of illustrators appeared on the title pages: Wanda Gag, Boris Artzybasheff, Feodor Rojankovsky, Gustav Tenggren and Ingri and Edgar Parin d'Aulaire, for example. The richness and vigor of foreign lands began to show up on book pages with wonderful effect. A varied and original use of many different media came into being, making our children's books on the whole the most beautiful in the world.

Of course, many of these artists worked and are still working in other fields of publishing. They do illustrating for adult books, magazines or for advertising agencies, sometimes all three. Even a stage designer has entered the field. But most of them love to do children's books, even though the monetary gain may be less per unit of work turned out and time consumed.

There are two reasons for this: *the human one* — the majority of children's books are lots more fun to illustrate than an advertisement for a bar of soap or a glass of beer. Most artists love children and are generous in contributing to their pleasure, and they themselves realize that they get a spiritual reward and satisfaction from so doing. *The material one* — if royalties are allotted an artist, even though they be small, they are apt to mount up handsomely over the years, because good juveniles are long-lived. Furthermore, even without royalties, it is excellent publicity for an artist's name to appear on a book published by a reputable company. One job leads to another, and though $300 to $500 may not seem much for doing the complete art work for a book, ten such jobs might come as a result, some paying royalties.

Nowadays there is considerable emphasis on fine illustration — for instance, the Caldecott Medal, named for Randolph Caldecott, one of the earliest English illustrators of children's books, is awarded every year to "the most distinguished picture book of the year." You may wish to refer to Part III Chapter 5, "Awards," for more details about that prize. Another honor now open to children's illustrators and designers is that of inclusion in "The Fifty Books of the Year," an annual selection by the American Institute of Graphic Arts. And every two years the AIGA has a Children's Book Show, which includes about one hundred books chosen for artistic and typographic merit.

Partly because of the rising interest in literary fare for children and the money in it and partly because of the high standards of the editors, art directors and designers in children's book publishing, the beauty of juvenile publications has reached a high peak in this country. Also, since World War II, exciting and beautiful books are being produced in Europe and some countries in the Far East.

Most art directors and many editors have an extensive art background and training and have become experts in selecting, guiding and planning the reproduction of art of all kinds. Their insistence on quality in art work and printing has been a determining factor in the past and present of children's books in this country and abroad.

Another contributing element has been the high standards of the artists themselves. The outstanding men and women in the field of illustration expend much time and interest in studying and experimenting with the different processes of art reproduction. Lynd Ward, for example, who is one of the great leaders in both the juvenile and the adult art field, with his work consistently inspiring and beautifully executed, took the time to go to the Academy of Graphic Art in Leipzig. Here he learned to work on lithographic stone with beautiful effect.* Other topflight artists who have given more to children's books than the art work in the many volumes they have illustrated are Robert McCloskey, Kate Seredy, James Daugherty, Clare Newberry, Warren Chappell, Garth Williams, Maurice Sendak, Marcia Brown, Roger Duvoisin, Leonard Weisgard, Barbara Cooney and many others.

I could name a hundred, so rich has this genre of art become. Instead, let me give some examples of beautifully illustrated books that may help a beginning artist to see what kind of thing does well in this field. And by "does well" I mean it has both high artistic quality and appeal for children.

The term *appeal* must not be confused with the sugary presentations one used to see (and sometimes still does) in magazines or in chain-store merchandise. By appeal I mean that which conforms to the most exacting principles of adult art but which by its conception and rendering is especially adapted and interesting to children. Furthermore, in illustration as in writing, children deserve and appreciate the best. There is none of the "that's-good-enough-for-the-kiddies" feeling in the books I am going to mention. Instead these artists are convinced, I am sure, that they are working for the most important audience in the world — the chil-

* See *The Mexican Story* by May McNeer (Farrar, Straus).

dren — and are guiding them toward a lifetime of appreciation of good art.

I have read the following books with my own or other people's children and recommend them all for diverse reasons. Just as there are many different kinds of good writing, so are there types of good illustration. One should be able to enjoy them all. My list could be much longer, because there are now so many volumes from which to select; but, as I said, you will find plenty of other books on the subject and many lists by greater authorities than I am. Also, you should do your own research in the children's room of your nearest public or school library. Please note that in the following list all ages are approximate.

Here are qualities to consider if you are illustrating books for:

VERY LITTLE CHILDREN, AGES 1 TO 3

Simplicity of concept, line and color is necessary for this baby age. There should be no exaggeration or emotional conflict. Pictorial content should be uncluttered in detail and easy to grasp at a glance.

Nothing But Cats and *All About Dogs,* written and illustrated by Grace Skaar (Scott), are good examples of modern drawing, embodying two essentials for the age: simplicity and clarity.

Two other Scott publications that are surefire are *Everybody Eats* by Mary McBurney Green with pictures by Edward Glannon and *Mr. Tall and Mr. Small* by Barbara Brenner, illustrated by Tomi Ungerer.

The *Jean Marie* books by Françoise (Scribners) are gay and inviting and in excellent taste.

The Little Auto and others by Lois Lenski (Walck) are effective in two colors, and their strong, firm use of black halftone is noteworthy. They also exemplify appeal for the youngest reader, especially small boys.

A Tale of Tails by Elizabeth MacPherson, illustrated by Garth Williams (Golden) has large, bold pictures, a lavish use of color and simple rhymed text.

Whistle For Willie by Ezra Jack Keats (Viking), shows a different and dramatic technique. *Little Bear's Visit* done by Maurice Sendak (Harper) and the other *Little Bear* titles are hard to resist for many reasons: humor, originality, just plain fun.

Where Have You Been? by Margaret Wise Brown (Hastings House), illustrated by Barbara Cooney, is delightfully fresh and simple and completely satisfying in two colors.

The Runaway Bunny also by Margaret Wise Brown and illustrated by Clement Hurd (Harper), has a wonderfully soothing tone to it, a very nice quality for this age.

THE REAL PICTURE BOOK AGE, 3 TO 6

More varied fare is possible here, but again clarity, simplicity and directness are desirable. Freshness and individuality are nice extras. Color can be used with flair and fury, but often a quiet contrast is as effective as the bright pinks and oranges so in style at the moment.

Nothing At All by Wanda Gag (Coward-McCann), and the other Gag books are perfectly attuned to the little child's sense of the ridiculous. They are also models of design and distinguished line work.

Mr. T. W. Anthony Woo by Marie Hall Ets (Viking), is

an impressive example of how satisfying black and white can be for this age. The rhythm of the text is cleverly matched by the rhythm of the drawings. Her other books, like *Little Old Automobile*, are great fare for youngest gentlemen readers.

The *Babar* books by Jean de Brunhoff (Random) combine marvelously funny stories and pictures that have become classics for this age. Note the attention to detail in all of them. They are also good for quite tiny children.

Little Toot and *Hercules* by Hardie Gramatky (Putnam) are especially dramatic in their use of color. Mr. Gramatky is one of several former animators in the Walt Disney Studios who have since worked out their own style and technique with excellent results.

Blueberries For Sal, Make Way For Ducklings, One Morning In Maine by Robert McCloskey (Viking) are, to my mind, almost perfect picture books. They combine originality with distinction in execution. They achieve their compelling effects with only one color and are realism lifted to great heights by an artist who obviously loves life and children.

Little Tim and the Brave Sea Captain (Walck), is the work of an English artist, Edward Ardizzone. Like all his books, it is characterized by a free, flavorful touch that would make it stand out in any group.

McElligot's Pool and others by Dr. Seuss (Random House), are some of the most beloved of all picture books. An extravagant originality and humor characterize them along with a gaudy but somehow delightful use of color. I'm not sure that Dr. Seuss's latest books are quite as successful. Sometimes too much of a good thing *is* too much.

Mike Mulligan and *The Little House* by Virginia Lee Burton (Houghton) are two immortal books that are worthy of ending this section with flying colors. Miss Burton's work has exquisite design and tonal patterns plus a vigor that children love. They are also fine for the next age group.

AGES 6 TO 9

This group is beginning to read, but still the children love to have many books read aloud to them. They require pictures, preferably on every page, to keep up their interest. Color is not an essential but is enjoyed.

Dash and Dart (Viking), *The Apple and the Arrow* (Houghton) and other fine books by Mary and Conrad Buff show the exquisite halftones and glowing full-color pages that make Conrad Buff's art always vigorous and memorable. A painter of the old school, he is known for carefully prepared work, which provides an interesting contrast with that of more modern illustrators.

Poo Poo and the Dragons by C. S. Forester, illustrated by Robert Lawson (Little Brown), and others both illustrated and written by Mr. Lawson, like *Rabbit Hill* (Viking), combine skillful drawing with a delicious sense of humor.

Benjamin Franklin and others by Ingri and Edgar Parin d'Aulaire (Doubleday), are outstanding contributions to juvenile illustration and books in general. Their beautiful lithographs were executed directly on stone, and the reproductions have the quality of original paintings.

Daniel Boone by Esther Averill is illustrated by Feodor Rojankovsky (Harper). This artist is famous for many handsome books, but none is more striking than this, comparatively speaking. When it first appeared in Paris in 1931 it marked a step forward in the clear, positive use of color and the successful marriage of text and illustration in children's books.

Little Leo and others by Leo Politi (Scribners), are light-hearted, brightly colored books, echoing Mr. Politi's Italian background and charm.

The Story of Serapina by Anne H. White, illustrated by Tony Palazzo (Viking) shows how well Mr. Palazzo can match his mood of illustration to someone else's story. His own books, like *Charley the Horse,* are full of artistic gusto and individuality.

Many Moons by James Thurber, illustrated by Louis Slobodkin (Harcourt), is fantasy beautifully interpreted by a most responsive artist.

Joan Balfour Payne is a wonder at writing and illustrating for this age. There is no limit to her imaginative ability to draw, which is happily coupled with an inborn storytelling sense and striking command of language. Her drawings in *The Leprechaun of Bayou Luce, General Billycock's Pigs,* and *Pangur Ban* (Hastings), show the impact of a unique talent for halftone illustrations and a wonderful capacity to use it briskly and humorously.

THE 9 TO 12 AGE

Illustration for this group has been confined for years to indifferent or just adequate line drawings, making the exceptions very welcome indeed. These "middle-aged" children do not need as much illustration as when they were younger, but they still welcome and appreciate quality. There is a new feeling of freedom in their books, and we can look forward to the use of quite modern techniques as well as the old standbys.

The Good Master and others by Kate Seredy (Viking) show the deep sensitivity of the artist. She has become justly famous for her exquisite halftones. Her art is quite liberal but very lovely.

Minn of the Mississippi, Seabird and others by Holling Clancy Holling (Houghton), have become classics for this age group. Note the page makeup in his books. The close interrelation of text and pictures is nowhere better shown than in Mr. Holling's books. Part scientist, part author, part painter, he combines all his skills in these outstanding volumes.

George Washington's World and others by Genevieve Foster (Scribners), exemplify expert authorship and creative illustration plus good bookmaking. Like Mr. Holling, Mrs. Foster has much to say, and much to say it with. Her dynamic presentation of history owes its success partly to her striking art work.

Daughter of the Mountains by Louise Rankin, illustrated by Kurt Wiese (Viking) is another example of Mr. Wiese's talents and versatility. This is a beautiful volume.

Twenty-One Balloons by William Pène du Bois (Viking), was an epoch-making piece of work when published in 1947, largely because of the irresistible humor and absurdity in both text and pictures. It is very individual in appearance. He has influenced many present-day artists.

Garth Williams' drawings for E. B. White's *Stuart Little* and *Charlotte's Web* (Harper) are small, delicate line drawings that just could not be better. Critics might say these books are for younger children, but really they are for all ages and deserve special mention because they exemplify the continued success of pen and ink as a medium. (Many modern artists would not be caught dead with a pen.)

King of the Wind and others by Marguerite Henry, illustrated by Wesley Dennis (Rand) should be an inspiration to would-be painters of horses. Mr. Dennis, an expert on equine anatomy, could create a mood of drama and beauty and hold it, which made him a valuable partner for an author. He told an amusing story about his desire to study the bone structure of a horse. He bought a very old animal that had just been killed for humanitarian reasons. He expected the buzzards to pick the bones clean, after which he could study them. Instead an unusually cold night came along and froze his prospective source of information, and when it thawed weeks later, the neighbors insisted it be buried! . . . Ah well, it was a good try.

There has been the beginning of a breakthrough toward the use of unconventional contemporary art work in books for this and other ages. Maurice Sendak's drawings for *Where the Wild Things Are* (Harper) are dramatic, true to the subject and yet free and powerful. *Fly Away Goose,* written and illustrated by Fen Lassell (Houghton) and Margaret Green's *Big Book of Wild Animals* with Jan Grabianski's drawings (Watts) are also worth studying in this regard.

Miroslav Sasek's *This Is Edinburgh* (Macmillan) and the others in his picture-travel series are delightfully alive and new in their interpretation of scenes and yet give a true impression of the cities visited.

THE HIGH SCHOOL AGE

The aesthetic standards for books for this age are not as high as they should be. Perhaps that is because these older boys and girls are supposed not to like pictures with their literature or perhaps they are being prepared for the relatively unillustrated and often undesigned realm of adult reading. The following books are outstanding in the pains that were taken to make them look purposeful as well as handsome.

Big Tiger and Christian by Fritz Muhlenberg, illustrated by Rafaello Busoni (Pantheon), is an unusual-looking book.

The Eagle of the Ninth by Rosemary Sutcliffe, illustrated by C. Walter Hodges (Oxford), has a traditional flavor. Her *The Mark of the Horse Lord* has no pictures but is a simple, handsome example of type design like that in an adult book.

Of Courage Undaunted by James Daugherty (Viking), gives a real lift to the spirited account of the Lewis and Clark expedition.

Americans Before Columbus by Elizabeth Baity, illustrated by C. B. Falls (Viking), has both beauty and exotic richness that fit in perfectly with Miss Baity's impressive portrayal of this continent in its earliest inhabited days.

The Legend of Sleepy Hollow by Washington Irving, illustrated by Leonard Everett Fisher (Watts), is a superb job of projecting an author for this age group via arresting design and drawing.

BOOKS ON SPECIAL SUBJECTS

The day of drab cookbooks, gloomy science books, and forbidding grammars has gone. Some of the best artists have been challenged by nonfiction subject matter that yesterday would have been turned out prosaically.

Construction Ahead by Henry Billings (Viking), shows how attractive a book on roadmaking can be.

A Book of the Year by Fritz Peters, illustrated by Ilonka Karasz (Harper), is about the changing seasons — a lovely piece of illustration.

All Around You by Jeanne Bendick (McGraw-Hill), is modern and lively-looking. It gives the simple scientific facts within a format that is right for a small child.

Frontier Living, written and illustrated by Edwin Tunis (World), is a volume as full of handsome drawings as it is of facts about our frontier life. Anthony Ravielli's drawings are few but perfect for the text of Katherine Shippen's *Men, Microscopes and Living Things* (Viking), as are those of C. Walter Hodges for his *Shakespeare's Theatre* (Coward). And if photographs can be included as a form of art and illustrations — as, of course, they are — those of Ross Hutchins for *The Amazing Seeds* (Dodd) should be given special mention.

In other words, intelligence, thought, time and talent are now put into all phases of illustration, whether it be for use by the general public or by schools and colleges. The smallest book or the biggest project is now worthy of the artist's fullest capabilities and knowhow. Truly we are in a creative era — one that gives full scope and full credit to the illustrator.

Walter Lorraine, inspired designer of Houghton Mifflin juveniles and a very capable artist in his own right, said in *The Horn Book* of December 1963, "There is, happily, much art in illustration today. It is art that serves well the basic function of illustration yet transcends that function. It stems from the integrity and efforts of many individual creative artists."

The above sketch by Andrew Wyeth was made at the age of 13 for my uncle, Joseph Hawley Chapin, art director of Scribners. A frequent visitor at the Wyeth house, my uncle became friends with "Andy." See also page 114.

2 · The A.B.C. of Modern Illustration

Everyone admits the importance of the illustrator in the field of children's books, but few readers or even authors know much about him. And in turn he often seems similarly uninformed about the field and its practical requirements.

For an editor to put his or her requirements for illustration into so many words is almost impossible, because requirements differ with every book. Also editors vary somewhat in their demands. However, for the sake of the hordes of students that every year pour out of art schools and into publishers' offices in search of work, an attempt will be made to outline in a general way the necessary qualifications for illustrating children's books.

Before doing so, though, I would like to have all artists who seek to be illustrators keep in mind what Marcia Brown said in her Caldecott Award acceptance speech June 19, 1962:

> Painters today have unlimited freedom in the choice of techniques, and an almost fetishistic interest in sensuous ma-

terials. But no matter how fascinated an illustrator is by techniques, illustration must still be that — a servant charged with elucidating the idea of the book. It involves a very different mental process from painting and arises from a different level of sensibility.

The rest of this speech is well worth reading, especially the part about the growing commercialism of children's books. See *The Horn Book,* August 1962.

Here are some other points of view on the subject:

Maurice Sendak, in the Sunday *New York Herald Tribune Book Week,* Fall Children's Issue of November 1, 1964, says in an article entitled, "The Shape of Music,"

> Vivify, quicken and vitalize — of these three synonyms, *quicken,* I think, best suggests the genuine spirit of animation, the breathing to life, the surging swing into action, that I consider an essential quality in pictures for children's books. To *quicken* means, for the illustrator, the task first of deeply comprehending the nature of his text and then of giving life to that comprehension in his own medium, the picture.

Incidentally, there is a very interesting "profile" on Mr. Sendak and his life and personal beliefs as an illustrator in *The New Yorker* for January 22, 1966.

Another good article is Roger Duvoisin's "Children's Book Illustration: The Pleasures and Problems" in *Top Of The News* for November 1965.

Both these gentlemen, Sendak and Duvoisin, are Caldecott Medal winners and are very prominent in the children's book field right now.

Fritz Eichenberg in the same 1964 *Herald-Tribune* Fall *Book Week* issue states his high ideals when he says,

. . . A book has an obligation to build taste, to cultivate a sense of lasting values. It should be a work of art and beauty, created with love and produced with care. It should convey a sense of quality, inside and out, through the harmonious blend of art work and attractive colors, through the use of good print on the right paper. What an object lesson in esthetics this could be to a child, painlessly and easily absorbed by him.

So, to start with, I would say the artist would have to be *genuinely enthusiastic about illustration as a form of art*. It is one of the great arts — different from other forms of painting and drawing because it is for a purpose and because the finished illustration is really only a working drawing. The final *printed* picture is the work of art and the proof of the illustrator's pudding. My chosen artist knows this and is deeply interested in this art form, the message it conveys to the public and especially the enjoyment it gives to children. More and more artists are drawn into the children's field by this genuine enthusiasm. So they pass the first test.

The second requirement is *inspiration*. That is more difficult to define because of its intangibility. Some critics see individual distinction in the work of one man, while some see it in another. On the whole, however, most present-day editors have a sound idea of what is good art and what is bad, and they will settle only for the best. As in writing, the best is rather obvious. A man has something to give in his painting or he does not, just as with authors. Of course, there are as many different ways of giving — i.e., styles — as there are artists. But they are not too important. The distinction or inspiration is there — call it *genius* in great artists; *talent* in those not yet fully developed. As a quality, distinction is hard to describe, being a combination of innate ability, plus imagination, individuality and that spark that has been called divine.

Men like Beni Montresor have the right idea. Here is a paragraph from his Caldecott Award acceptance speech of July 6, 1965:

> We have to be open to the marvelous adventure of books made of images, because it has already existed for a long time, and because now people are searching for it more than ever. At this time only one thing should occupy us: to work for images of the highest quality — full, rich and provocative images that carry the imagination to new heights that will be launching pads for new and always more daring discoveries.*

So much for that intangible: *inspiration*. Glance at the list of books ending the last chapter. Their artists were all inspired — in many different ways and in many different moods. That is one reason why illustration is so fascinating.

The third requirement is *training*. The very variety of illustration makes this important. Artists use all kinds of techniques, but whatever they use, the result must be art work suitable for reproduction in a book.

An editor usually presupposes an art school training. The day of the self-trained artist or one who has learned his craft as apprentice to a master is largely over. Especially is the day over when the work of an untrained amateur, no matter how sweet and pretty it is, can be considered for juvenile illustration. Many beginning authors unwisely obtain the services of such people because they live close by or are friends, and send in their amateurish effort with the manuscripts. This

---

* *The Horn Book*, August 1965. The prize-winning book was *May I Bring a Friend?* by Beatrice de Regnier (Atheneum).

should not be done. Unless a manuscript is written and illustrated by the same person, an editor almost always selects the artist. I have spoken of this elsewhere but am mentioning it here again because poor art cannot help but make a reader feel that the manuscript itself will be of the same quality.

Present-day art schools vary greatly in the training they give artists. As with other educational institutions, their worth is measured by the knowledge, experience and teaching talents of their faculty. However, even those with a first-rate staff have been slow to awaken to the possibilities of creative work in illustration and are just becoming aware of the need for practical training of their students for a career in this field.

All illustrators should be familiar with or have taken courses in the fundamentals of design, drawing and color. Design usually includes the theory and practice of composition, perspective, balance and so on. Drawing concerns both techniques and their application, with emphasis on still life and life drawing, landscapes and portraits. The use of pencil, pen, crayon, watercolor, tempera, casein or oil paints is taught here, and probably the instructors in these media determine to some extent whether a man will belong to the "natural" school or whether he will depart from realism and go into a freer style. Much of the illustration in present-day children's books is a good example of a free interpretation of the text. Some is inept, but some is very exciting. There is a new look to books these days.

Color, its theory and application, is taught all art students, although its usage can be as diverse as human nature. Color mixture is extremely important for a young illustrator to know. If he is imaginative and able, he can achieve a rainbow of different shades from the use of two or three colors and black.

A definite *technical training* is called for in the illustration of children's books, just as it is in adult books.* There is more varied use of color now and more opportunity for picture sequences — which is fun but again demanding. Here are some of the technical essentials that an editor would expect from an illustrator.

I. A KNOWLEDGE OF THE MOST COMMON METHODS OF PRINTING, such as LETTERPRESS and OFFSET LITHOGRAPHY (see Chapter 5) and how to prepare artwork specifically for them.

A. LINE DRAWING (Letterpress or offset): how to execute pictures in pen and ink (using black India ink), scratchboard†, air brush, etc., that will reproduce clearly.

Some use is made today of Bendays (screened sheets that can be applied to parts of a drawing to obtain a halftone effect), and an artist should know how to select and apply them. Collage is a new and interesting medium.

B. HALFTONE (Offset): how to use wash, tempera, casein paints and other material.

Oil and watercolor are not used a great deal by modern illustrators, because they are difficult and expensive to repro-

---

*A most valuable book on this subject has just come to my attention: *Preparing Art for Printing* by Barnard Stone and Arthur Eckstein (Rheinhold). It discusses among many things the printing processes, typography, one-color and multi-color printing, necessary tools and materials, and the steps in preparing copy for the camera. It is well illustrated.

† Barbara Cooney's article *"Scratchboard Illustration," The Horn Book,* April 1964, gives a detailed and very useful view of this method.

duce. A halftone can be printed by letterpress, but the screen required is so coarse that the effect is undesirable.

II. A KNOWLEDGE OF REDUCTION AND ITS EFFECTS. Most editors do not care whether drawings are executed in actual size or for one-third reduction, but it is the exception for an artist to ask for more reduction than that. For example, it is unwise to expect huge canvases to reduce to a 9″ by 6″ page size without tone loss, sacrifice of detail and thickening of line. No matter what reduction is desired, it is vital that each drawing be reduced the same amount.

III. AN ABILITY TO SEPARATE COLORS BY ONE OF THE METHODS MOST WIDELY USED. Most books that contain any color are printed in two, three or four colors. By overprinting various percentages of the four "process colors" — black, red, blue and yellow — almost every color in the palette can be obtained. A wide range of tone can also be achieved with two or three. For evidence, glance through a printer's ink book where these percentages are shown in combination.

When you have become a famous artist, for instance like Andrew Wyeth, son of the renowned N. C. Wyeth, you might be invited to illustrate a book in "full color" —*
meaning that you can use pretty much any medium you wish and any combination of colors, and the printer's camera will separate the colors with filters. The publisher is willing to pay the high cost of this method, because your name on a book sells so many extra copies that he can afford to do so. This expense may be decreased in the future, because there has been a breakthrough in the direct repro-

* As mentioned before, Andrew Wyeth was a friend of my uncle's as a boy. The previous drawing and the following letter and sketch point out that artists often show their talents early and should be encouraged by parents and friends to obtain professional help and training.

Chadds Ford Pa
March 27, 1931.

Dear friend Porthos
I received "The Three Musketeers" I think it is great.
I like the illustrations especially the one in which you are presenting the book to me I don't know how to thank you for such a book,
I am sending you a drawing I did. I hope you like it.
You must come down soon I will have more pictures to show you.
Your old friend
D'artagnan
(andy)

ONE FOR ALL AND
ALL FOR ONE

duction of color with the introduction of new electronic machines, the Klischograph and the color scanner.*

* The Klischograph I saw in action in Edinburgh, Scotland, and the Time and Life color scanner in New York. The first makes a plastic plate direct from the original color copy (which might be watercolor, tempera, or oil) while the second requires that this color copy be reduced to transparencies, and hence is used mostly with color photographs. When I wrote the first version of this book I described these processes in detail but since then it has become obvious that both machines need refinements before they can be used to any great extent for children's picture books. Perhaps in the next edition of this volume I can say that they have revolutionized color printing as I hope eventually they will.

As a beginner, however, and probably for years after you have passed that stage, you will be called on to make color separations so that your work may be reproduced more inexpensively. You also have more control of it. Here are various methods:

A. *ACETATE SEPARATIONS*

These are made by executing a black "key" drawing, usually in ink or dry brush on heavy white cardboard. Over this, sheets of acetate (a cellophanelike substance, smooth and shiny on one side and rough with a slight "tooth" on the other) are placed with each color area indicated in *black* — a sheet for each color.

Black overlays are preferred by engravers, because they reproduce best under the camera. In the actual press run colored inks are employed in these areas according to the artist's specifications. Hence illustrators should take pains to supply accurate color swatches and thus avoid corrections or disappointment with the finished job. Color proving is expensive, time consuming and not always economically feasible. Incidentally, be sure your color swatches are done in a flat, even manner. It is most difficult to match watercolor or tempera swatches that may vary by several tones in the space of a square inch. Actually, when it is possible, the artist should be asked to select his colors from a printer's ink book and specify the exact number of the ink. Be sure that the swatch selected is printed on uncoated stock. The effect is quite different from that on coated stock (shiny paper); and ink books give both, since many magazines and advertising flyers are made of coated stock.

By the use of register marks these overlays are fitted accurately on the key drawing so that the final picture will be neat and satisfactory. These register marks are extremely important and should be drawn very carefully on each sheet as well as on the key drawing. A light table is useful in doing this. (See page 117.)

When plates are made from these acetates, "progressive" proofs may be pulled. These show progressively how the addition of each color adds to the total effect. By these proofs, also, it is possible to tell what plate is at fault if a particular proof differs from the desired effect.

The ability to make a neat, accurate set of acetate separations is a skill that editors prize. It often means that an artist can graduate from straight line drawing in books for older children to color work in picture books. It takes a professional knowledge of color mixing and overprinting — also time and patience — but it is a craft a young artist should master if he wants to illustrate children's books.

1. *DINOBASE SEPARATIONS*

Dinobase is a special kind of acetate* that eliminates camera work, because the artist is in a sense making the plates himself; and the drawing can be reproduced in line instead of halftone, at a great saving. These transparent sheets are exposed by direct contact with film plate in a vacuum frame. The resulting negatives record every minute element in the drawing with great fidelity. However, the drawings must be done *actual size,* as no camera is used. These sheets are equally good for key drawing and color overlays. They are expensive to buy, but the reproduction is excellent and a variety of effects ranging from soft halftone with many gradations to crisp line can be obtained with an ordinary pencil

* Word has just come that Dinobase is no longer available but another similar sheet will be shortly. Ask your art supplier.

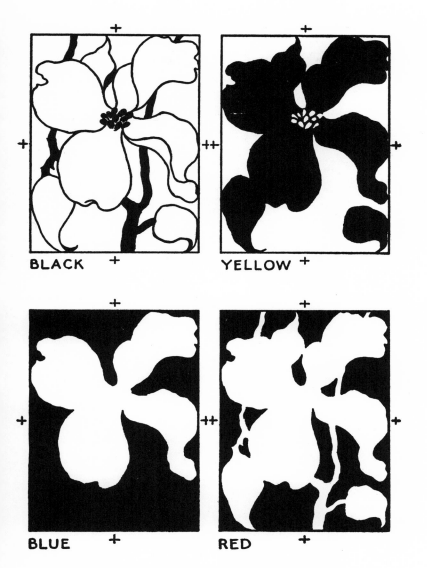

BLACK

YELLOW

BLUE

RED

Acetate separations for four-color reproduction.

Four-color separations by Antony Maitland from *A Proper Place for Chip* by Anne Molloy (Hastings).

10   RED

10   BLUE

or crayon. Genevieve Vaughan-Jackson, artist of the Hastings House *Preserve Our Wild Life* series, uses this method with great success. See *The North American Wolf* by Mary Adrian.

For the use of Dinobase for color overlays see *The Little Juggler* by Barbara Cooney and *A Proper Place For Chip* by Anne Molloy, illustrated by Antony Maitland (Hastings House), reproduced on the preceding two pages.

In *The Horn Book* for February 1966, Dahlov Ipcar describes how she combines Dinobase and watercolor paper for "elusive freshness." In her *The Calico Jungle* (Knopf) she started with collages made out of fabrics with little bright designs, and like many modern artists she likes "a fine sable-hair brush rather than a pen." But on Dinobase she uses "plain lead pencils for delicate lines and two kinds of wax pencils for shading."

Adrienne Adams gives an excellent idea of the separation process and the whole preparation of artwork in her article "Color Separation," *The Horn Book,* April 1965.

2. *BOURGES OR COLORON SHEETS*

The use of colored acetate sheets like these is common, because they are helpful in visualizing color effects in relation to the black key drawing and give a good indication how colors react to each other when overprinted. Often an artist is limited in the number of colors allotted to his job, and these sheets show him what he can do with what he is allowed.

Artists differ greatly in their likes and dislikes for these media. As editor I usually let the artist select his way of doing the art work as long as it is acceptable to the art director and economically feasible. Perhaps eventually with the help of electronic devices it will be possible to tell the artist to "just paint." Meanwhile we have to cut corners because of the high price of printing in this country and also (something that is not as well known as it might be) because camera work on full-color art is often far from true even though it costs a fortune.

B. *COLOR SEPARATIONS BY THE BLUEPRINT METHOD*

The execution of a black key plate is the first step in this method, also. One is made for each illustration in the book that is to contain color. This set of black-and-white drawings is sent to the lithographer who is going to print the book. He photographs it and sends three blueprints of each key plate back to the art director, who in turn gives them to the artist. On these prints, guided by the lines of the key plate, the artist indicates the color areas in black, usually with a wash effect in ink or tempera. There is a blueprint for each color on each page, so that when properly executed there are three prints for each picture, plus the black drawing, which has remained at the printer's awaiting the return of the blueprints. From these prints a plate is made for each color just as from the acetate separations.

This method has one disadvantage over the acetate method. The blueprints are apt to shrink a little, and so the plates sometimes are not absolutely accurate. This is a real difficulty if the artist has planned his color areas to "trap" (close up tight to a line). It is a feasible method for artists whose work is more free.

There are several commercial processes available that facilitate the separation of color and lessen its expense — for instance, patented masking sheets. I have had artists use each of these processes in picture books with a degree of success, and I generally leave it up to the illustrator to select the one he likes best.

IV. COMPLETE, DETAILED KNOWLEDGE OF THE MANU-SCRIPT ITSELF. Barbara Cooney in her article, "An Illustrator's Viewpoint," *The Horn Book,* February 1961, says, "The first duty of a good illustrator is to know his manuscript cold. No illustrator worth his salt makes factual mistakes, substitutes blonde hair for brown or shirts for jackets."

V. A CAREFUL, EFFECTIVE AND EVEN ARRANGEMENT OF PICTURES throughout the book. They should not occur immediately after a chapter opening, because they would look bad there; and they should not be clumped together, leaving long sections of the book without any illustration.

VI. THERE SHOULD BE A NICE FLOW OF THOUGHT THROUGH THEM, completely in keeping with the tone of the book, never stopping its onward progress or distracting from it.

VII. A BUSINESSLIKE ATTITUDE IN THE PREPARATION OF WORK AND THE MEETING OF DEADLINES.

The old days when artists were supposed to be flighty, disorganized creatures have gone. They are still characterized by more joie de vivre than most other groups in the publishing world, but their art training and their association with the businessmen and women of publishing have shown them that if they want a part in the big enterprise of illustration, they must act accordingly.

The next chapter will give an idea of the vital part time plays in the book-production scheme and how it concerns the illustrator. The frequent complaint of the artist is that he is not given enough of it, and that is true, I'm afraid, owing to the lack of clear planning that still exists when a book is contracted for. That is the point to outline step by step the progress of its manufacture, allowing the artist enough weeks or months to do his job carefully and thoroughly. However, I have known a few artists, even when given this consideration, to wait until the last moment to do the work anyway — which is poor planning and not conducive to bringing many assignments to that particular person.

A common fault with well known artists is to say "yes" to too many jobs. This obliging attitude sometimes makes their lives very hectic and is not conducive to peace of mind or their best work.

Deadlines are important in publishing just as they are in every business, and most artists of today are conscientious in meeting them.

Artists are also conscientious in the preparation and final presentation of their work. I recall especially the package of art work that arrived from Polly Jackson for Helen Kay's *Summer to Share.** Each key drawing was neat and clean, carefully marked for register and with the page number indicated. And on each key drawing was its set of Dinobase separations, each one taped in place so that each individual acetate could be examined without disturbing the others.

Furthermore, the entire art work was there, complete with cover die and jacket. There were no missing parts to come "later." Every sheet for every page was marked, and there need be no guessing as to, "Is that the yellow plate? No,

---

* This is the book I described in my article on censorship in *The Top Of The News*, April 1965, in which a Negro child had to be changed to a white child because of pressure from the sales force. This was a short-sighted as well as a prejudiced point of view because the book, published in 1960, would have antedated by five years the move toward books on integration. It is still a good book and has a worthy point but the main impact of the story was changed by making the "cast" all white.

that must be the blue." It was a very impressive, satisfying sight. I wish I could have kept it to show artists what "complete and satisfactory" art work (the contractual term) could be.

WHAT TO EXPECT FOR FEES

An artist's start in illustration depends quite naturally on his capabilities. It also depends on the kind of work that is available. Most editors know even before they contract for a book how they want it illustrated and by whom. That is almost always true of picture books, so that the jobs that are open to beginners are mostly occasional jackets or assignments of a few line drawings and a jacket. The latter usually calls for separations in two or three colors, which is why the knowhow to make them is so important to the newcomer.

Fees for single jackets ("single" meaning without other art work) generally start at $150 and go up, depending on the complexity of the job and the ability of the artist.

Fees for a half-dozen line drawings or chapter headings plus jacket usually start at $300 and increase accordingly. I put that figure low because it is sometimes best for an artist to take almost any job so as to get started, and this would be a very fair amount to ask for. After the artist has done a few jobs creditably, he can request $450 or more, although to set any price is questionable, because the requirements for each book are what really decide the fee.

The actual amount of money is always agreed on by the editor and artist before the work is started. However, sample rough drawings may have to be approved first, before the artist is given the final green light. If the artist has an agent, such arrangements must go through him, and all fees are paid directly to him. There are several excellent art agents. See the *Literary Market Place* (Bowker).

The actual payment of the fee is usually after delivery of "complete and satisfactory art work," the extent of which has been previously agreed on. Sometimes, in the case of a large fee and a complicated book taking many months or years to complete, half the fee is paid on completion of half the art work.

The artist's fee for children's books is paid by the publisher, not by the author, with the exception of scientific or technical books, in which necessary photographs and charts are supplied by the author without charge.

An artist may not expect a share in the royalties of a book unless he makes a major contribution to it and unless his part in the final product is as important or almost as important as the author's.

Of course, when an artist is also the author of the book, he receives all the royalties. He may also be given a separate outright fee for the art work, depending on circumstances.

When the artist's contribution (to a book he has not written) is a major one — for instance, in picture books requiring an illustration on almost every page — he is usually given half the royalties. This also means that he receives half the amount agreed on as an advance on signing the contract and half the subsidiary rights as well.

When his share of the book is proportionately less than in a book that is largely pictorial, he receives a smaller share of the royalties. This is especially true in the books for the 6-to-9 age, which carry a large number of pictures but are not essentially "picture books." Many such contracts call for 7½ per cent royalty to the author, and 2½ per cent to the artist. Again there is a proportionate sharing of the advance and other monies.

There are exceptions to the practice of paying royalties to the artist for a picture book in color. In many of the inexpensive series, the work of the artist is bought outright just as is the author's, and he receives no further payment.

All in all, the financial outlook for the beginning artist is not exactly bright, but it may become so if he perseveres, keeps his individuality and distinction and gradually climbs the ladder of hard work to fame. Once he has "arrived" and is known for his fine work and his artistic integrity, many books are offered to him, and he can command a high fee and resounding royalties. Not too great a number arrive at that peak any more than they do in other professions, but there are plenty of comfortable places close to the sun where an artist can earn a very respectable living from illustration. As I have said, there is a new and exciting emphasis on art in children's books for all ages today.

HOW TO GET STARTED

This is difficult, but not any more difficult than getting started in writing or any other line of work. I have tried to outline the necessary qualities of talent, imagination, individual distinction and technical ability. The beginner will have to add to these, perseverance and courage. Often it is hard to keep going against a succession of shut doors or, "No, thank you, we have no books for you," but it can be done. Again I have to say that everyone was a beginner once. One prominent illustrator told me the advice he gave to youngsters: "All you have to have is talent and guts and a good pair of shoes."

Albert Dorne, formerly of the Famous Artists School in Westport, Connecticut, now deceased, had this to say on the subject in the *Famous Artists Magazine,* Volume 10, Number 3, Spring 1962:

> The careers of many of your Faculty members [i.e. the F. A. School] are indeed rags to riches stories in the best Horatio Alger tradition. But none of us went suddenly to riches through some lucky break. It was a slow transition — in which we continually developed ourselves as professional artists. . . . We had no special advantages . . . but we all had a lot of drive and singleness of purpose.
>
> We didn't begin our careers doing covers for the *Saturday Evening Post,* or creating illustrations for slick magazines. All of us began by making local names for ourselves in much less demanding art markets, doing small line drawings — sometimes very menial jobs — that all beginners must start with and continue doing for quite a few years. Gradually, as we showed we could do bigger and better assignments, we got them. We had to work our way up to the big-time illustration jobs.
>
> Quite naturally, the big important assignments are given to mature, experienced professional artists.
>
> . . . The fact that you can't start at the top is no reason to be discouraged — nobody does. What's important is that the creative satisfactions and financial rewards in store for the ambitious, dedicated and well-trained artist are worth all the effort along the way.

Well, let's suppose you have all the necessary qualities, either as outlined in the foregoing paragraphs or summarized above. How do you sell your wares?

The majority of artists pack their portfolios with samples of their work and go the rounds of publishers. The editors do not often see people who come unannounced in this way, because they do not have the time. In most offices, though, there are art directors and their assistants who can spot talent and originality and, if interested, will ask for photostats of samples to be left on file or will request that you leave your portfolio and pick it up another day. You should comply with these requests willingly.

This is the usual method of trying to get a book job. I am not sure it is a good one, although occasionally artists are hired that way. The trouble is that you may arrive at a terrible moment when the department is preparing for a sales conference or a dozen other things. Secondly, it is extremely difficult for a person to judge your work with you yourself standing right there pointing out its virtues.

Furthermore, the samples themselves are apt to be poorly tuned as far as salability goes. For instance, the majority of budding artists appear with a sheaf of oversized paintings in full color on some completely adult and often weird subject. It is hard for an editor or an art director to judge what these will look like when reduced to a 5″ by 8″ page size. In addition, no one hires an unknown artist (or very many known ones) to do full color work nowadays, because full color reproduction, as I have explained, is so expensive.

The adult tone of most samples is another point against them. It is impossible to judge whether an artist who is good at adult stuff will have the right touch, warmth of feeling, and directness that attracts the juvenile audience. Many artists have difficulty in actually drawing children. (One told me that he thought all little children looked alike! I protested loudly both as an editor and a parent.) Others do not have the action and esprit that is part and parcel of drawing for children.

At this point you may well ask, what *should* an artist have in his portfolio? Here are some suggestions:

1. He should have some sketches of *children*. Believe it or not, they occur frequently in juvenile literature and cannot be avoided or always drawn "back to."

2. If the artist must paint on a big scale, he should come with reproductions reduced to some suitable book size, such as 5½ x 8¼, 6 x 9 or 6⅝ x 9½.

3. He should have samples of a black-and-white halftone drawing, and some clean-cut (no wash used) line drawings in pen and ink or other medium like scratchboard. The reason for the latter is that many of the books for the 9-to-12, and 12-to-16 age groups are still printed by letterpress, and the art work has to be reproduced in line. All in all, any artist who can get appeal, individual flair and a graphic quality into a one-color picture, be it halftone or line, stands a good chance of being seriously considered.

4. He should have an accurate set of acetate or Dinobase color separations done in black, showing how he would separate the colors in a sketch so it could be reproduced by this method.

5. He should have several samples of two-color work, both in separations and in sketch form. Many artists can get wonderful effects with two colors, and they are the boys that are being hired today for the usual run of picture books. Two colors are a lot cheaper (50 per cent, to be exact) than four colors.

And here is further advice that, if followed, will set you apart from other fledgling artists:

Have a rough dummy of a well-known fairy, nursery* or

---

* Look, for example, at what William Stobbs has done to *The Story of the Three Little Pigs* (McGraw-Hill).

folk tale, with the typewritten text pasted in place and some nice-looking rough sketches in black-and-white and color showing how you would lay out this story in picture-book form if you had a chance. Be sure the dummy adds up to thirty-two or forty-eight pages, complete with title page and front matter, to show that you are a "pro" or almost.

Let the editor (or interviewer) know that you have been to printing plants and understand the different processes.

Let the art director know that you have a working knowledge of type and type layouts. Carry some layouts with you.

Know something about artists already famous in the field.* In other words, show that you are familiar with the scope of children's books and their wide artistic range. To do this you should spend many hours reading in the local public library. Yes, I said *read*. Such knowledge will help you judge future manuscripts.

Keep your courage up. The day will surely come when you will get your chance. The boom in children's books and the modern emphasis on superior design and general appearance is bound to result in an increased demand for capable artists.

* A new book, most useful in this regard to artists interested in the picture book field, is *the art of Art for Children's Books* by Diana Klemin (Clarkson Potter). Unfortunately, it arrived too late to be included in the bibliography and index.

3 · Picture-Book Timetable

The requirements for illustration can be shown most clearly by describing what actually goes on between the artist and the editor, the author, the production manager and the printer in the course of producing a book. We will take as our example an offset picture book in four colors done by the separation process (see preceding chapter) because that is more complicated than a letterpress book illustrated with black-and-white line drawings. The latter usually is a clear-cut case of art work ordered, approved, plated and printed with the text. A picture book in color, printed by offset, is quite different, not in being any better but in being harder to do, technically speaking.

Let us also suppose for the sake of complication that the text of the book has been written by one person and the pictures are to be done by another. This is in contrast to the book written and illustrated by the author, who can consult with himself if the words have to be changed for some reason and who has no one but himself to blame if the pictures do not exactly fit his conception of what they should be.

As is usually the case, the manuscript of this hypothetical book appeared first. It was enthusiastically singled out by the first reader as having picture-book possibilities and thus came immediately under the editor's discerning eye.

Yes, the editor thinks the first reader was right. The script is good: it has a firm little plot for its twenty typewritten pages, a worthy point and wonderful pictorial possibilities. Its style and subject matter remind the editor strongly of one of her favorite artists, whose work might be perfect for it. The editor again reads the manuscript and decides tentatively that it could go into forty-eight pages, that it ought to be an oblong shape to fit the contour of the countryside that is so prominent in the story and that it ought to be rich with color because the tale is laid in Mexico. The illustrations would have to be done by separations, because full color work is too costly.

At this point the editor makes two phone calls. The first is to the production manager. She would like an estimate on a sixty-four-page picture book printed by offset in halftone, four colors both sides of the sheet, trim size 9½ ″ by 6½ ″, endpapers in four colors, jacket ditto, all art work to go on one sheet and to be done by separations on acetate or on Dinobase. A cloth binding is to be included, the whole to sell at $3.50, with the library binding priced accordingly.

The second call is to John Linsky (to coin a name) the painter, who she knows has made several trips to Mexico. How is he? *Fine*. Is he very busy? *Yes*. Would he like to do another picture book? *Yes*. It has to be done by separations. *Oh*. It is a very good story, and it is laid in Mexico! *Well, that helps*. The art work would have to be done in four months, finished by August 1 — forty-eight pages, trim size 9½ ″ by 6½ ″ plus ends and jacket making sixty-four pages in all, 4 colors throughout. *Any royalties?* Yes, 5 per cent. *Sounds possible. Send it along for a quick reading.*

The editor mails the manuscript, putting as many measurements, production requirements, contractual details and deadlines as she can at this point into an accompanying letter. She also asks in the letter that rough color sketches as samples be submitted within two weeks — that is, if the artist likes the story. She hopes he will, because she thinks he is just the one to do it, he has been to Mexico, and he knows how to make separations. (She is cognizant of all this from having known him and worked with him before.)

In a day or so the artist telephones back and is very enthusiastic about the story. He agrees to most of the details in the letter but would like a larger page size if he can get one.

The editor calls the production manager and relays the artist's request. The production manager promises to go into a huddle with his lithography expert or possibly with the representatives of one or two offset printing companies. In a couple of days or a week, depending on how busy he is and how successful he has been in finding an economical sheet size, the production manager drops in to see the editor. He may talk as follows:

"I can put it on the big four-color press at Sutherly Company and give you a 10½″ by 7¾″ trim size, but you would have to run twenty thousand copies to keep the price below $4.50.

"Or you could run a 10″ by 7″ book at Fairfax Press on their two-color press, but you would have to consider the extra expense there, too, because the cost of the binding on a book that size would be excessive. If you want as big a size as that I suggest running four colors on one side of the sheet and one on the other."

The editor explains she would prefer to have the whole book printed in four colors.

133

"Well," says the production manager, "I can get by on the unit cost of sale (cost of the individual book) with two colors on both sides on a 9½ " by 6½ " size, or two colors by one on 10" by 7". Let me know which you prefer."

This is just a sample of what their discussion might be. Or they might be able to plan the book just as the editor wants it then and there.

The editor calls back the artist, and they talk over the various possibilities. The artist prefers to have the larger size and to limit his color to one side of the sheet. The editor may reserve final judgment until the artist's rough dummy comes in.

Now at this point the editor asks the artist to send in sample color roughs and black-and-white sketches. These are partly for the author, who wants to see how the artist is going to treat his work, and partly for the editor, who wants to be sure that the artist is heading in the right direction. At any rate, with either letterpress or offset books, it is always a good idea to get the artist to rough out two or three pages to "set the scene." Often this procedure helps him to jell his own feeling about the book, and it certainly is insurance against disappointments when the final art work comes in. Some famous artists are not asked to submit sketches, because their styles are well known. However, no matter how illustrious they are, samples are always useful, especially when the manuscript is radically different from the others they have worked on.

So let us suppose that sample color roughs are made. They probably include one of an important scene and one of the jacket. The latter is a definitive and vital piece of work. It is important to have its concept approved from the beginning, not only by the author and editor but by the sales manager, as jackets are often the only things some buyers will look at. Let us assume that author, editor and sales manager like the roughs very much. And now, with that off his chest, the artist turns to making his dummy.

This dummy is a blank book of forty-eight pages cut to the right trim size — usually twenty-four sheets of paper or light cardboard — numbered carefully from 1 to 48 with the pages for color illustrations plainly marked. To get all the colored pages on one side of the press sheet, these pages must appear only on alternate openings: i.e., every first, third, fifth, etc., set of facing pages; or every second, fourth, sixth, etc. Color must alternate by twos with black and white in these openings so that they will fall in the proper order on the press sheet and so that color plates are necessary for only one side.

The artist, who has been sent a carbon copy of the manuscript by this time, then sits down to one of the hardest jobs in bookmaking. He must fit text and pictures in the required number of pages in this dummy to gain the effect he wants and to display the high points — and the low points — of the narrative. To do this he cuts up the typewritten manuscript* and pastes it roughly in place on the pages with a vague indication in pencil, ink or what-will-you of what he is going to draw. He may have to shift paragraphs and lines (never altering the text), change pictures from this page to the next and generally grapple with his problem until he solves it. Then he takes his brush and gives a clearer idea of

---

* Whenever possible, I have the manuscript set in type by this time so that the artist makes his dummy with the galley proof and thus the space left for text will be exactly like that in the printed book. If that is not possible, the script is typed with the same number of characters per line as there will be when it is set in type.

Sample distribution of color in a book that has black and white on one side of the sheet, and color on the other.

what the color pages are going to portray and generally smartens up his little "book" for presentation to the editor and probably to the author, too. This dummy is his interpretation of the book in roughest form.

Incidentally, in or with this dummy are eight extra pages

(beyond the forty-eight) on which he sketches his conception of the jacket and endpapers. The book now adds up to:

48 pages of text, of which 24 are in color, 24 in black and white.

8 pages of endpapers, sometimes in color, sometimes not (4 of these are at each end, 2 of them pasted down on the cover). They are the same back and front, so he only makes one endpaper drawing.

8 pages of jacket, with each jacket flap counting for 2 pages of the 8.

64 pages total, and all to go on one press sheet.

The first thing the editor does when the dummy comes in — at least it is the first thing I do; practice varies — is to flip through the pages quickly to see what the over-all impression is. Usually this moment is very exciting, because the artist has been selected carefully in the first place; and he usually manages to convey some of his enthusiasm for the book in this little preliminary volume.

After that, the editor slowly checks the dummy page by page to be sure the number of pages has not been exceeded and that color is indicated only where it is allowed. She sends the dummy to the production department to have it checked again against the estimated cost. Then, when it is returned, she goes over it carefully for actual interpretation and detail. Usually she calls in the artist and the author, and they enjoy it together; or when that is impossible, she mails it to the latter. Changes of tone, scene or treatment are suggested if necessary, and then the whole dummy goes back to the artist.*

* I understand that some editors do not consult the authors about the illustrations in their books, but I always do as a safeguard against mistakes. Practices differ in this respect.

In the interim of the examination of the dummy, the artist has been making up a sample set of separations for a color page. If his technique varies from the last book or if he is new at the separation process, he especially needs to do this. Much time and money can thus be saved by forestalling costly changes later. So he selects a particularly difficult color page and sends in his black key plate and three acetate overlays along with color swatches in tempera or some other flat color for the four inks he wishes used in the proving. The editor and the art director and possibly the artist, too, if he lives near by, select the exact inks from a printer's ink book or direct the printer to match his swatches.

While the printer is proving up this sample page, the editor has started the artist working on the black key drawings. These will not have to wait for the sample color proof. And while he is working on the black drawings and the production department is proving the sample page, the editor and the author are putting the finishing touches on the manuscript, unless this has been done before. The actual type face and its size is decided by the editor, the artist, or the art director or all three — whoever is designing the book. Sample text pages have been obtained while all this discussion has been going on, and they are approved by the editor, the author and the artist. The final copy-edited text is sent out to be set in type, and suddenly the heat of time and deadlines is on. The artist really cannot make finished drawings without knowing just exactly how much space he is going to have on the page, so everyone waits for these first galleys with ill-concealed impatience.

The galleys arrive and are whisked off to both author and artist. The former reads them for typographical errors (few changes are allowed authors in picture books!) and the latter quickly cuts them up and pastes them in his rough dummy — or in a fresh "printer's" dummy, which will go to the press with his completed art work — to see how they fit. Usually a word and character count have been taken previous to having the manuscript set, so the text fits fairly well; but there are always a few adjustments an artist has to make to have the text look exactly right.

For added space he may need to lose a line or two on one page that cannot be added to the next or pushed back onto the previous one — so words have to come out. Usually short lines on the ends of paragraphs are easy to "lose." Or he may be stuck with a "widow." This is a short line (half a line or less) at the top of a page. Such lines look unattractive and must go back on the preceding page somehow. To leave them in would be poor bookmaking. He may want to change a small detail that will make his picture more effective. For instance, he may want a colt to be standing up instead of lying down as the text indicates. If this change does not interfere with the recital of the story, it is justifiable.

All these corrections are checked with the author and editor, added to the author's and proofreader's corrections and final galleys are obtained. These are gone over again, and this time special attention is paid to poor type — i.e., broken letters, alignment of lines, etc. When everything seems to be perfect, reproduction — called "repro" — proofs are pulled.

So much for the text. These proofs are combined with the final art work at the printer's.

Meanwhile, our artist has been working very hard. He has his final text pasted in place in his dummy, so he knows just what the dimensions of all art work should be. He has the proof of the sample set of separations from which he can tell how to execute his other acetates and key drawings. Gripping his pipe firmly between his teeth, he plows on.

During the correction of the galleys and the proving of the sample separations (or perhaps before), the production department has been busy obtaining final figures on the book. The sample separations have indicated that Mr. Linsky is going to add a few more color furbelows and complications than they expected. Plates or films are going to be more expensive, and the company that is going to print the book has raised its original estimate on seeing the sample art work.

At this point there are usually two choices, but only one answer. Another printer can be called in, more sample proofs made and the whole process repeated. In other words, right now the whole book can be rethought and replanned. That sounds logical, but often it is not. The book has been assigned to a spring list; doing all this work over again would mean postponement until fall. Neither author nor artist wants that; nor does the editor. She has counted on this book for the spring and she has no room for it in the fall. It MUST come out in the spring.

Consequently, some way has to be found to offset the first printer's rise in price. The retail price can be increased, the binding changed or perhaps the number of color pages cut down. Perhaps all three measures are taken. At any rate, the added expense is compensated for by some definite saving somewhere in the book. New figures are obtained, and a new estimate drawn up. This is approved by an official — usually the general manager of the company — and the book can go into production.

In this interval the artist may have completed half the art work and sent it in. Sometimes this can be given to the printer and the cameras started up, but usually it is best to wait and hand over the whole job when it is completed.

In longer books, when time is really desperately short, the printer may let the editor know what pages are needed to complete the first form, and the artist is asked to jump around in the book and finish those first. That is harum-scarum publishing; but sometimes it has to be done, and rarely does a book suffer from it.

Let us imagine, however, that this is an ideal book and that the artist has time to complete his work in peace. He has not been desperately sick, nor has his wife had a baby, leaving him home to take care of the other children, nor has he undertaken an additional job from another publishing company that he thought he could squeeze in while doing this one. All these (except the last) are legitimate reasons for a delay in agreed delivery of art work, but they can throw an editor's time schedule greatly awry, and they are most likely to occur at this stage in the progress of a picture book.

But these difficulties have not occurred in the production of this book. On August 1 the complete art work including the jacket and a line drawing for the die on the cover,* is placed on the editor's desk. She exclaims with pleasure and has a quiet half hour enjoying the pictures and the precise, workmanlike way the artist has presented them. Then she calls her production assistant, the art director or the production manager, or both, and they carefully go over them page for page. They are measured and checked for production

* With the present library bindings, this is not necessary. The jacket art is printed on the cover by lithography or silkscreen.

and compared with the rough dummy that has been included in the package.

If the artist has also made the printer's dummy, that is included too. Usually, however, this is done in the art or production department. This final dummy contains the corrected galleys or reproduction proofs accurately pasted in place on each page. The front matter (including title page, copyright page and dedication) is also pasted in; photostats or van Dykes (blueprints) are made of each piece of art work, reduced to page size, and those are pasted in. A correct printer's dummy or mechanical is very important, because it insures the proper arrangement of art work and text in a book. Drawings cannot appear in the wrong order or upside down; paragraphs cannot be omitted or incorrectly placed, and so on. Anyone who wonders why so much care is taken with dummies should hear the tales of woe about certain mistakes that have occurred. Thousands of dollars have had to be spent to reprint signatures (parts of books) or to put in erratum slips; publication dates have had to be postponed. The correct imposition (placement of the pages on the press sheet) of a book MUST be checked at this time, and the best way to do it is to supply the printer with an accurate printer's dummy. Nothing should be left as "understood."

When the complete art work has been handed in, and the artist is celebrating in the nearest bar, the production department takes over until color proofs are obtained for the whole book. I have before me a production manager's directive that is illuminating at this point:

> When complete art is turned over to this department measure, count, and check it against the signed estimate.
>
> Give order in duplicate to the printer.

Set up a tentative schedule and place it on the board. [Every publisher has a board or rack where each title in production is listed. The different production stages are marked by pegs or divisions until the book is printed, bound and delivered to the stock room.]

Order paper for definite edition. Keep checking order to be sure it is ready by the time plates are ready to print. Keep checking the schedule for plates.

Obtain a proof date on color plates and inform the editor. Keep checking this date.

When color proofs* are delivered by the printer to the production department, they are taken at once to the juvenile department, where there is generally a big consultation over them. Among those present are the editor, her assistant, the art director, the production manager and the printer's representative. The purpose of this huddle is to approve the proofs so that the final corrections can be made and the first edition run off. Consequently every part of every picture must be scrutinized carefully for color, register, clarity and inaccuracies. The original drawings are always there for comparison.

The actual color reproduction is what gives the most trouble. Sometimes the reproduction is way off because the printer has not matched the artist's color swatches or because the plates have been run with ink that is either too strong or too weak or because the ink density varies from one side of the proof sheet to the other. Or the artist's separations may not be strong enough. Often the overprinting of the colors gives the wrong effect, and that is hard to correct,

* Color proofs are not absolutely necessary if the artist has done a book or books by the same method. However, they are always helpful to him and to the art department and editor.

because although you can "pull down" (lessen) the amount of red, say, in a picture of a man with a red coat, so that his face will not be so red, you will also decrease the red in his coat so that it looks anemic.* In such a case the printer may suggest "opening the screen" on the coat, which will allow more ink to flow on the paper — or the red plate may have to be remade. Possibly all the plates will have to be remade. Fortunately this drastic action is not often called for because the printer is not likely to appear with proofs that are so far from the originals, especially if a color proof has been obtained first.

Let us suppose then that these proofs are fairly good. There are some corrections to be made. The red is too strong in the plates on the upper half of the sheet. The green in the sleeve of a man's shirt has been omitted. The register in the bottom half of the sheet should be corrected by sliding the yellow plate a bit to the left. All these corrections are written on one set of proofs for the printer and also on another set for the art director, the production department and the editor.

Because there is not time to prove and deliver a new set of proofs, it is agreed that the editor or juvenile production manager will go to the printing plant to check the color proofs when these corrections have been made and the book is ready to run on the press. Some editors do not do this, and occasionally it is not necessary; but if there is any question about the end result, being on the spot is a good idea. Thousands of poorly printed sheets are hard to dispose of.

At this time, or sometime earlier, the printer also brings to the production department a "salt print" or "van Dyke" —

* See Chapter 7 for an example of this problem.

144

which is really a big blueprint like those used by architects — of the whole book. This again, like the dummy, is for a last-minute check on the imposition of the individual pages. It is folded, compared page for page with the printer's dummy and the whole book is carefully read from stem to stern for the last time by someone in the juvenile department. That reader should not be the editor, because by now she has read the text so many times that she has become conditioned to it and would not be able to spot an omission or an error nearly as well as some less interested person.

During the conference over the color proofs, the artist may be present or called in, or he may not be. This depends on whether he is geographically near by, whether he knows color reproduction well enough to be of help and also whether he is a levelheaded, rational fellow or a fussy, excitable one. The latter type can be too particular or too easily discouraged to be of use.

This holds true in the ensuing visit to the press at the time of the actual run. An artist who knows his printing processes can be a pleasant and valuable adjunct on such a trip. At least, the privilege of seeing his book on press is one that is highly esteemed by professional artists, and it is one that should send untrained artists running to the nearest offset plant so they can learn and act intelligently when their own picture books are printed.

Let us suppose, however, that the editor goes alone.* She arrives early in the morning as requested and waits for a clear sheet to come off the press. The first sheets are usually a mess, until the plates are properly in place and the ink flow is regulated. Finally, a sheet the head pressman approves of

* Some actual visits to a press are described in Chapter 7.

is obtained and put out on a big board. If this inspection sheet is good, she checks it for color and compares it with the first proof sheet, which was marked for correction in her office. If these corrections have all been made and a sheet reasonably close to the art work has been obtained, she approves it, and the press run is on. Sometimes each color has to be proved separately, taking all day and often into the night. Sometimes even then it is not right, and new plates have to be made; and the whole process repeated. This should not happen if the editor and the art director have checked the art work with the printer before plates are made.

A striking example of the necessity of this occurred with a four-color book on which the preliminary art had been okayed. However, when the total and final art was delivered to the printer, he called up and said something was wrong with the white that had been used for highlights. I immediately drove to the plant (Halliday Lithography Company in Hanover, Massachusetts), where Harley Stone showed me what was wrong. A fluorescent substance had been added to the tube of white paint used by the artist, and the camera had picked it up as another color. Mr. Stone had a special light that, when turned on in a darkened room, made the fluorescent spots glow in an odd manner. He previously had had the same trouble with other art — the paper some photographs are printed on, for instance. If undetected, these photographs when printed would have looked quite different from the others (developed on ordinary paper).

In the case of our book, the artist had run out of her usual white paint and unknowingly had bought a new tube containing the fluorescent substance to finish the work.

This is a good instance of how much a printer can help you if you consult him in time. Mr. Stone also helped me plan a book, *Pangur Ban* by Joan Balfour Payne, in two colors that the art director and I believed could not possibly be done in less than three. And, if you have to have three colors for a book, you might as well have four; because most color presses used for picture books are two-color, and if you have to send the sheet through twice, you might as well use the full capacity of the press. Four-color presses *can* be used for picture books, but the register problem where you are printing four colors at once is difficult, and it is very hard to control all the colors over the whole plate surface. It can be done, of course.

To go back to our hypothetical book, now the sheet looks reasonably good after a couple of tries. The printer and the editor go out for lunch and then come back to look over the proofs of the black art work for the other side of the sheet. These have been proved on another press and, of course, may have been submitted for approval by the editor and the art director long before this. The same comparison of original art work and proof is made and corrections indicated. Possibly these are few, and the editor decides that the printer can go ahead with that side of the sheet on his own. She departs reasonably well satisfied.

The printer heaves a sigh of relief, and word passes around the pressroom that all is well.

Now if this four-color book is run on a two-color press, the editor — or whoever goes from the production or art department — will either have to make two trips to okay the color side of the sheet or she may trust the printer to put on the first two colors before she gets there. She then okays only the printing of the last two colors.

After the full edition of the color side has been run off, then the next day the plate for the black-and-white side of the sheet is put on the press. The corrections the editor has indicated are carefully made, a sample sheet is approved by the head pressman or official in charge and the run is completed. Our book is printed.

As soon as these sheets arrive in the bindery — or possibly before — a sample set is folded and sent over to the editor for final approval before binding. Hopefully she looks through it. It is all right. She puts her initials on it and sends it back to the bindery. Machines are started up and the book emerges as a bound volume — at long last. May it sell and have to be reprinted many times!*

---

* In which case (I hate to say it) the editor, or some other responsible person, should again go to the plant to okay the first sheet before the book is run. I have seen some sorry-looking second and third editions of lovely books.

4 · Typography and Book Design

Authors in general are interested in the appearance of their books, but few are concerned with the technical aspects of production and design. This is also true of many booksellers, librarians and reviewers, whose primary concern is in what the book has to say.

However, there is new interest in appearance, and it is now acknowledged that a book can be beautiful in design, with or without illustrations. It is also true that good-looking books cost no more than poor-looking ones — at least in general layout. Expensive paper, very wide margins and a deluxe binding do add to the cost, but a completely utilitarian book in a compact size can be handsome. There is no excuse any longer for dreary-looking textbooks or prosaic novels. In fact, some textbooks today are quite beautiful.

Of course, design is particularly important in the children's book field, because it determines much of the reader appeal. In an age when reading has to compete with radio, television, hi fi, the comics and the movies, everything should be done to make books *look* attractive. Also, in an age when color work is expensive and when the text of almost any book has to be compressed into as few pages as possible, intelligent, creative book design is again important, even vital.

There are many courses given and a good deal has been written on this subject. There are also many schools of thought, almost all of which are sound if they stem from actual experience. Book design is a *practical* art. A few special books are designed each year for parlor ornaments or for big companies to give to their big customers, but on the whole most books are laid out and printed to be read. This is especially true of children's books, which makes their design a truly exacting and rewarding realm to work in.

I have been interested in both typography and design, because my famous uncle, Joseph Hawley Chapin, to whom this book is dedicated, tried to educate me in both subjects at a tender age. He was a confrere of many renowned artists, among them Howard Pyle, Edwin Abbey, Everett Shinn, Charles Dana Gibson, N. C. Wyeth and Reginald Birch, some of whom I met as a little girl. Certainly I remember several heated arguments carried on in my uncle's office at Scribners or his home on Central Park on the virtues of this illustrator or that, and this book designer or that. And often the format of particular books was discussed at great length. I can remember, too, taking down the books later in my uncle's library and looking at them with wide-eyed interest and respect in the light of what had been said about them.

But a lot of water has gone over the book-design dam since that day, although the fundamentals of good design remain the same. Contrast the *Scribner Classic* series, which my uncle designed almost in its entirety, with such books as

The Rainbow Classics (World). On the one hand you have a realistic use of rich color and shading and classic type, while on the other, flat color, bold design and unusual type treatment compete for your attention. In other words, illustrations and book design have turned modern just as advertising and architecture have, and there is so much that is new and different that one hesitates to voice an opinion or to say what is good and what is not.

Instead, one had best pay primary attention to the fundamentals so that one can do one's own judging. But keep in mind again that book design is a practical art, that books are written and illustrated to be read and looked at — and in our field, read and looked at by children, who are natural lovers of beauty but whose tastes are for the most part unformed and impressionable. Hence, one should realize that design is not an end-all;* the book's contents, be they largely pictorial or largely prose, are most important. Design should simply present them in the way they can best be appreciated by the reader.

DETAILS OF DESIGN

Design consists of the selection of the following items in the format of a book:

1. Size of the page.
2. Kind and size of type face for the body of the text.
3. Kind and size of type face for:
   Title page

---

* As Carl Zahn, designer for the Boston Museum of Fine Arts, said at the Trade Book Clinic of the AIGA, November 12, 1964, "Design is not something that is put on top like icing; if it is worthy of the name, it is an intrinsic part of the product."

Front matter: copyright page, dedication page, half-title, acknowledgments, etc.

Chapter headings

Running heads: the topmost lines of type on each page, usually spaced somewhat above the body of the text. (Not all books have running heads.)

Folios, or page numbers

Footnotes — if any

Back matter: index, bibliography, etc.

Binding

Jacket

4. The placement of this type on the page or on the binding or the jacket. This includes the measurement of margins and other use of "white space" on the page.

5. Leading: the amount of space between the lines in the body of the text.

6. The placement on the page of all illustrations unless the illustrations are full-page ones and "bleed" (come right up to the edge of the paper).

7. The placement and choice of all decorations, such as large initial capital letters beginning each chapter, ornamental borders, and so on.

All these details go to make up the format of a book and are the job of the book designer or art director of a publishing company. He may work on all the books, or there may be a special person delegated to the juveniles. Whoever he is, given a book-design assignment, he must read at least part of the book himself, consult with the editor, study the sample art work and then face up to his drawing board.

He probably starts with layouts for a sample text page. These are made on strong, transparent tissue and show all the details that I have mentioned for a general page of text taken out of the body of the book. Following that, he draws

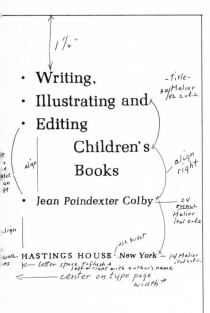

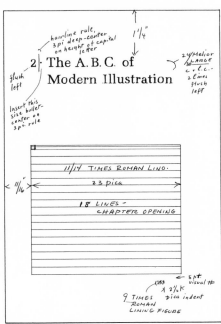

Title page and chapter opening layouts for *Writing, Illustrating and Editing Children's Books.*

up more layouts for a typical chapter heading, an illustration page, the title page, the front matter and so on. Nothing is left for the typesetter to guess at. Every word in the whole book, even if it is just the date on the copyright page, is exactly described as to size and type face and location on the page.

LAYOUTS

Layouts are rather fun to do, if somewhat exacting and time consuming unless you are an expert. Everyone in the juvenile business should try at least one, if only to acquire the firsthand information on and respect for these items of bookmaking, which are so often overlooked.

On these two pages are sample layouts by Al Lichtenberg, art director at Hastings House, for *Mountains of Fire,* written and illustrated by Genevieve Vaughan-Jackson, and printed sample pages and illustration. See how well they all go together and help to point up this forceful non-fiction book on volcanos, designed for older boys and girls.

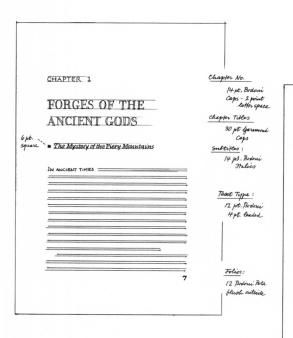

down the valleys, drowning between five and six thousand persons. Since the disaster a tunnel has been bored into the crater so that never again can the lake forming in it drain away in such a terrible fashion.

Papandayan volcano erupted in 1772, but this time the cause of deaths was the enormous quantities of volcanic material ejected from the crater. So much was thrown out that, like Mount Mazama, Papandayan collapsed on itself, leaving a gap five miles long and six miles wide. The countryside was devastated, including all the coffee plantations and forty villages. Three thousand people died.

Galung Gung is yet another Indonesian volcano capable of spreading death and destruction. In 1882 the mountain was forested from top to bottom and there were many villages strung around it. In October of that year there was a terrific explosion. The earth shook; columns of hot water, boiling mud, ashes, and stones were hurled up from the top of the mountain like a tremendous waterspout. The rivers overflowed and the entire countryside was buried deep under a flood of blue mud. Villages and plantations disappeared without a trace, all in the space of five hours. Four days later came another violent eruption, accompanied by an earthquake. The top of the mountain fell in, changing the landscape to hills where before there had been level land. Rivers altered their courses and two thousand people were drowned overnight.

The northwestern arc of the Ring of Fire around the Pacific contains the volcanos of the Philippines and Japan. In the Philippines there are two active volcanos, Taal and Mayon (Mayōn). In 1911 Taal had a violent eruption of rather an unusual kind. All the usual preliminaries took place—earthquakes increasing in intensity, columns of black smoke pouring

125

MOUNTAINS
of FIRE

An Introduction to the Science of Volcanos

WRITTEN AND ILLUSTRATED BY
Genevieve Vaughan-Jackson

HASTINGS HOUSE PUBLISHERS · NEW YORK

[Editorial markup in margins:] 48 Garamond No. 3 — 18 Bodoni Italics U. & L.C. — small caps 14 Bodoni U. & L.C. — 12 Bodoni Caps

volcanos can be very large indeed. The Hawaiian Islands are magnificent examples of this type of volcano.

The amount of gas in magma can vary considerably. The more gas there is, the more explosively the magma will erupt. It no longer flows as liquid streams of lava; but comes bursting out of the volcanic vent in blobs and spatters or even as lava froth. These fragments of lava cool very rapidly as they fall back to earth and gradually build a cone around the vent. Such a *cinder cone* usually grows very quickly and is comparatively short-lived. Paricutin (Pa-reé-koo-teen) volcano, in Mexico, is a symmetrical, smooth-sided mountain some fifteen hundred feet high with a crater at the top. It was active for only nine years and grew to its present height during the early part of its existence. Many smaller cones have an even shorter life than Paricutin.

The Church Tower
of San Juan

155

TYPE

Needless to say, to make these layouts or to do any part of book work, the designer must know a great deal about type itself. Actually, anyone dealing with books should have some knowledge of it. It makes a fascinating study.

The first letters of our roman alphabet were all capital letters and were cut in stone and then eventually handwritten on scrolls. The early printed letters followed this calligraphy closely, and just as handwriting developed lower case or small letters to save space, early printing followed suit. However, in the fifteenth century, when movable type first was used to any extent, different type faces came into being, and printing moved slowly away from the calligraphic form. This change was brought about through the influence of scholars who became printers and did much of the work themselves at their own small presses. Certain of these master printers of Italy, Holland and France contributed a great deal to type styling in the sixteenth and seventeenth centuries, and although Caxton started English printing late in the fifteenth

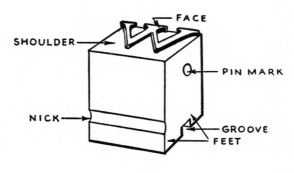

A piece of type

century, it was not until the eighteenth century that English-men came to the fore in type design. For instance, around 1720, William Caslon cut his famous Old Face, which has been used with variations ever since. Here are two lines of it as it can be ordered from a type book today:

"Type comes from the Greek word *typos* meaning blow or impression." Webster's Dictionary.

(Incidentally the word *typos* is set here in "italic" or slop-ing type, which was first cut by an Italian printer named Aldus around 1500. This is in contrast to roman or upright letters.)

Another English master printer of the eighteenth century was John Baskerville of Birmingham, whose type face was so beautiful and yet so readable that it is still very popular today. Here are two lines of it:

"Type comes from the Greek word *typos* meaning blow or impression."

At first, each type face was measured separately, which was extremely confusing to any one wanting to use more than one kind in a book. But in the eighteenth century, the present point system was developed in France, and it has gradually been adopted for all kinds of printing.

A *point* is roughly 1/72 of an inch. Twelve points con-stitute a *pica*, which is the measuring unit of the printed line. The only other measuring term that is in common use is the *em*,* which is actually the square of any type body size, but which is generally used to mean pica or 12 pt. ems. An

---

* This word is used, since the letter *M* is the widest character in the alpha-bet.

em is a blank piece of lead cast as a space unit in every size of type. For instance, when you want to indent a paragraph or a group of lines, you mark the indentation so many *ems*. The paragraphs in this book are indented one em. (Smaller spaces are called *ens,* which is half an em, *en quads* and *spaces,* but their exact definition and use is too technical to go into here.)

So much for spacing within the type lines.

To space the lines themselves, a printer uses *leads,* (pronounced like the metal) whose thickness is also specified in points.

These lines are *one point* leaded:

> "Some of the types best suited to children's books are those designed by John Baskerville and William Caslon, both 18th century Englishmen."

These lines are *two point* leaded:

> "Some of the types best suited to children's books are those designed by John Baskerville and William Caslon, both 18th century Englishmen."

These lines are *four point* leaded:

> "Some of the types best suited to children's books are those designed by John Baskerville and William Caslon, both 18th century Englishmen."

Machine leading is available in multiples of one point. Half-point leading is to be discouraged, because it must be inserted by hand. The width of a type line is measured in picas; 6 picas equal 1 inch. Pica width is to be specified in units of no less than ½ pica.

Spacing, or leading, is very important, because it regulates to an extraordinary degree the readability of any given type area. It is therefore of special significance in juveniles.

Type itself is very interesting, both its history and its selection. A beginning artist, author or editor would do well to get a type book from a nearby foundry and study the different kinds and sizes as they look in the many faces available today. Such a book would be divided between the faces available for monotype machines and those for linotype, and those with *serifs* (small lines at top or bottom to finish off the main body of the letter) like that in which this book is set and without serifs (sans serif) like this spartan type. As you can see these two types are very different and are used for widely varying purposes. A third section of the type book would include *display type,* which is usually 24 point or larger and set by hand.*

> Capitals ABCDEFG
> Lower case abcdefg
> Small caps ABCDEFG
> Italic caps *ABCDEFG*
> Italic lower case *abcdefg*
> Numbers 123456
> Oldstyle numbers 1 2 3 4 5 6 7 8 9

A few kinds of type can usually be obtained in **Bold Face Like This** also.

With this simple information it is possible for you to understand the layouts of the full text and chapter opening pages from *Tom And The Red Coats* by Barnett Spratt (Hastings House) as shown on page 160 and possibly to look at the layout of your own books with more appreciation.

Certainly the layout or format of children's books is particularly interesting, because there are so many more govern-

---

* You will find a good, basic description of type, its makers and its uses in Marshall Lee's *Bookmaking* (Bowker), pp. 78-102.

ing factors than in adult books. For example, a juvenile book designer must keep in mind the following items besides the purpose and actual content:

1. Age group
2. Illustrations
3. Length and page (trim) size
4. Nature of the contents: e.g., a nonfiction science book on shells, a romantic historical story or a poetry collection. They would all be designed quite differently.

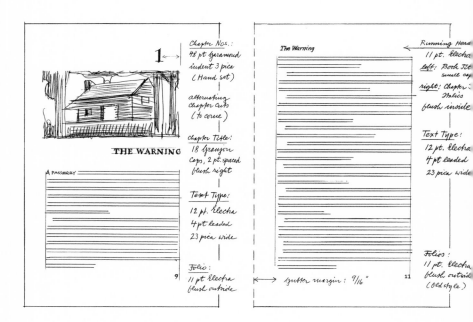

Chapter opening and full text page layout for *Tom and the Redcoats* by Barnett Spratt, illustrated by Lloyd Coe (Hastings).

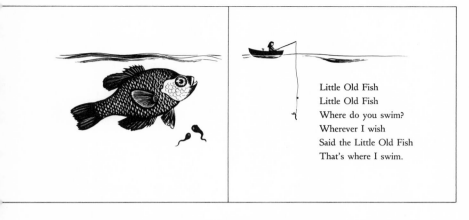

Little Old Fish
Little Old Fish
Where do you swim?
Wherever I wish
Said the Little Old Fish
That's where I swim.

Two facing pages from Margaret Wise Brown's *Where Have You Been?*, illustrated by Barbara Cooney (Hastings).

AGE GROUP

The age group for which a children's book is intended is important in the selection of page size, kind and size of type and almost every other detail of format.

AGES 2 TO 5. Large-sized type, 14 or 18 or even 24 point, is usually used because these manuscripts are short and often have only a few words or a line on a page. A very clear, readable face is desirable.

Well-designed books for this age group can act as an early stimulus to the small child's interest in reading.

Lots of white space in margins and plenty of leading between lines (4 points or more) are necessary for simplicity and restful effect. Large-sized pages offer obvious display advantages, but small books have their own appeal too.

AGES 6 TO 9. The actual page size of a book for this beginning-to-read age is not too important, although some chil-

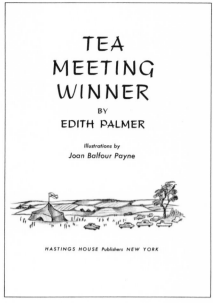

Half title, title page, copyright page, and first page of text from *Tea*

dren want to get away from large-sized, babyish-looking possessions even in their literature.

Large type (14 to 18 pt.) is desirable if the book is intended for children to read to themselves. Also the type must be readable and not fancy. These children should put all their attention on word content and not be distracted by type effects. However, their books need not be ugly and "schoolbooky"-looking. Some of the most beautiful types are the easiest to read.

Ample margins will enhance the appearance of any book, even if the paper is of only average quality. By putting the reader "at ease" they will heighten his or her receptivity.

Here is an example of type appropriate to this age group.

1

I T WAS THE day before the Tea Meeting. Jane and Larry Bell could hardly wait, for it was their favorite day next to Christmas. There were no presents but all of the boys and girls from the nearby farms would be there, and they would have fun.

This August event had taken place near their home in New Andrews, Nova Scotia for over a hundred years. When there were no telephones or automobiles, it had brought farm families together before the autumn harvesting. In those days, no meal was complete for grown-ups without tea. That is why it was called the Tea Meeting.

Their great-grandfather had selected the place where it was always held, a beautiful meadow on the bank of the French River. Here there was plenty of room to park cars where once the horses and buggies had been tied under the trees.

5

Meeting Winner by Edith Palmer, illustrated by Joan Balfour Payne (Hastings).

He was Jane and Larry's Great-uncle Angus, who played the bagpipes. Everyone loved him, just as everyone loved to hear his old tunes floating across the New Andrews hills.

Four lines of type taken from TEA MEETING WINNER by Edith Palmer (Hastings).

Page size: 6½″ by 9¼″. *Type:* 14 point Baskerville, 3 point leaded.
Text: 27 picas wide by 39 picas deep, 28 lines a page.
Gutter margins: 1 1/16″.
Top margin: 1⅛″.

163

AGES 9 TO 12. The page size for this group is usually dependent on content and illustration and may be large, like the Holling Clancy Holling or the Ray Bethers books. However, the standard 5½ " by 8¼ " format or some variation of it is usually used, because these children want longer books than the preceding age group; and this size is the least expensive.

The type should still be fairly large, at least 12 point, and well leaded. These children usually read fairly easily, but they have not mastered the art completely and need to be encouraged by frequent illustrations and open, easy-looking type lines.

For an example for this age group, see the four cuts on the opposite page of the title page, text pages, and illustration from Clem Philbrook's *Captured by the Abnakis* (Hastings), illustrated by Joshua Tolford.

JUNIOR HIGH AND HIGH SCHOOL AGE. Although size may vary according to content, it is best psychologically to make these books look as nearly adult as possible. Hence, the 5½ " by 8¼ " or the 6" by 9" sizes are usually selected.

Type need not be larger than 11 or 12 point (a larger size looks as if it were meant for a younger age level) but there should be at least a 2-point lead between the lines so that a tight, heavy, hard-to-read appearance is avoided.

Much can be done with chapter-opening decoration, drop initials and other typographical devices for this age. For the most part the books for these boys and girls contain no illustration, and hence it is up to the designer to liven up the format and make it look interesting.

Look at the chapter opening from *Five Artists of The Old West* by Clide Hollmann (Hastings) designed by Al

CAPTURED
BY THE
ABNAKIS

BY CLEM PHILBROOK

ILLUSTRATED BY JOSHUA TOLFORD

HASTINGS HOUSE, *Publishers* · NEW YORK

I

Isaac Bradley swung his ax with uncommon vigor. There was a decided nip in the harvest-scented air. There was something else in the air too. Ike couldn't quite name it, but he could feel it.

Joseph Whittaker, Isaac's rotund companion, put it into words. "Trouble with Injuns is, they're sneaky," he said from his perch on a nearby stump. "They been peaceable quite a spell now. But that don't mean they'll stay peaceable, does it, Ike?"

Ike drove the bit of his ax deep into a pine and left it there, straightening to take a breather. Short, compact, quick of mind and body, Ike was fifteen. He tried to remember that Joe was only eleven, but sometimes it wasn't easy. Joe was extra big for his age—almost as big as Ike himself, who was extra small. But extra strong too, Ike was, and a willing worker. He could swing an ax from "daybreak to backbreak" with the best of them.

Joe was a neighbor of Ike's, and the two families often swapped labor. First Joe would be loaned out to Ike's pa a few days, then Ike would be loaned out to Joe's pa in return.

7

Kohokas nodded. "The Fat One will go first."

Joe turned to Ike imploringly, a stricken look on his grimy face. His shoulders sagged, his arms hung limply at his sides, he was scarcely able to place one foot in front of the other. He was just about done in.

In a flash of inspiration, Ike saw the answer to Joe's problem. "The Fat One will not go first," he corrected. "The Fat One will not go at all. I, Mosbas, will go for him."

Kohokas scowled fiercely. "And who will run the gantlet for Mosbas?"

Ike glared back defiantly. "Mosbas will run the gantlet twice!"

A hubbub immediately arose among the braves, as they noisily discussed this proposal. Bomazine, Ike could see, was strongly in favor of it. There was a triumphant glint in his beady black eyes.

Ike had counted on that. Bomazine would relish two opportunities to strike him down. But how about the others? How about Kohokas?

The solemn chief studied Joe for a few moments, then turned to Ike. "Mosbas is brave," he admitted, "but Mosbas is also foolish. He cannot run the gantlet twice."

Ike's eyes held his. "The Fat One cannot run it once," he said flatly.

Kohokas stared at him impassively for some time. Then he inclined his head. "It shall be as Mosbas wants. He will run the gantlet twice—down and back."

Now that it was done, Ike began to doubt his sanity. What had he let himself in for? Most captives considered themselves fortunate to survive the ordeal once. How could he possibly survive it twice?

He was even more apprehensive a short time later when the well-worn path led them from the deep forest to the edge of a vast field. Before them lay Pigwacket, an In-

43

Title page   First page of text   Full text page Illustration

165

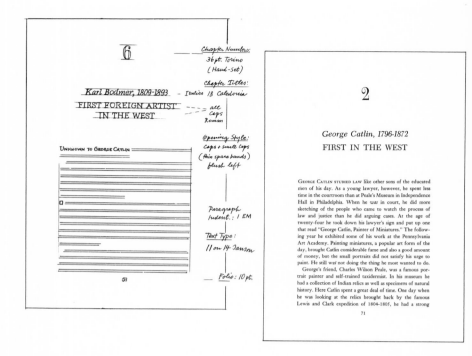

Layout and printed chapter opening
page from *Five Artists of the Old
West* by Clide Hollmann.

Lichtenberg. Note the placement of the initial number and
the simple but effective choice of type and decoration for a
book about our early art and western history.

ILLUSTRATIONS

These determine to a large degree the size of the book, the
length and particularly the type face, as well as the selection
of paper stock. No good designer would think of laying out
a book without studying sample illustrations and selecting
just the right type to go with them and with the story itself.

166

The specifications drawn up by the designer for *Five Artists of the Old West* are as follows:

TEXT: 11 on 15 Janson

CHAPTER HEADS: 18 Caledonia

CHAPTER NOS: 36 Jarvis

RUNNING HEADS: 10 Janson

FOLIOS: 10 Janson — flush outside

CAPTIONS: 10 Janson Italic

TYPE PAGE: 24x43

TRIM SIZE: 6x9

MARGINS: Head 11/16; Gutter 1″

ESTIMATE OF LENGTH:

Total characters 195,000

Characters per line 60

Characters per page 1980

Lines to a page 33

Lines to opening 19

Text 98 pages

Front & back matter 10

Illustrations 20. Total 128

All these data are given on this one book so that you can see how very definite a designer has to be on each item of format.

It is obvious that this is a good choice of type to go with the subject matter and the reproductions of the classic paintings.

LENGTH OR NUMBER OF PAGES, AND TRIM SIZE

Length and trim size are all important, economically speaking, in most books. Picture books are apt to be in large trim size and short in length, yet they present tough problems of type choice and type allocation so that the right paragraphs fall with the right pictures and so that there is room enough for both without crowding. In the 6-to-9 age group, trim sizes are more conventional and smaller, but length is important in a different way. The size of type must be large, but at the same time a book with many pages (say, over ninety-six) should be avoided. It is poor psychology for beginning readers.

This age shies both at small type and at volumes that are heavy to hold. It is far better to cut the text than to give a crowded appearance, and it is better bookmaking to use a 12-point type, well leaded, than to crowd a 14-point type up against the gutter, leaving scanty margins and a breathless pushed-together look.

CONTENTS

This, like the setting, helps to determine the details of the format. The design of a quiet English story would be quite different from a fiery South American one. All of which would seem self-evident, except that occasionally one sees a book that seems to disregard the whole "feel" of a story, with the use of flamboyant type faces when the obvious need is for quiet distinction — or vice versa.*

For appropriately matching type and setting see *The Wildlife of Africa* by Jocelyn Arundel, illustrated by Wesley Dennis (Hastings) on the opposite page.

This type face, 11 point Baskerville, is small, because it

---

* Seth Agnew of Doubleday said in his review of the 1963 AIGA exhibition of children's books: "Many of the books submitted and some of the books in the show, appear to have been assembled from unrelated components by people who did not speak to each other. It is hard to imagine that one person or group of people thought ahead and planned the book as a complete unity. . . . Some few of the books seemed to me, too, to be actually shells; exhibitions of virtuosity on the part of the illustrator, the designer, and the publishers' staff. Like the bookseller [previously mentioned] I am not convinced that the child would know or care and can almost be persuaded that he was not greatly considered in their preparation." *Publisher's Weekly*, April 8, 1963.

from grass roots and, with the action of wind and burning sun, former grazing lands became deserts. Valuable acacia trees, robbed of the vegetation that protected their shallow roots, withered and died.

Wild animals in this region of Somalia began to search for new grazing and water. Herders had to whack down shrubs and trees to provide fodder for their own animals, now that grass had become scarce. More bare land was exposed to the sun as patch after patch of bush and dry forest vanished. Today the same areas of the Somali Republic that supported both man and wild animals verge upon stark lifeless desert that can support neither.

Illustration by Wesley Dennis and sample of type from *The Wildlife of Africa* by Jocelyn Arundel was necessary to limit the length of the book to 128 pages; but its 3-point lead and the ample margins make it readable, and the nice definition of this type face goes well with Wesley Dennis' animal drawings. The whole format is in keeping with the African setting of the book and the high school boys and girls who will read it.

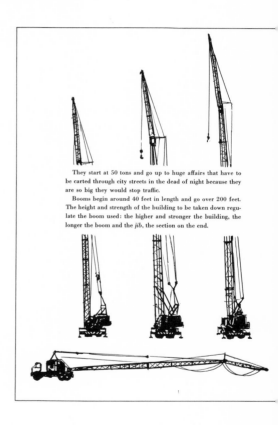

They start at 50 tons and go up to huge affairs that have to be carted through city streets in the dead of night because they are so big they would stop traffic.

Booms begin around 40 feet in length and go over 200 feet. The height and strength of the building to be taken down regulate the boom used: the higher and stronger the building, the longer the boom and the *jib*, the section on the end.

Doublepage spread from *Tear Down to Build Up, The Story of Building Wrecking* by Jean Poindexter Colby, illustrated by Joshua Tolford

Below is a double spread from my book, *Tear Down To Build Up,* illustrated by Joshua Tolford (Hastings).* This book on building wrecking, intended for the 9-to-12 age group, shows a nice choice of type, giving the art work full play, but standing up to its vehemence and strength.

What with the high rates for hand composition, a working

Most of the cranes, whatever their size, operate in the same way except for minor differences. Here is what the inside of most of the cabs looks like:

There are four main *levers*:

1. Controls either the crawlers or the swing of the house.

2. Controls the main hoist, to raise or lower the bucket or anything being lifted.

3. Controls the secondary hoist. This can open or close the clam shell bucket.

4. Controls the boom movement, up or down.

Note: there is a 5th lever to the left of the driver's seat which, when engaged, first moves the crawlers; when disengaged, it moves the house.

1.
2.
3.
4.
5.

There are two *foot pedals:*
1. A clutch
2. A brake
These are like those of an automobile.

11

* Please note that most of the examples in this chapter are from Hastings House books simply because of the convenience of reproducing the art. I would have liked more examples from the books of other publishers, but time did not permit this.

designer should explore available machine type faces to the utmost and reserve the use of hand type for chapter headings and title pages.

Here is a list of generally available machine type faces according to their origin and application. They can usually be had in 6- to 14-point sizes and a few in 18 point.

OLD STYLE	MODERN	
(for historical or	*Serif*	*Sans serif*
traditional effect	Caledonia	Futura
Caslon	Century	Spartan
Garamond	Cheltenham	News Gothic
Janson	Electra	Grotesque
Baskerville	Times Roman	
Kenntonian	Bodwin	
Granjon	Primer	
	Weiss	

All this and much more a book designer must know, but again, like the artist, the important thing is for him to be vitally interested in his work. In the old days, children's books supposedly were not worth any particular trouble or thought, and their appearance in the early twentieth century was stodgy, unattractive and unreadable. Designing, like illustrating, has been slow in reaching its present heights and still has a long way to go in some respects to be of over-all good quality.

One of the best investments any firm can make is the hiring of an intelligent, well-trained designer. Book designing demands interest, imagination, artistic ability, mental integrity, and professional training if it is to be good. It is first and foremost a creative task, and an essential one in the book business.

5 · Printing Methods

Note: This chapter is for the neophyte in publishing — the newcomer in writing, illustration or editing. There are many books on the subject, some of which I have listed in the bibliography. I especially recommend *Bookmaking, The Illustrated Guide to Design and Production* by Marshall Lee (Bowker), but no book or books can be a substitute for a visit to a printing plant. Everyone even remotely connected with the book business should go.

In the last chapter the preparation of a manuscript for the compositor was described. Now let us follow the actual process of changing into book form a manuscript on which a designer has worked.

This process is often confusing to many people, including authors and artists, because it is technical and little publicized. They do not realize that there is more than a slight gap between the final acceptance of a typed manuscript and its bound, jacketed debut. We have closed part of this gap by following a script through the design department. Now we will watch it change into book form.

There are three general ways a book may be printed: on a *raised* surface, which is called letterpress; on a *flat* surface, which is called lithography or offset lithography or simply offset; or on an *indented* surface, which is called intaglio or gravure. In letterpress the paper is printed by direct contact with inked type or an inked plate. In offset a mat or roller is passed over a plate and then over the paper so that the printing is not direct — it is "offset." In intaglio or gravure the surface of the plate is etched. When the plate is wiped, these etched portions hold the ink and are what make the imprints on the paper. (I hope that experts will pardon this oversimplification.) There is a fourth printing method called *silkscreen*, in which ink is forced through treated portions of a fabric screen. This used to be silk and was a hand method, but now nylon and other synthetic materials are used, and machinery does the work. It is still a method used mostly for small runs or for copy that requires a great density of ink — for example, the printing of white on a dark book cover.

PRINTING BY LETTERPRESS

Let us consider letterpress first, since it is the oldest and still probably the most common method of printing, although offset is catching up fast.

We have arrived at the point where the copy-edited typescript lies before the editor in its final form. By this time the author, the artist, the art director, the designer, and the production department have agreed on its size, shape and number of pages. In other words, it has been estimated as to length and designed as to trim size, type and so on. In this case a "stock size" has been chosen — one that is known to be economical from the point of view of both paper and press bed. (This is the flat surface of the press, where the plates are placed.) The artist has sent in his completed line drawings consisting of — shall we say — eight full pages, endpapers and three-color jacket. (The jacket will be printed separately.) We are ready to go into production.

One of the commonest book sizes is 5½" x 8¼", because a 33" x 44" sheet of paper can be used, which will allow 32 pages to be printed on each side with no wasted, unused paper. There are many press sizes, but it is economical to plan books for a press on which 32 or 64 pages can be printed at once. (See the explanation of a 32-page form on the next page.) The odd shapes of some children's books are sometimes expensive to produce, because they often have to be run either on small presses or on large presses, with a lot of wastage. In the old days this was not as costly as at present with pressmen getting higher wages than editors and with paper itself a distinct item of expense.

The planning ahead of a book is a most important phase of bookmaking. If enough thought and care are put into its production *in advance*, a good-looking, well-made book results, and many headaches are avoided. One of the "in advance" stages in bookmaking is the laying out or design of it.

As you have seen in the previous chapter, layouts are pencil diagrams, showing exactly the type to be used, the size of the page, the dimensions of the text area, illustrations, captions, folios (page numbers) and leading (amount of space between the lines).

A rough character count has been made on our manuscript to determine the approximate number of words, lines and pages so that the book can be made up into even "forms." A form is a rectangular metal frame and the plates or type it holds, which is placed on the printing press bed; 32- or 64-page forms are the most usual in book work, since it is cheaper to print that number of pages at a time. How-

175

ever, 16-page forms, and even 8-page forms are sometimes necessary.

Now the script is ready to be set in type. Type is set by linotype, monotype or by the new computer composition method. This method plus the entry of electronics in other phases of printing mark a major breakthrough in this busi-

A modern computer composing machine.

This photograph and that on page 178 were supplied by The Mergenthaler Linotype Company.

176

ness. An operator does not have to be specially trained, the machines cost less than the old-style ones and take up less space. Also they produce copy via paper tape, which is changed to magnetic tape,* for the computer setters without having to go through the reproduction proof stage. At present, the justification of lines is somewhat of a problem; authors' corrections are another and the human element of running a computer is a third. Hence the new method is mostly used now for newspapers, textbooks, dictionaries, telephone books and paper backs. However, it won't be long before all composition will be done by this method and great should be the saving in time, and perhaps, money.

Meanwhile let us concentrate on the usual methods of composition: linotype and monotype. These are called "hot metal" typesetting in contrast to "cold metal" or setting from tape.

In linotype a whole line of type is set at once by an operator sitting in front of a linotype machine. In monotype a man operates a machine that punches a series of dots and dashes on a roll of paper, and the type is set from that by another machine or "caster." Linotype is less expensive but when corrections have to be made, a whole line must be changed to correct one letter. In monotype, a single character or phrase can be fixed without disturbing the rest of the line. However, linotype has nearly supplanted monotype in most shops in this country† because of its greater speed

---

* This step may be eliminated soon.

† Oddly enough, it is the other way around in England. At the huge plant of Thomas Nelson, Ltd., that I visited in Edinburgh, Scotland, they had fourteen monotype machines to two linotype. They had the very modern Klischograph, though, for color work.

An old-fashiond Linotype machine

and lower cost, so that it is important for an editor or a designer to see that manuscripts are laid out in type faces available in linotype. These are clearly indicated in type books.

Film type, the recent development I have just mentioned, is also set up by the punch-card method, which is then directly exposed on a film negative, avoiding the use of metal altogether.

178

Large type sizes (24 point or more — see preceding chapter), like those used on title pages or jackets, are set by hand, one letter at a time, from a case that looks like this:

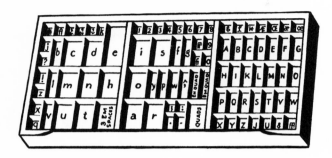

The type is dropped in a little rack or "composing stick" by the typesetter, who fills in the specified space between the letters with blank lead pieces. I have set type by hand, but never became very good at it. An experienced operator knows his case by heart, and his hands fairly fly between case and stick.

Sample pages are set up according to the layouts of the art director and are sent to the editorial and production departments for approval. If the visual effect is not good — for example, sometimes the type chosen looks too heavy or too hard to read — new layouts are made. Added leading can easily be handled. Correction at this stage can thus do wonders. Or if the book is discovered not to fit in its entirety into even forms, new layouts are made with a different size type, with more lines on a page, smaller margins or some other change. New sample pages are then obtained.

We will assume that sample pages have already been approved; so this time the whole manuscript is set up in type, and galley proofs are taken on long rough sheets. (A galley is a shallow metal tray with raised edges on three sides in which the type is placed for proving.) A set of galley proofs containing the whole book is sent to the author after having been proofread at the press. Final corrections are made when the author sends the proofs back with his revisions. It is important for the onward progress of the book that he not make too many. Wholesale rewriting is very expensive and causes delay, especially with the new electronic computer typesetters.

At this point the copper or zinc engravings of the illustrations arrive. These engravings or "cuts" are inserted where they belong with the type if they are half pages or spots. The galleys are divided up into pages; then the full-page cuts are placed so that each one goes with the appropriate text and each appears on a right-hand page if this is at all possible. Then the "pages" are locked up. This means that each page is placed inside a framelike iron case, and from this locked-up type, page proofs are pulled and approved by the production and the editorial departments. Then plates are made.

If the type and cuts are plated, an impression is first made in wax, and this wax mold is coated with graphite and placed in a bath of copper sulphate, through which is run an electric current. This liberates negative and positive ions with the result that the copper fills in the wax and makes an exact reproduction of the type. (Nowadays, more modern shops use terraplate instead of wax. This is a mixture of lead and graphite, a molding medium backed up with tin.) This copper shell is quite thin and has to be backed up with metal, mostly lead. The resulting plates are trimmed and beveled. When that is done there is a set of plates all ready for the presses.

During the last few years plastic has been used to make

plates, and the saving in cost is considerable. Long runs of fifty or a hundred thousand copies were not feasible at first, but now such plates are successful even for long runs.

Our book next arrives in the press room, and the forms are locked down on the press beds. The paper has been brought up in huge piles and has been loaded on the feeder of the press. The press is started up, and off she goes!

Several sheets are inspected for color — or amount and evenness of ink — okayed and the run is on. As soon as that form is printed, the pages are dried and sent back to the presses to be "backed up," or printed on the other side. At that time each sheet is put on a "light table" (glass lighted from underneath) and checked for alignment of text areas and folios — or page numbers. Proofs are scrutinized and okayed, or last-minute corrections are made, and away the presses clatter with their deafening shuffle and drone.

So the sheets of our book, 33" x 44", are printed and trundled off to the inspection room, where they dry and await delivery to the bindery.

I had a minor internship in printing during the run of *The Song of Robin Hood* by Anne Malcolmson, illustrated by Virginia Lee Burton (Houghton), at the Riverside Press. The book was only 128 pages long, but, contrary to most, many of the text areas were different in size and had to be centered, measured and arranged exactly so on the press bed. This was a honeycomb affair, which you attacked with a big key (it looked like a roller-skate job). A turn here and a turn there shifted the plates so that eventually the beautiful designs were rightly placed in the exact spot the artist wished them. She also regulated the flow of ink so the sheet was evenly printed. That was most important, because there was a large amount of black in the illustrations.

PRINTING BY OFFSET

In the last section I described rather sketchily a typical children's book being printed by the letterpress method. It is to be hoped that the inadequate description convinced you, as I said in the introductory note, that you ought to visit your nearest letterpress printing plant. Such an excursion is an absolute essential to any artist, author or editor.

In this section I shall try to give you a brief and extremely elementary view of another kind of printing: offset lithography. Offset is particularly interesting, since most of the modern colored picture books and also books with photographs or halftone illustrations are produced by this method. Two of the reasons for using this type of printing are that offset is cheaper on long runs (editions of twenty thousand or more) and that coated stock or shiny paper does not have to be employed for halftone pictures as it does in letterpress. A third and most important reason is that the artist can use a fine wash or halftone technique as well as line and thus create many different and soft effects. Line drawings can be very beautiful, but they do not fit the mood of every book; and variety in illustration is both stimulating and gratifying.

Lithography is based on the age-old fact that oil and water do not mix. The process had its beginnings many years ago, when artists actually prepared their work upon stones that had previously been leveled by grinding to produce a flat surface. The artist was required to work in "reverse," so that when the paper was pressed against the surface, the image that then appeared was "reading right."

This was largely a hand method of printing, and as time went on and more copies were required, the same stones were locked in presses in much the same manner as type is placed in letterpress printing. It was then found that production was excellent* but still slow, and with the advent of high-grade photography, methods were worked out whereby it was possible to photograph the art subject (done separately on drawing board) by a large camera; and the resultant negative was then transferred to the stone. After the possibilities of stone had been exhausted, a grained zinc plate was employed. This was flexible and meant that the zinc plate could be strapped around a cylinder — and so the present-day method and equipment evolved.

The basic chemistry of lithography is still maintained, however, and the principle of the antipathy of oil and water is the basis for the entire industry. For the moment, let us concern ourselves only with the reproduction of a piece of black wash art work, which will be combined with type to produce an entire page. The reproduction proofs of the text and other type matter, together with the art work, are sent to the lithographer. He makes a negative of both the type and the illustration in his camera and then strips the two units together as shown in the dummy that has been prepared by the publisher. This has to be "flopped" so that the text and pictures are not in reverse, and generally a complete positive is made of this combined art and type.

To get the dark and light variations of color, the film has been "screened." This screen, composed of hundreds of cross lines ruled on glass, is put between the picture and the film with the result that different parts of the picture are broken

---

* Lynd Ward describes this method in a very lucid, interesting manner in the February 1964 issue of *The Horn Book*. He did for me the handsome *Mexican Story* by May McNeer (Farrar, Straus) on lithographic stone. We had one of the stones at our sales conference when I presented this book. It created a lot of interest and admiration.

up into large and small dots depending on the density of the color. These dots actually control the appearance of the final picture, because they make up the printing surface of the plate.* Thus commercial artists who do the correcting after the first proofs are drawn and the areas to be changed have been indicated are called "dot etchers." They actually correct these tiny dots so that the reproduction in the book will be more like the original art work. I understand that in some cases computers can now make such corrections — which is again a large saving.

To return to our positive plate, this is next put close to a sheet of sensitized metal in a vacuum frame and exposed to a strong light, which goes through the transparent parts (the actual "drawing" of the picture) and hardens the surface underneath. The dark parts of the film keep the light off the remainder. Etching ink is then poured over this plate and eats into these exposed parts. The result is a picture etched on the surface of the metal. The plate is then ready for the press.

Now the plate is strapped around the press cylinder, and the paper is placed in the feeder mechanism. The press is started, and the cylinder revolves, causing the plate to contact first an inked roller and then a second cylinder, which is covered with a rubber blanket. The blanket is used as a transfer agent only, since the paper is brought in direct contact with the blanket, and not the actual plate. (Hence the term "offset.") This insures longer life for the plate and at the same time lends a soft quality to the final result. In the areas where the light has been exposed through the transparent areas of the positive, the emulsion is hard and will

* In another field a more recent application of the dot system can be seen on any television screen.

184

not allow the ink to adhere. This means that the ink stays only on the plate areas containing the illustration and type.

If it is a four-color book, there are four plates for each page obtained by using a filter in the camera for each particular color; if it is a three-color job, there are three plates for each page, and so on. With one set of these plates the text must be combined — usually the black one, because it is easy to read black type. But the text may be printed in blue with the blue plate, or in any dark color used in the pictures. Thus, one set of plates combines the text and one color of the pictures — usually black, dark brown or dark blue — or possibly this one color is the *only* color of the book.* This plate is all ready to go to press, or, if more colors are used, the other sets of plates are, too.

Lithograph presses used for picture books are mostly two- or four-color presses, so that if the book is a two-color job, it will need to go through a two-color press twice — once for one side of the page and once for the other. In the case of a four-color book, two colors are printed on one side and then these two colors on the other. After that the same sheet is sent back through the press again for the addition of the other two colors on each side. Or, on a four-color press, all four colors may be put on in one run, then the sheets dried and turned over for the four colors to be put on the other side. There is always a register problem, though, with four colors printed at once. You seldom can get them lined up exactly right.

Production speeds of from three thousand to ten thousand

---

* A delightful example of the success of one color is *Blueberries for Sal* by Robert McCloskey (Viking) in which both type and pictures are printed in a deep, blueberry blue.

sheets per hour are common at the present time, and research is continually being advanced with an eye to increased press speeds. Such equipment makes longer press runs not only advisable, but in many cases almost necessary, if the publisher is to take complete advantage of present-day technology.

Altogether the cost of first-rate color lithography is tremendous. There is the expense for the camera-focusing first, hours and hours of it to get the art work reduced to the right size and to photograph faithfully all parts of the picture. Then there is the large amount often spent on color correcting, as described. More dollars go into "salt prints" or van Dykes.

The greatest outlay, though, is for the "plates" or films. This is understandable when there are sometimes four plates for each picture. For a picture book the cost of these varies from $2,000 to $10,000 on up. The total investment a publisher often has to make in a picture book before he sells a single copy can run anywhere from $10,000 to $50,000.

For this reason as well as many others, an editor carefully investigates the art work of a proposed picture book before a contract is issued. A lot of work and a lot of money have to be spent above and beyond the remunerations to author and artist before the finished book appears.

To get the final effects they desire, all artists should know the offset printing process thoroughly. The best way to learn this is by working in or visiting an offset printing plant. Then the problems in color work become clear or at least clearer.

6 · Bindings and Jackets

On each of my many visits to printing plants and binderies, I have wondered if I was not in the wrong end of publishing. The process of actually bringing a book to its final, printed and bound form is such a satisfying one, perhaps more so than the editorial operation, where the pleasures often seem small and sometimes questionable.

My doubts are probably caused by the age-old feeling that the other fellow's grass is greener, but I defy anyone who has read thus far to visit a bookmaking plant and not be fascinated by the whole process. To me this feeling is especially strong in a bindery. The different machines are extraordinary, albeit rather old-fashioned, and the men who work and oversee them are excellent craftsmen.

Part of the fascination comes from the many different *kinds* of equipment in a bindery. First of all, there is the folding machine. The printed sheets — whether printed by offset or letterpress or whatever — are delivered to the bindery from the printer and are folded up into signatures, or groups of 16 or 32 or 64 pages each, depending on how

many pages are printed at once. This folding also depends on the imposition, or placement, of pages on the sheet and the way the book has been planned for binding. For instance, a short 24- or 32-page picture book probably will be center-sewn, or saddle-stitched, which means that a long series of looping stitches will run down the middle of the book. Such sewing allows the book to lie flat and permits a good view of double spreads (pictures that stretch over two pages). In juveniles, however, it has the disadvantage of leaving an end of binding thread exposed at the bottom of the book where it is cut off from the next volume. Young children often find this an irresistible temptation. Also the middle pages can come out with a good pull.

This center stitching or center wiring (in a cheap book) calls for a different press layout and different folding from Davis side-stitching, or from Singer-stitching, which is the

binding most commonly used in schoolbooks and in the library binding of trade juveniles, because it is strongest. With the Singer machine the folded signatures are laid flat in a pile and stitched straight up and down through the whole thickness of the book just as you would sew several pieces of cloth together on a sewing machine. Such a book will seldom shed a page or loosen under wear, but it has the obvious disadvantage of being impossible to open flat, so that some of the art work is wasted. You can get around this somewhat by asking the artist to keep important material out of the gutter and by allowing at least ⅜ inch between the pictures and the gutter. This insures quite a good-looking double spread. See pages 40-41 in *Pangur Ban* by Joan Balfour Payne (Hastings). The wolf comes together nicely in the middle.

As the experts say, side sewing results in "mouse-trap"

books — they snap shut on your hands. Regardless of this, it is the binding required by most librarians for books up to 128 pages, and library binding is something all publishers have had to go into to keep institutional sales.*

Our book, however, is not a picture book. It has 160 pages and is going to be reinforced Smythe-sewn, the usual type of binding for books of 160 pages and up that will receive a normal amount of wear. Just previous to the sewing, the signatures are "gathered," or collected in order (another admirable machine). They are "smashed," or flattened (stay away from this one) and piled up ready for whatever sewing has been ordered by the production department.

Smythe-sewing means that each signature is sewn to the next group and the whole held together by the glue of the backing, a strip of cloth reinforcement on each side of the signature and the cloth cover.

Now our book is beginning to *look* like a book. Its edges are trimmed so that there will not be any uncut pages, and it is ready for the cover. The machines from now on are efficient — but again in great need of new automated techniques. For example, after the edges are cut, the back of the book is glued and rounded and backed. Then it is ready for the casemaking, or covermaking, machine, which does a complicated job slowly and carefully, if you can call a machine "careful." This is also true of the casing-in machine.

---

* Another example of a picture book in color with one or more double spreads is *Shaun and the Boat* by Anne Molloy, illustrated by Barbara Cooney. It was vital that these pages be checked in the "mechanical" or printer's dummy. They all had to be individually cut apart to leave at least ⅜ inch on each side of the gutter so that the stitching would not cut in on the art when it was bound. We checked this at the press again before the book was run.

Signatures
sewn together
and covered
with glue

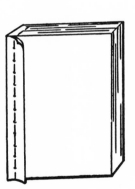

Smythe Sewing

STITCHES

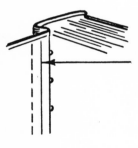

Saddle Stitching

Reinforcement
pasted to cover
under endpaper

Singer Stitching

Let us watch a casemaking machine in action. It takes cardboard that has been cut to the right size, places the pieces correctly on the cover cloth, cuts the corners, folds down the sides and cuts the cloth off at exactly the right place for each book. Then it folds down the new edge and proceeds to the next one. These covers may already have been treated with pyroxylin and printed by offset with a design and the title. This is required of the so-called "library binding." Books for the trade are simply stamped with a cover die that has a design taken from the illustrations or especially drawn and with appropriate lettering. This die has previously been cast in brass or some other metal by a diemaker, usually in a separate shop.

At this point the casing-in machine takes cover in one hand (it seems almost that human) and glued signatures in the other, presses the two together and delivers the final product for flattening in the hydraulic presses. The winger or "windmill" casing-in machine requires a man to split each book in half (open the pages at the middle) and place it on an arm, whence it is swung into the cover, but a newer machine splits the book mechanically and causes it to come up through the saddle and through the paste rolls and then anchors it to the cover by the backstrip. The strip of reinforcing fabric is now glued to the signatures and to the cover. It may be exposed or covered by endpapers. These "ends" are now added, which also helps to hold the book to the cover. They are glued to the cover in front and in back and may have been separately printed with a design beforehand.

So, there is our book, complete except for jacket, being pressed down so that it will not warp when shipped out to the stores and eventually to individual customers. (Needless to say, one of the first copies goes to the eager but apprehensive editor.)

All these details have been semitechnical and hence possibly uninteresting. And they certainly are incomplete, for it is impossible to describe everything that goes on in a bindery.

Again I urge you to see the whole business yourself if you have the opportunity and I do hope that there will be some modernization in it before too long.

Kenneth James, general manager of A. Horowitz & Son, binders, spoke as follows at the Trade Book Clinic of the American Institute of Graphic Arts. The following excerpt is quoted from *Publishers Weekly*, May 2, 1966:

> The first use of cloth for bookbinding was in 1820. We are still using book cloth today; it may be natural finish, pyroxylin-impregnated or unsupported vinyl but the concept of cloth over boards remains the same. On the other hand I have been told of advances being made in printing . . . whereby manuscripts are typed once, corrected by computer, projected through cathode ray tube onto film and printed electrostatically. When I ask what happens to the printed sheets I am told they will be bound in the conventional way. All this talent and money to improve the relatively few operations involved between manuscript and printed sheets, but no comparable advances for the many start and stop, pick up and put down operations in binding!

Some variations of binding are of particular interest to artists, designers and others planning to go into the field professionally. For instance, there are several ways of dressing up a book. One is by the use of headbands, those colored pieces of tape that appear on the top and bottom of the backbones or shelf-backs of expensive books. These increase the sturdiness of a binding to some extent but are really there almost entirely for the sake of appearance.

Another extra that can add glamour is tinting the top cut edge of the pages of a book. Since most editors of children's books have to pare their costs to the bone, you do not often see this practice in juveniles.

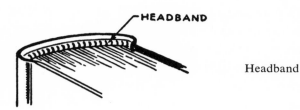

HEADBAND

Headband

Still another variation is the use of the three-part binding, in which the sides of the book may be bound in printed paper while the shelf-back is bound in cloth. This may save money because the amount of cloth is cut down, but occasionally one sees two colors of cloth used in this manner. The effect can be very attractive and is a pleasant change from the usual all-one-color binding, though few are those that can afford it. Not all binders are equipped to do it, either.

Gold or silver stamping on the cover and shelf-back is another beauty touch that one can have for a price. This is not much more expensive than a one-color stamping, yet enough so that if you have to cut corners, it is an extra to omit. Also, it is not always appropriate to the contents.

Stamping in two, three or four colors is another way of adding eye appeal. Beautiful bindings are sometimes achieved in this way, or as is common practice nowadays in library bindings, the binding cloth is printed in two or three colors by lithography or silk screen.

Endpapers are probably the most accepted way of enhancing the appearance of a binding. They are an additional expense to be sure, but not a large one, and they often do contribute a great deal to the attractiveness of a book. Sometimes endpapers add valuable information, too, like Barbara

Cooney's diagramatic drawing of the curragh in *Shaun*; or they supply a panorama of the countryside that sets the place and tone of the volume, like those by Wesley Dennis for *The Wildlife of Africa* by Jocelyn Arundel (Hastings). Incidentally, in that book, at the request of several librarians, we used *two* sets of endpapers: 1) plain white (this is pasted down) and next to it, 2) the double-spread lion picture. In this way, when the book is rebound, the art will not be lost, as it frequently is.

This is only one of the practical criticisms of binding that have come from librarians. Naturally they, more than any other group, are interested in the durability of books. Through their insistence much more attention is being paid to the quality of the binding of juveniles and the materials that go into them.

In fact, to meet their requirements, most publishers have to put on bindings that outcost and outwear the interior pages. This does not make sense and is not done in England or European countries. At present the cost of so-called library binding is tremendous. It is partly responsible for the price of children's books today and for a good deal of extra and expensive accounting work at the publishers', who have to bill and keep track of two editions of each book.

Besides cloth of various grades there are several bookbinding papers used mostly on adult books and sold to the general public rather than libraries and schools. These differ widely in wearing capacity and other qualities and should be used with caution because of the library requirements cited above. However, some of them are of excellent value and wear better than the cheap cloths. Some indeed are more expensive than cheap cloth.

195

Books bound in "plain" (i.e., not binding) paper are not good investments if you want long-lived possessions, unless they have *cloth* shelf-backs. When there is no cloth in the binding and the paper goes over the hinge — a practice in some of the inexpensive picture book series sold in chain stores — it wears out quickly, and the book comes apart. Still, most of these books sell for a relatively small price and are not intended to be everlasting treasures. Sometimes their low binding cost allows the publisher to price them for a large public sale, enabling parents to buy more books than they otherwise could. There is something to be said for both expensive and inexpensive bindings, and certainly the essential thing to keep in mind is that the *insides* of a book are most important. No book should be bought only because it is attractively or staunchly bound, although I am all for both attributes.

JACKETS*

The value of good jacket design should be self-evident, since jackets are responsible for the first impression a book makes on buyers and readers. Nevertheless, in some cases and when time runs short they are not accorded the planning and attention they deserve.

Though the jackets of picture books will invariably bear the mark of the illustrator, either by repeating an inside illustration or featuring one in a kindred spirit, the typography may depart from the book itself if the requirements of strong

---

* On some library bindings, the jacket is omitted. The binding is stamped or printed in several colors and hence is attractive to the young customer, and the flap copy is incorporated in the book itself. This seems an excellent idea, because it keeps prices down, but jackets are widely used for display purposes by librarians so perhaps this saving is not a warranted one.

display and poster impact demand it. Muted colors and static type arrangements do not make for effective book jackets and should be avoided. Jacket illustrations and typography are best when they symbolize the spirit of a book in its entirety.

In the case of a book that is to be printed by letterpress, the jacket is printed on a separate small press, because it is usually in color. Also letterpress color printing has to be done on coated stock (paper having a shiny surface of china clay) so that a letterpress jacket could not be run with the book anyway. It is therefore a separate item of expense and an important one, as I have explained above, because this outer sheet that wraps around a book is the first thing a reader or buyer sees. It may prejudice him for or against the book at once. Consequently, money put into good-looking jackets is well spent.

If a book is printed by offset, the jacket may be printed with it — that is, included on the same press sheet — if there is room for it and if the colors of the jacket are the same as those in the book itself. If not, the jacket has to be run separately either by letterpress, offset or silk screen. Art directors, book designers and those who check imposition try to plan offset books on press sheets that will be large enough to include the jacket and still not have waste space.* Sometimes, if a book is run in one color, the first color of the jacket may be printed at the same time. Then, after the press run, the jacket is cut off and run through another press to add its other colors. This method is not recommended.

* The demand by jobbers for extra jackets is one objection to this practice, but often it is cheaper and better to give them the five hundred or so extra jackets that they seem to require and throw the books away than run an extra jacket separately. The book business is amazing in many ways like this one.

The preparation of art work for letterpress and offset jackets is the same. Both can be done by the full-color or by the separation method. Those that are done by letterpress usually are in line or flat color, although they may be done by halftone if desired, using a coarse screen. Separations save on expense and insure the jacket's looking the way the artist intended.

The kind and weight of paper is important in jackets, because they take a good deal of wear and tear. The actual selection of paper, however, is a study in itself, and one that is too technical for inclusion in this volume. Like other aspects of production it is fascinating, and every artist, editor and production man should know something about it.

A jacket is often proved like any other color printing job, and the art director and editor are usually responsible for the acceptance or rejection of this proof. Occasionally jackets have to be sent back two or three times to obtain the desired result and to be sure the title and other lines of type are clear and effectively displayed.

The wrapping of the jacket on the book is part of the binding process, and therefore it is important to have the jackets printed and in the bindery ahead of time. *A jacket should always be ready for the semiannual sales conference on each title to be presented.* Salesmen feel lost without jackets. Often they would rather have them than books — less heavy to carry and less to read.

If the jacket is to be varnished — which helps to give it sparkle and prevent soil — this is usually done outside the bindery. For a small and often quickly discarded object the jacket requires a lot of work and money.

7 · Production–Close Calls

There is one important item to be pointed out before this section of the book is ended. It holds for illustration and any other part of the publishing business. Every week there is a crisis, and it is always a new and different one.

As I have pointed out, it is vital for the editor, the art director or the production manager — or all three — to check the final art work of a book before it is put into production. It must be correctly done for reproduction, it must be right for the particular chapter it is in, it must be located on the proper page in that particular chapter. For this purpose each piece is numbered or cued in some way and the galleys so marked. When it is delivered to the platemaker or the lithographer, it is counted and signed for. The editor and the art director are satisfied that everything has been done that should be done, and this part of the book is completed.

So that you can learn by my experience, I will describe a few unexpected happenings that will serve to show that you cannot guard against the unknown, and in publishing there always *is* an unknown.

First of all, the complete art work of my book on building wrecking, *Tear Down To Build Up,* was lost. Supposedly we had sent it to the printer via his messenger on a certain date, but after a couple of weeks his representative called to ask where it was. My consternation over that telephone call was considerable, as was everybody else's. The production office was turned upside down for the missing package. The receptionist was quizzed. For some reason there was no receipt signed when it left our office, so it seemed it must still be there. But it was not.

The printer insisted he had never received it, and there was no proof that he had. I asked for permission to go to his plant and look around, but editors are not allowed to do things like that.

Another week went by. Fortunately the company was insured for such losses, but I certainly felt foolish when I called the artist, Joshua Tolford, and had to ask him to do the whole thing over. It is a semitechnical book, and there were over forty pieces of detailed drawing in it. Fortunately, Josh is a wonderful fellow and a wise one, too, for he had kept his tissue roughs. But even at that it took him another six weeks to do the job. Of course, he was paid for it, but there were other things he would have preferred to do; and furthermore, the book had to be postponed until the next season.

MORAL: to artists, save your roughs until the book is printed.

MORAL: to editors, be sure there is a signed receipt for anything of value leaving the office. Check the receiver to be sure it arrives. In this case, the art was finally found (too late) at the printer's. They never said just where.

The only good thing about this incident was that it concerned my own book. If I had had to confess to the author as well as the artist that we had lost the art work, it would have been rough.

Another story concerns art work that was being completed. Lynd Ward was the artist on the *America's* biographical series at Houghton Mifflin and had warned us that he would be in Mexico for the winter and would be shipping the illustrations for *America's Robert E. Lee* by Henry Steele Commager from there. Apparently at that time the Mexican postal department was lax and also often grabby, especially with parcel post shipments. The loss of paintings sent to the United States was almost routine, so Lynd suggested he mail the art piece by piece by airmail.

This was fine with me, and soon it began to come in. The black and whites arrived in fine shape, but the color panels, done in casein paint, were packed carefully in layers of wax paper. The first one I opened had a small piece of paper firmly stuck to General Lee's nose, and when I tried to take it off, it was obvious the nose was coming too. This was true of other parts of the paintings also.

The production department and I decided that if we let the paint dry, the paper might come off easily. So we waited a week. Meanwhile other color panels arrived, similarly wrapped and decorated with wisps of paper. The paint never dried, because, on the advice of a magazine article, Lynd had added wet varnish to the casein to prevent chalkiness; and the varnish had softened up en route because of being tightly wrapped. I cabled him about our predicament, and he sent the remaining art framed by strips of rough wood, from which little pieces of sawdust came off and stuck also. The only thing to do was to buy several pairs of tweezers, with which my helpers and I spent many a lunch hour, picking minute particles of paper and wood off the handsome paintings.

Actually, we did not mind doing this because it was such a magnificent job, but — as Lynd Ward's wife, May McNeer, said, "We all waited for the Robert E. Lee — and waited and waited!"

MORAL: wrap your art well; insure it, and entrust it to the mail department only when you have to.

The following incident will serve to show my ignorance, but it has another important point, too. Conrad Buff did the art for his wife Mary's *The Apple and the Arrow* (Houghton) in oils. (Those were the days when you could still afford to use this method.) The paintings were rich and glowing with color, and I can remember driving to the lithographer in Providence with great anticipation, because I loved this book and was looking forward to seeing it in its final form.

When you go to a press to check a book before the final run there is always quite a wait, because the plates have to be adjusted, the amount of ink, and so on, has to be corrected, before the pressman shows you a trial sheet.

This particular side of the sheet did not look too bad, except there was something wrong with the red. The uniforms were fine, but the faces of all the people, even the boy, looked apoplectic.

They cut down on the red, and then the faces looked fine; but the uniforms had turned a strange, dirty pink, and off in one corner a face did not have any color at all. Well, to shorten up this obvious tale, we had to compromise. Sometimes you do. I had the white-faced dead man taken out completely, and no one ever missed him, I hope.

It took all day to get a good proof, and then I had to go back the next day for the other side of the sheet. This was more of the same, but I take my hat off to those printers and to all the others who have had to deal with my particularness: they never complained (at least where I could hear it) and they seemed as anxious as I was to get a beautiful book.

MORAL: and, please listen, all you artists who would just like to sit down and paint your pictures instead of separating the colors in them: camera separation is not guaranteed perfect. Possibly with the new color scanners and the Klischograph, the situation may be improved, but until their equipment can be used economically, you had better do your own separations — that is, if you know the exact effect you want.

The next incident is not as flattering to the printing industry as the last one. It concerns the press-proving of *The Little Juggler* by Barbara Cooney (Hastings). I always ask Barbara to go with me when one of her books is on press, because she knows her printing and her colors and exactly the effect she wants. Furthermore, she does not irritate the printers and is wonderful company (for me).

This particular April day was a beauty. We started out in Barbara's Alfa Romaeo, which was fun in itself, and as we drove through the early lacy green of the Massachusetts countryside, the drive seemed more like a quick trip through the Elysian fields than a business one. However, we arrived at the press and were soon looking over a sheet. The register was good, and so were the colors except the red. (Reds are difficult; there are so many. So are blues and greens!) Barbara wanted a particular medieval red, and the one they had was almost orange. Well, again the printer was patient and daubed on test paper various combinations of colors until by the middle of the afternoon we had the red we wanted. I signed a press sheet, gave one to Barbara and took one with me — the usual procedure.

The book was printed and bound, and one day the art director proudly showed me the first copy. I nearly dropped dead. There was the whole book printed in the original orange-red with which we had started!

MORAL: for prospective editors and art directors. I had my okayed sheet. It was very different from the printed book. Theoretically we could have refused the whole printing, but by so doing the title would have had to be postponed a season. Since it was obviously a Christmas book, that would have meant postponing it a whole year. It was quite a decision. In the end, thanks to the sales force saying they never would have noticed the difference (sales forces always say that, and I'm sure they never do) we let it go. And go it did. So that a second edition came up very quickly, and you may be sure that that one was printed with the right red. In case you have reordered on this title, you might be interested in comparing them.

Incidentally, the excuse the printer gave was that the night crew came on just as we left and the foreman paid no attention to what we had been doing. He just went back to the original ink that was marked on his work sheet.

MORAL: there is none, except to realize that sometimes you just cannot win.

During twenty years of editorship and approximately two hundred picture books, I have only had to ask twice that a book be reprinted and the first sheets thrown away. The first time it was the printer's fault; the next time it was ours.

A four-color book was to be reprinted for about the fourth time. Since the first three editions had been satisfactory, there seemed no reason for any of us to go to the press for the occasion. When the printed sheets had been shipped to the binder, the usual sample folded and gathered sheet was sent to the office, and I looked at it.

The printing job was unbelievable. Not only had the colors been changed just enough to make it look like a Sunday comic paper instead of a book, but the register was extraordinary. The green stockings of the little girl were a quarter inch in front of her bare, white legs. The blue of her eyes had landed on her cheeks and a bridge, which was important to the story, had become two bridges: one in black line and the other in color.

The printer agreed with us that a new batch had to be done, and it was; but we lost our binding date and customers had to wait another two months.

As commented on previously, *reprints are important* and are not supervised enough by some companies. This is especially true right now when federal money has resulted in large orders of back-list books so that reprints are jamming up in both letterpress and offset printers. Needless to say a lot of them are going through with a minimum of care. For instance, I saw a reprint of quite a famous title in an author's house last week. He complained about it to me and showed me the original edition. The comparison was sad indeed. The first printing had nice fine lines and lovely highlights. The new book had page after page of blobs of black ink.

Probably the plates were worn out, but there was also too much ink on the sheet. Anyway, the point is that publishers should not put out this inferior merchandise. Authors and customers should complain. I honestly think that neither the editor nor the production manager saw this pathetic book, but they should have.

A new printing of a new book had to be made owing to a series of unfortunate circumstances that bear repeating, because it shows there should be a backup man on every book who knows the editor's, the author's and the art director's wishes. We had had a preliminary proof pulled on this title, *Pangur Ban* by Joan Balfour Payne. It was almost faultless; at least good enough so that I was prepared to make any small variations at the press when it was run.

Unfortunately a week before the press run I had to be rushed to a hospital for an emergency operation. Even then, I did not worry, because the proof had been so close to what we wanted.

In my absence, however, the art department had sent to the printer an order for a different ink "to pep it up a little," thinking I would be at the press to change it if I wished. The book was printed in a wild green and had to be reprinted completely.

Perhaps the most amusing printing of a picture book took almost twenty-four running editorial hours. The reason for the rush was that the sales conference was the next day. If Hardwick Moseley, sales manager of Houghton Mifflin during my editorship there, ever taught me anything — and he did, a great deal — it was that at each conference you must have a complete folded color sheet on a picture book for every salesman, or you postpone the title.

The black-and-white side of this particular book had been run, but the four-color side was the problem. So there I was at 8 A.M. to see the first two colors go on. By 10:30 these were okay, and the run was complete by about 4 P.M. Then the sheet had to be dried and the rollers washed up for the next two colors. This is a lengthy process, because the rollers are huge; and care must be taken to remove every speck of the previous inks. Finally, about 10 P.M., the last two colors were ready to go, and we looked at a trial sheet. The green was completely wrong!

We had had no proof run on this book, partly to save money, partly to save time, but mostly because we thought with a careful selection of colors from the Glen Killian ink book, we would not need a proof. However, instead of getting a nice spring green, a chromy, bilious color showed up. It might have been the proximity of large areas of blue that changed its value from that in the ink book, but anyway it was dreadful. We had to have another green. Even the head pressman agreed.

He scooted around, and the next two hours were consumed mixing up batches, combining this and that, until we found what we wanted. Then the press had to be washed up again for this different color, and another problem appeared.

It seemed that all the ink was stored in a separate locked building, which was surrounded by a high link fence, also locked. (After all, it was nearly midnight, and the custodian of the ink had long since gone home.)

The key to the building itself was found after an emergency phone call, but how to get over the fence? The night watchman did not have the key; the day man did not choose to answer the phone. I could not blame him. Suddenly the ink appeared. I never knew how, but two of the pressmen were young, long-legged and full of ginger. They ran some trial sheets — perfect. The run was on, and enough folded, trimmed sheets were delivered to the New York office that morning so each salesman had one.

I drove home at 4 A.M. with a huge January moon hanging in the sky like an iridescent platter. The northwest expressway, which is usually five abreast with slow-moving traffic, did not have a car on it. I was so happy over the final result of the book that I drove from side to side, singing "Night and Day" (appropriate) until I realized there might be a policeman around even at that hour. When I reached home, I showered, got breakfast for myself and the family and left to take the shuttle to New York. I was in the office by 11 A.M. — only fifteen minutes after my appointed time to present the juvenile books.

MORAL: 1. Printers are wonderful men.

MORAL: 2. Publishing is sometimes a lot of fun.

PART III

EDITING

1 · Diagram of a Publishing House

A great many people are interested in books and writing, but they know less about them than almost any other American business. And I use the word *business* advisedly, because that is what it is, in spite of visionary misconceptions on the part of those outside.

To be sure, publishing has its visionary side, its glamorous past and its occasionally exhibited high ideals, but these did not and do not flower without dollars to support them and organizations to produce them in tangible form. Furthermore, any publishing house that does not make more money than it spends, in the long run (meaning a reasonable number of years and measured against the initial investment) has to close its doors.

The financial part of publishing will not be discussed here except as necessary to show in a small way how a publishing house functions and how books come to be.

211

For some reason many authors and the majority of readers think a book is produced without effort and by some very speedy process. I wish to prove otherwise and to show that publishing is a complex business with a lengthy and time consuming method of operation. And that a book, once it has left the hands of the author and editor for the last time, is nothing other than a piece of merchandise, produced in as routine a way as possible.

Having worked for a large, a medium-sized and a small publishing house, the facts I am presenting will be a kind of mélange of all three. Naturally, each company differs from the others to some degree, but I believe that most companies follow the general pattern outlined below.

Here are the various divisions of a publishing house listed in the order a manuscript reaches them:

1. Cataloguing Department
2. Editorial Department
3. Production Department and Art Department
4. Sales Department
5. Advertising Department
6. Promotion, Publicity and Mail Order Departments
7. Shipping Department
8. Treasurer's Office
9. The Executives

In smaller publishing houses some of these divisions may be consolidated, while in larger ones they may be subdivided further. The results and duties are usually the same, with just more people doing them.

Let us start and outline in general the duties of each department as a manuscript passes through it.

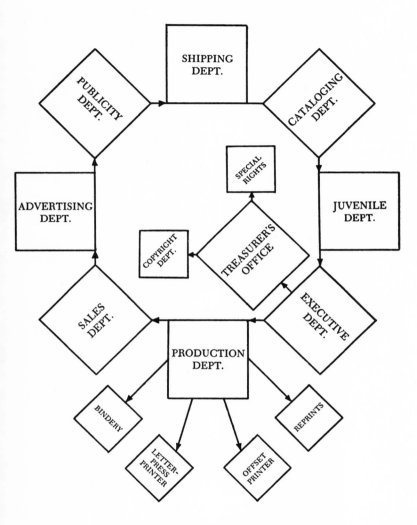

Diagram of a Publishing House

CATALOGUING DEPARTMENT

When a manuscript first comes into a publishing office, it goes to the Cataloguing Department, where it is given a number. Then a slip is made out noting this number, the author's name, the date, how it was sent (by express, first-class mail, etc.), the amount of return postage enclosed, how it happened to come (through an agent, directly from an author or through an editorial connection), what editorial department (juvenile, adult, educational) it should be assigned to. This slip always comes back to the Cataloguing Department and is filed there with the editors' vote and reasons for acceptance or rejection. In this way it is possible to keep careful track of authors and their manuscripts over the years.

EDITORIAL DEPARTMENT

Here, then, we have a fresh manuscript that has just been catalogued and sent to its proper editorial department. If the material has come in through the personal contact of any one editor, it is immediately assigned to him. If it has come in "cold," that is, directly from the author, unexpected and unsolicited, it is assigned to an available editor. If the piece of work falls into a particular category, history or science, for example, it goes to that editorial specialist.

Now, properly assigned, the manuscript gets a first reading with the results noted on that slip originally made out by the cataloguing department. A really poor manuscript dies here and goes back to the cataloguing department with a rejection slip or brief letter, both to be returned to the author. If the work has merit, it is usually passed on to another editor for reading and is discussed in a meeting of all the editors with possibly the addition of the sales manager and other officials.

At this point, after these two readings, a questionable manuscript is often rejected, but usually an encouraging note instead of a rejection slip is sent to the author, sometimes with suggestions for revision.

But here comes the manuscript that makes the grade. It probably is read by nearly all the editors in that department. It is discussed by the sales manager, and the production manager is called in to see if the book can be manufactured profitably. A word count is taken, rough cost figures are drawn up, an estimate of the probable edition (number of copies in the first printing), retail price, and so on, is made — often with the help of one or more salesmen, who report what the book might "do" in their territory. One particular editor writes up the book for presentation to the executive committee. There it is voted on, and if accepted, the contract is drawn up according to the agreement with the author, which has already been settled verbally or by letter.

We shall skip the ensuing editorial problems: the countless revisions, the continuous research, the preparation of bibliography and indices, the endless discussions between editor and author, editor and artist, editor and production department, editor and art director and agree that we have a finished manuscript, neatly typed and carefully copy edited for punctuation, spelling, and all other vagaries. (The proofreading and copy-editing department may or may not be part of the editorial department.)

PRODUCTION DEPARTMENT AND ART DEPARTMENT

Next the completed, copy-edited manuscript arrives at the production department. Here the production manager, his secretary and one or more assistants hold forth. One of the assistants estimates the length of the book very exactly this time: that is, he counts the numbers of characters (letters, punctuation marks and spaces) and approximates the number of pages according to the kind and size of type chosen by the book designer. This designer may be art director and head of a good-sized department if the publishing company is large. Or he may be just a person in the production department who has other duties besides "laying out" the manuscripts as they come in. (Book design and layout are described in more detail in Part II, Chapter 4.)

The manuscript is then sent to the printer or the company's press, if they have one of their own. Then, on the basis of the production department's specifications, a definite cost estimate — in contrast to the preliminary one before contract — is made. If the prices quoted are acceptable, the manuscript is then set in type. Proofs, known as "galleys" — to be precise, galley proofs — are "pulled" by the printer and sent to the publisher.

The galleys are proofread for the many errors that are apt to occur in typesetting even when done by tape. After these corrections are marked, the galleys are then sent to the author. Sometimes authors hardly read them; other authors may read them so carefully as to decide to rewrite practically the whole book in the margins. If an author does that, he has to pay for the changes, since most contracts prudently allow for a correction margin of only 10 per cent of the original composition cost. In other words, the manuscript should be agreed on by both author and editor as good and right *before* it goes to the printer. At least that is the theory.

Now we have the galleys back from the author. The editors often fret over his revisions, but finally they are made. The galleys are proofread again and returned to the printer for paging. At this point the illustrations are added. The page proofs are carefully read. If the book is to be printed by letterpress the plates are made, plate proofs are checked, and the plates put on the press.

All these operations are overseen by the production department. The manager follows the life of each book with elaborate time schedules that are continually being changed. Usually a big board in his office shows exactly the position in production each book has reached.

SALES DEPARTMENT

After the book is printed, the sheets are shipped to the bindery. Now, with the book on the way to being bound, the sales department comes into the picture. This department almost always consists of a sales manager, assistants who receive and correlate orders and a corps of salesmen who come two or three times a year to sales conferences to hear about the new books and then fan out over the nation to sell them in their particular districts. The sales manager himself is usually based in the home office and may or may not do direct selling by personal calls on large accounts. He ordinarily covers the accounts in eastern key cities like New York, Boston, Philadelphia and Washington. But whether he does or not, he is the king pin, the boss of the book, after it has made its conference appearance. He keeps daily sales figures on each new title and monthly or bimonthly checks on all titles in print and is in constant touch with each salesman.

Needless to say, the sales department is a most important

cog in the publishing wheel, because no matter how brilliant the books an editor can find and publish, they will not sell if the salesmen do not cover the important stores, libraries and jobbers (wholesale booksellers) in the country. Some sages say that a good book will come to the top regardless of the amount of publicity, advertising or the prominence of the publisher. But in this age of intense competition and of thousands of volumes published — many often on the same subject — a good number are lost in the shuffle. Personally, I think this is inevitable, but intelligent, comprehensive, aggressive salesmanship can do much to prevent it.

Therefore, the sales department and the sales conference are of primary importance to the individual book and to the company as a whole. It is at the sales conference that our new book is "presented." This gathering is usually held twice a year — in June for the fall books and in December for the next year's spring books. These conferences include the entire group of salesmen (some on full time for the company; others on commission who sell this "line" and those of other companies). The heads of all departments are present, as well as the company's officers. The book is described in detail by its editor, and then its sale and publicity possibilities are discussed thoroughly. The salesmen are asked to speak about the sales potentialities in their territories.

With juveniles every effort is made to have bound books for the conference, or at least folded press sheets. That is because illustrations and format (size of type, etc.) are of prime importance in a children's book. Naturally, complete books are a great asset in selling juveniles. Salesmen always bless an editor who provides them and object when they are missing. For instance, it is difficult to sell a picture book from a sample page or jacket. Illustrations, margins, length of text, kind of type — all these physical details when exhibited *in their final book form* help to raise a book's prepublication (or advance) sale and have a great deal to do with launching it properly.

It is quite an occasion, a sales conference! There is drama in the air, friction between individuals, outbursts of scorn and also outbursts of humor. My aim has always been to have *all* books ready for each conference, but that is extremely difficult because of leisurely authors and artists and because of production hazards and holdups.

In the case of the majority of adult books, and those for the upper age groups, bound books or press sheets are not available at the sales conference. Therefore each salesman is given a sample page set in type, a table of contents, a sample illustration (if there are to be any) and a finished jacket in color. These sheets are put in a transparent binder. When a salesman represents several companies, he may have to carry fifty or more of these.

After the sales conference is held, the salesmen go out to sell the new books in their territories. These territories add up to the whole of the United States with the exception of Hawaii. (Canadian representatives often attend sales conferences, too.) Soon the reports of sales begin to come in. And they happily mount as each man continues on his allotted tour.

The sales manager and the editor usually have most of the say on publication dates. These are important for juveniles as well as for adult books. For instance, it is foolish to publish children's books in June, when most people who are responsible for promoting the books — reviewers, librarians, booksellers — are either attending conventions or are busy preparing for summer schedules. Also the salesmen could not have covered their territories in that short time. Remember, the sales conference for fall books is in the preceding June. June publications would have had to be sold at the December conference and therefore presented to the bookstore buyers in February and March. See the Publishing Calendar at the end of this chapter.

And there are other factors: adult book publishing, for instance, is a matter of delicate timing. That is not true so much in the juvenile field, and there is much more around-the-calendar issuing of juveniles than there used to be.

To an author a delay on publication is aggravating and hard to understand. He delivers the manuscript and expects publication in a month or two. In some cases I have known this to happen — production departments can rush things through if there is some extraordinary reason.* But it's a risky procedure! Either that book misses a formal presentation at a sales conference (and this is, as we have seen, *very* important, because talking about a book and pushing it personally with the salesmen means a great deal more than a letter or announcement sent to them en route) or it means the book comes out before the salesmen have a chance to finish their tour. Either way sales are sacrificed.

The bête noire of publishing is a change in publication date. This upsets the salesmen, the stores, the reviewers, everyone. But the sales manager or the editor may decide it must be — either because the actual production of the book has become snarled and bound copies will not be available in time or because he may believe it would be advantageous

* See "Operation Instant Book" by Janet E. Babcock, *Book Production,* January 1966.

to publish the book sooner or later than originally planned. Sometimes a change is made when two *big* books might conflict. In fact, there are really many reasons for publication date changes, but few of these satisfy an author.

A publication date change means so much trouble that I think an editor is justified in asking an author to turn in a manuscript, finished and ready to set in type, at least six (and preferably eight) months before publication date. This gives time to plan and execute a bound book of handsome, salable format that will be ready for one of the two annual sales conferences.

Before we leave the sales department, let us look at one further duty fulfilled by its sales manager: *keeping the book in print.* This calls for sagacity, second sight and alertness, since many a gravy train has been missed by having a book suddenly flash into best-sellerdom only to have the stock give out just when the wave of popularity is approaching its peak. To prevent this calamity a sales manager watches the daily sales total and the reports of stock on hand with wrinkled brow and drumming fingers. Shall he recommend another printing while there are still six thousand copies in stock? How large a second edition will he need? After all, it is just as bad to get stuck with too big a second printing as it is to miss the boat by not having books to sell at the right time. I have known of instances where a book seemed to be going over with a bang only to have it suddenly stop selling. The transition from best-seller to "remainder" (books sold to a remainder house for ten cents or so on the dollar) may be swift — unless you have a crackajack sales manager. And it sometimes happens even when you do.

Reprints in juveniles are easier to judge, but harder to

manufacture because of the intricacy of production, especially of picture books. As has been shown, offset picture books are really complicated, because the color has to be checked carefully. So, if you are an author of one, do not grind your teeth if your book is out of stock for a month or so.

The sales department naturally has charge of all sales campaigns and therefore can be excused for looking at a book entirely from the sales angle. Well, why not? The salesmen *know* that publishing is a business and that everything depends on their success in pushing their merchandise, just as it would if they were selling a line of socks or electric beaters. The fact that children's books are merely another form of merchandise is hard for authors, artists and even editors to believe. It is true, though, and hence there should be the closest contact between a children's book department (or any editorial department) and its sales department.

A sales manager can often be helpful in pointing out sales possibilities or sales deficits in book ideas before they are published. He may bring in an occasional good manuscript, as can the regular salesmen. He can give support when most needed, and nine times out of ten he is a good fellow with a fund of stories that help to break up an editorial depression caused by any number of things.

ADVERTISING DEPARTMENT

To some extent, advertising is planned at the sales conference. The advertising manager and his assistant takes notes on each book, including the main points of interest, and plans are drawn up for imprinted folders, bill stuffers, posters and so on. Big campaigns are usually planned beforehand, however, and outlined to the salesmen at the conference. As a matter of fact, the advertising department does a lot of work before a conference, so this is probably the best place to describe its function in the publishing picture.

The advertising department and/or the juvenile promotion director handles display material, special brochures and jackets. It is a busy place.

In some companies the advertising department designs and writes the ads. In others this is done by an outside agency, whose representatives attend the conference. Nowadays most companies have a juvenile promotion director who writes the juvenile catalogues, releases and advertising. The amount of money to be spent and the size and placement of ads is decided on at a meeting. The copy is written, laid out, proofs read, and the amount spent is carefully placed against the title of each book. In this way you can check back on the planned program and its results and also answer authors' complaints about too little advertising for their books, which appear as surely as birds in the spring. I might add that they are the most futile of all complaints, because there is little an editor can do about them.

I do not know one author who thinks his or her books are advertised enough; and it is important to say here for everyone's peace of mind that probably no two books have exactly the same amount of money spent on them, although a tremendous effort is made to be fair. Some authors would like a page in the *New York Times* (cost $2460.00) but wise ones appreciate separate mailings on their books to librarians, ads in the library or education magazines and representation in the many exhibits that travel around the country.

The amount of money allocated to a book is usually in direct proportion to its sales possibilities. Naturally, if after publication it looks as if a book is going to exceed the estimated sales, more money is voted or given it. In some companies there are meetings of the advertising department with the company executives to determine the exact amount of money to be spent on each title, and the whole amount has to be within the annual advertising budget. In other companies the arrangement is less binding, and it is possible to get more money for certain books and projects without going before the executive committee. The advertising manager customarily holds the purse strings, but there is always some higher authority to whom he must answer.

PUBLICITY, PROMOTION AND
MAIL ORDER DEPARTMENTS

At the sales conferences the publicity or promotion department (in most companies they are one and the same) springs into action. The publicity manager is always present and makes notes on such pertinent matters as where authors live, what the chances are of feature pieces or interviews on TV or in the local and national papers, what publicity tie-ins can be arranged, what can be done to make authors happy and introduce them to reviewers, bookstore owners or key librarians. He also discusses with the salesmen any public appearances in panels or luncheon meetings that might be arranged.

Generally the publicity department is responsible for making special contacts for the author and for meeting important people, although often editors help on that. The publicity department or the juvenile promotion man or girl must keep photographs, biographical data and reviews on file and send this material out when requested by librarians, bookstore owners, reviewers or lecture bureaus.

The publicity department is also supposed to issue releases to the press or flyers to the trade telling about the most newsworthy books, the authors and the illustrators. The purpose is to stimulate interest in the bosom of a reviewer, TV program editor, bookseller or jobber for that particular title. However, because there are so many of these from so many different companies, the receivers sometimes find their sheer numbers baffling. Consequently releases or flyers should be issued sparingly and only when there is something extra special to be said.

Sometimes the preparation of the semiannual catalogues (spring and fall) comes under the advertising department and sometimes under the publicity or promotion department and, as I have said, the promotion director of the juveniles, if there is one. Then again, they are often in the province of the mail-order department. Company procedure here differs widely. But, make no mistake about it, catalogues are important. They are read and filed carefully away for future reference by all the up-and-coming store buyers and librarians in the country. A good catalogue is hard to compile and to check and expensive to print and circulate. But when one has been done well, it is worth its weight in gold, both to the authors and to the publisher.

The work of the mail order department is obvious. The extent of it depends on the amount and kind of catalogues, circulars and advertising done by the company. Many publishers prefer not to handle small orders; others have a system set up for them. This department is often under the promotion or the sales department. Of course, it concerns both.

Before we leave the advertising and publicity or promotion departments, let us look at them in relation to the whole publishing company's picture. They are important in that they bring the author and the book to the attention of the public. They operate on budgets allocated to them, which are part of a big program. The proportion of income devoted to these departments by most companies is hard to estimate, because it differs widely, but it is a real slice of each publishing dollar.

THE SHIPPING DEPARTMENT

Before publication day the shipping and billing departments have been alerted on each forthcoming title. They receive the advance orders from the sales department and pack the books so that they will be received prior to publication date. Their job is not as easy as it sounds, because with changes of price and date and with variation in bindings and in discounts, their work is complex and exacting.

Books may be mailed at a special rate, and this rate is uniform all over the country, but they can often be shipped more cheaply by truck or by express, which varies by zone. The time element is an important one, too, because West Coast accounts must receive their shipments at the same time as those near at hand, which often means juggling of schedules and frequent cursing at the whims of the editorial and production departments with their changes in publication dates of new books and bound dates of reprints. It is economical to ship several new or reprinted titles together, so that last-minute departures from schedules are really gruesome.

Then, too, after publication date has passed, the shipping department always has the headaches of rush shipments, delays, errors. The head of a shipping department has a nasty job, I think, because he can be blamed for almost anything (a store will kick more loudly about late, incomplete or badly wrapped shipments than almost anything else), and when deliveries are accurate and right on time, he is rarely praised. Also, the shipping department is often responsible for checking and counting stock, although that is largely computerized nowadays. Still it is very important to be able to know what is on hand in sheets and bound books of any given title at any time.

TREASURER'S OFFICE

This brings us to the treasurer and his office, the ramifications of which may be extraordinary, depending on the size of the company. Let us imagine a small company that has just contracted for a book and paid an advance royalty of, say, $500. Before this is paid, the treasurer, the president, the vice-president or whoever is in charge has worked out a cost and time estimate that is in keeping with the financial policy of the company. All this has been prearranged and is usually in the heads and the papers of one, two or three key men who know what they are doing and want to do. They have worked out in general the "publishing dollar" for their company. They know they can spend a certain percentage of it on production, on advertising, on royalties, on overhead and so on. Each book varies a little in each respect, but not too much, or their policy fails to work; and a figure in the red results. Usually, one book cannot do much damage unless a lot of money has been sunk in it, and most companies would not put all their eggs in one basket. But it is true that policies are important, that estimates must be adhered to and that money for advertising or publicity or advances cannot be given without a careful sizing up of the situation as a whole.

Advances, until they are paid off by earned royalties, are one of the great risks of a company. Whenever an advance is paid, money is set up in its place that cannot be used for any other purpose. This prevents a tailspin of deficit, although the tax picture has changed the policy of advances nowadays so much that it is hard to decide how to handle this part of a company's finances. Fortunately, large advances are not often required in the juvenile field.

Advances, of course, involve a good deal of bookkeeping. As may be the case in any business, bookkeeping is a first-class headache for the publisher even in this day of the computer. Withholding and social security notations are just part of the burden, because there are so many involvements in the present-day selling of books. In fact, in or connected with the treasurer's office is usually a man or woman who does nothing but handle what are known as "special rights and permissions." These have been partly explained in Part I, Chapter 4.

The treasurer is a busy man. He views the books from an impersonal point of view, but is occasionally jolted from his stony financial composure by having to sign a check for $500 for an advance on a book called *The Pinkest Elephant* or something equally irrational. However, most treasurers are well acquainted with the steady revenue that comes in from good juveniles over the years. And no one knows better how much can be lost on poor ones.

THE EXECUTIVES

The treasurer is one of the executives, as are the editors-in-chief of each department, on whose shoulders rest the final success of a company. If they cannot obtain good manuscripts, a company cannot last. And again, the responsibility of selecting the editors who pick out the books rests on some key man or men in the company. He or they may be the president, the vice-president, the general manager or all three. Let us suppose for convenience that there is only one in command.

If he is wise, he distributes his responsibility among many people, obtaining the best man for each job and thus bringing many good brains to bear on his problems. This may be carried on to such an extent that he may seem a remote personage, even a figurehead, but that is almost always wrong. In this business of publishing he formulates the final policy, sees to its general operation, watches it carefully, but does not interfere between author and editor or editor and production man unless something goes radically wrong.

In most cases he dominates the executive committee and the board of directors. He tells them what the company's plans are and its accomplishments since the last meeting. As in the British government, if the board goes against his policies, he is often removed or removes himself. He is IT.

The executive committee usually votes on the books to be published, sanctions advances or sudden emergency demands from authors, and decides the expenditure of other monies. Any important problems are brought before this group and settled there rather than by the board of directors, although procedure differs widely in this respect.

The duties of the board of directors resemble those of any business. Also, they vary tremendously, depending on whether there is company stock in existence and the manner in which it is held and by whom.

In closing, may I say again that this is a very general picture of a publishing house. However, it has been so widely copied in other books on publishing (as has the diagram beside it) that it must have some virtue.* (It appeared first in *The Children's Book Field.*) I have omitted a few people who have important functions, partly because they have little or no contact with a manuscript or its sale. For instance, in any company printing its own books, there is usually one man whose chief duty is to deal with the labor unions. These are very powerful in the publishing business, as there are few stronger groups than those run by the typesetters, foundry workers or pressmen.

In other words, publishing is not simple. Authors and artists should realize that though they are a vital part of the publishing picture, they are not all of this fascinating and very complex whole.

---

* An author never minds being quoted. It is very flattering. But when a section of a book is used, it is only courteous — in fact, it is safer, legally — to obtain permission to do so. We sent out over fifty requests to use the many quotations from authorities that appear in this book. . . . A few years ago, through sheer coincidence, I attended an author's lecture entitled, "How Not To Write." See Part I, Chapter 3. Sure enough, the lecture consisted of the points I had made in that chapter, one after the other, without mention of *The Children's Book Field*. I enjoyed being introduced to the author after the program.

PUBLISHING CALENDAR

SALES DEPARTMENT		EDITORIAL DEPARTMENT	PRODUCTION DEPARTMENT
		TYPICAL MANUSCRIPT	
SALES CONFERENCE for Spring Books	DECEMBER	*(Let us suppose ms. first received in November. Returned with advice on revision.)* Revised ms. received.	
	JANUARY	Returned with final changes to be made. Final ms. received	Layouts for sample pages made
Salesmen travel	FEBRUARY	Copy edited / Sample pages OK'd / Sample art OK'd — **THE ARTIST** Receives carbon of ms. Submits sample drawings, get them OK'd	Copy-edited ms. received and sent to printer
	MARCH	Galleys received and sent to author	Galleys corrected
Salesmen repeat calls on large accounts. Possibly sell books published in May or June	APRIL	Revised galleys received, changes OK'd — Works on final art work	Revised galleys corrected
	MAY	Art work approved / Proof of art approved and placed in galleys — Delivers final art work	Art work plated
SALES CONFERENCE for Fall Books	JUNE	Page proof received and OK'd / Ms. received for Fall Books / For further details, see Part II, Chapter 3	Jacket art received, plates made / Pages plated and printed / Cloth and cover die OK'd / Bound Books
	JULY		
Salesmen travel	AUGUST		
	SEPTEMBER		
	OCTOBER	Salesmen repeat calls on large accounts. Possibly sell books published in December or January	
	NOVEMBER		

This schedule varies with every book, but it will give some idea of the passage of time and will serve to show how publishing programs revolve around conferences and seasons.

2 · A Juvenile Department in Action

The job of being editor of children's books in a publishing house varies as much as that of being a housewife. If Mrs. B. Sterling Farnsworth has a cook, a nursemaid, a laundress and a chauffeur, her household duties are not as varied or arduous as those of Mrs. Tom Jones, who must cook, wash, iron, clean and drive the car for her family. There is a never-settled argument as to which life is more rewarding, but at least everyone will agree that they are different.

That is the way with so-called "juvenile" editors — a curious term but a permanent part of publishing lingo. So instead of considering it a cross to bear, wear the term proudly.

Some companies have departments composed simply of the editor (Mrs. Tom Jones) and her secretary, because the department handles only the work that is strictly editorial, i.e., the selection and editing of manuscripts and art work.

Other juvenile departments are larger, because they do the regular editorial work plus production and promotion detail as well. In the latter case the editor and her assistants (most juvenile editors are women, perhaps unfortunately) follow the books from the moment the manuscript is un-wrapped until it leaves the bindery — and they do not lose sight of it then. Thus their labors include not only the selection and editing of manuscripts but also obtaining an artist for the illustrations, establishing the format — which means selecting page size, kind and size of type, kind and weight of paper — doing page layouts, checking with the estimators in the production department on a score of items of expense, measuring the illustrations for the engravers or lithographers, checking sample pages and proofs, making up dummies, matching colors, checking galleys and front matter (titles, contents pages, and prefaces), deciding on the type of binding and on the color, kind and material of the cover. Then there is the manufacture of the jacket, which is more of the same.

By no means are all the steps in bookmaking included in the above enumeration, since each book has its own individual peculiarities that depend on whether it is to be printed by letterpress or by offset. These are the two most widely used printing processes (which were described in the last section), for they are the A and B of the publishing alphabet.

This partial listing will give you an idea, though, why a children's book department is often bedlam. A good many books are put out every year, and each one of them is a mass of detail, always in a slightly different stage of production than any of its brothers. In most publishing houses the production department for adult books also handles the juveniles. It acts only on the orders of the juvenile editor, however, and her specifications; and her department must check all proofs, make all changes and be an ever-ready go-between from the author and the artist to the press until the book is done.

Since children's books are often full of color and irregu-
larly arranged pages, the process is like following a very
complex recipe — except, as I have said, no one book is
quite like another, so it is up to the editor and her assistants
to shuffle around the different ingredients and come out with
a good result. Almost every editor has expert help all along
the production line — but the juvenile department assumes
the planning, the decisions and the responsibility for each
little detail.

The division of labor in this department is important for
doing work of such variety, although everyone usually is able
to do everything and is cognizant of the progress of each
volume. In this way one person can substitute for another
at almost any given moment, and this system prevents
any job from becoming uninteresting. For the editorial
peace of mind, though, the work is roughly apportioned as
follows:

The "juvenile" production manager is responsible for production progress and for layouts. She checks art work, makes
up dummies, reports that author Susie Snoozle can't get all
that text on page 9, as the picture of the giraffe up a tree
takes too much room. She keeps in close touch with the adult
production department and is the one who finds out that
artist Hiram Smrktovskytz's four-color pictures will cost
$8,000 for plates alone, and so the book will have to sell for
$4.50 — which it can't. She is the bad-news bearer, whose
job depends on finding out details in time to circumvent real
trouble. She is a very important person, who sees that production goes on more or less smoothly, reports snags and
helps in steering around them. She knows so much that she
can criticize anyone, especially the editor. Actually, in a
small juvenile department, she often *is* the editor. Then

again, her duties may be performed in part or in whole by someone in the adult production department.

The second assistant is in charge of manuscripts. Some fifty to two hundred or more manuscripts may be received a month depending on the popularity of the publishing firm — figure four to six for every working day. It is her job either to read these or get someone else to. The good ones go on to the editor, and if she, too, finds virtue in them, the author is advised on possibilities and suggestions. When the revised manuscripts come back, this girl and the editor reread them for progress.

After a finished manuscript has evolved out of the months of travail, she must go over it to check the facts. For example, in a recent biography my bright compatriot discovered that the hero was born in three different years if the author's figures and text were to be taken seriously. I had missed this variable age completely, so absorbing had been the progress of the narrative! She also may or may not do the promotion work I have arbitrarily assigned to the third assistant.

Number Three Girl Friday helps with the voluminous correspondence that seems to be necessary in an editorial department with a back list of established authors and with so many newcomers knocking at the gate. Her main duties, however, concern promotion. She either writes or oversees the writing of all catalogue, flyer and flap copy. She attends the library meetings the editor cannot attend and accompanies her to the big ones. She handles all promotion mail concerning exhibits and book fairs. She is a member of the Children's Book Council and goes to their meetings and other promotion meetings. (In some companies she is not in the juvenile department but the general promotion department and handles adult promotion as well.)

235

The fourth assistant, if one is lucky enough to have such, has another tossed-salad job. As secretary to the editor, she must type letters, obtain hotel rooms for her boss or for authors or mail off a batch of proofs to an artist. This petty officer also returns rejected manuscripts to authors. She deals with the review list, which is a long list of names of people who receive advance copies of all or certain books on the list. (In the juvenile field, some reviewers are interested in only one or two age groups or kinds of books, so you do not send them all your new books. For instance, you do not send books for girls to the Boys Clubs. Q.E.D.)

This hardy individual must always be packing up or filing outsize art work, for it goes back and forth to the artist, to the printer and to exhibits, and she has to know where the material is at any given moment. Sometimes she undoubtedly would like to get into the big boxlike art work file and stay there.

And now as to the editor. Obviously, if she is any good at passing out responsibility and seeing that it sticks, she has relatively little to do! There are a few small items, though, of intriguing variety that are hers, alone. I have gone into more detail on each of these in a separate section. This chapter merely correlates her work in a general way with the others in her department.

For instance, the actual choice of books to be published is up to the editor. At least it is in my case.* I never dictate a recommendation for a contract without wondering if I have launched a ship of state or a tiny sailboat.

* In some large companies there are special editors who handle projects like a biographical series or individual subjects like science or crafts or religion.

Secondly, there are the authors and artists — not only those who have books in production but those who have already been published. An editor must keep in fairly constant touch with them, and these meetings, telephone calls and correspondence are really fun for the most part. Authors and artists are people who have something special about them, some individual way of looking at life that is unusual and interesting. I feel very fortunate to have known so many so well.

Such contact with authors and artists and the selection of manuscripts can be both a joy and a headache. Some of the most wonderful people I know I have met through my editorial contacts. They have become lifelong personal friends. Keeping in touch with them is often quite exhausting but, as I have said — fun and rewarding.

Another editorial task is orienting the juvenile department with the other parts of the company, maintaining as close and pleasant connections as possible with the various departments outlined in the preceding chapter. I may think some of their people act rather strangely, just as they often wonder why anyone writes or is interested in juveniles. But we manage to get along nicely most of the time. I enjoy working with different kinds of people. Sometimes I have received very valuable suggestions from men and women in the office who seem far from the world of children's books but who are interested enough to want to help me and the cause.

I suppose the biggest editorial job is carrying out the company's general policy of publishing worthwhile books. In the juvenile department an editor is supposed to be the catalytic agent between genius and its physical form; that is, between the general and the specific. In other words, acting on the company's principle, my department produces books that are examples of it — I hope.

Publishing will always be a combination of the aesthetic and the mundane. Perhaps therein lies its charm. How difficult to find, to nurture and to polish good art — which good writing and good illustrating are, of course. How difficult, also, to produce this in distinguished format and to sell it at sufficient profit so that more good art can follow! Many prefer to have as little as possible to do with the production or business side of publishing. To me, acquiring this additional information makes the editorial side more rewarding and easier to do well. I have found all parts of editing fascinating. I just wish I have the time to keep up with the exciting modern developments in art and production. It is a rapidly expanding new world we work in, and editing is one of the most necessary, most demanding, most frustrating and most rewarding jobs in it.*

* There is such a thing as teamwork in publishing. Sometimes a whole company can feel an inner force, a consolidation of spirit, or a band of friendly accomplishment that will suddenly make enjoyable the hard work of publishing books. Or it can be a department that works together as a unit. I had the privilege of being part of such a unit at Houghton Mifflin. There were four of us: Greta Lyons was in charge of production in the juvenile department; Emilie McLeod was my editorial assistant; Isabel Hooker ran the secretarial end and kept us all in order; I supposedly was chief but that was only on paper. We all pitched in and published some great books. It was a team effort, hard work but great fun.

Greta Lyons is now Art Director at Charles Scribner's Sons; Emilie McLeod is editor of children's books at the Atlantic Monthly Press; Isabel Hooker is probably ordering some man around the way she used to order us. I hope every editor has the experience of working together as closely and as well as we did.

3 · Standards of Publishing

This chapter necessarily repeats certain material included in Part I, Writing, but is different in that all comments are made from an editorial point of view.

Most of this chapter was first written in 1952 as a speech given before the New England Library Association at their annual conference. I expected to have to rewrite it for 1966, but I find that although the over-all publishing picture has changed quite a bit the basic principles behind it have not. At least mine have not. Remember, though, the principles stated here are just *mine*. I am not speaking for other editors.

1. A BOOK SHOULD BE WORTHWHILE — worthy of a child's time, worthy of being remembered, worthy of being bought, worthy of being kept. It can be a vivid bit of history, a fascinating study of some aspect of science or a revealing story of present-day life that specializes in finely drawn characterization and natural situations. It can be any of a score of different things — sheer fun, for instance.

Humorous books to my mind are very important. I publish as many as I can find. Their publication stems from one of my most serious beliefs: that childhood is not what it is cracked up to be nor the golden period we ourselves remember. I am reliving my own childhood, somewhat, with my three children and can see that nowadays life's path (what a corny phrase!) is not easy for boys and girls. I wonder if it ever was!

I will not elaborate on the rough stretches of childhood. What meets my eye, however, is sufficiently rugged so that any time there is a chance to publish something truly funny, I do. A child needs to relax as much as an adult. When he really enjoys and laughs at a book, he will read it over and over and it will comfort him like an old friend. I do wish more writers would write more amusing books. Lots of authors — and this is especially true in the juvenile field — take themselves very seriously. They have lost that light, lovely touch, if they ever had it.

All of which brings up the second point:

2. A BOOK MUST BE ENJOYABLE TO CHILDREN. I do not mean that it must be consciously *amusing*, because a child has a complex emotional setup almost from babyhood and is capable of enjoying many, many things that are not funny to him. He enjoys quite serious history, for instance, if it is told interestingly and clearly. He is a pushover for books on science or nature if they are simple and straightforward. He loves books on foreign lands. He likes moral stories if the author can write without preaching. He likes all kinds of subjects, but he does so spontaneously, often without knowing why. He cannot be *made* to like anything, and only rarely can he be talked into reading, especially finishing, what he does not care for.

This, then, is a very important point in juvenile publishing in spite of the fact that adults do most of the buying of children's books. The final consumer is the child, and unless he reads a book with a fair degree of interest and pleasure, it is not a success.

Many editors know almost automatically what children prefer and so do not have to worry about this point. And in most cases I feel sure about each manuscript as it comes to my attention, but if there is the slightest doubt in my mind — either about a part of a book, or about the whole — I try it out on some neighboring children.

In most instances the children's comments, although innocuous-sounding, have helped immeasurably in making my decision. In others they have helped to point out needed revisions, offering suggestions that the author or artist has received most enthusiastically and incorporated in the book. And, conversely, they have often made me decide to reject the manuscript.

Let me take just one example: a picture book came in with wonderfully free, unconventional pictures, a new idea and some very amusing (to us grown-ups) scenes. There was not much plot or action, but still the pictures were *so* good, and *so* original! Since we had to make a fairly quick decision, I read it to a six-year-old that afternoon. Her only comment was, "When does something happen?" Then I took it to two young friends around the corner, aged four and six. Their mother, on bringing the manuscript back, said, "*I* thought it was clever, but Alice said, 'Well, the pictures are okay,' and Bill said, 'Now let's read something good!'" Wouldn't you as editor have been convinced that this manuscript should not be published? Incidentally the art director, who brought in the book, thought I might be missing a big thing. "A possible Caldecott or AIGA winner," he said. I never saw it published, although it may have been. I did put the illustrator down in my book as a future possibility, but when I called him a year later, he had moved away.

3. A BOOK MUST HAVE WIDE APPEAL. Here again contacts with all kinds of children and groups help, because by and large what one normal youngster likes very much, another one will, too. Except for regional books, tastes do not differ widely over the country. There is limited appeal for the book on an odd subject, the impressionistic book, the one presupposing an unusual, intellectual background or the very technical one. On the other hand, there is a wide appeal for books that are written for both boys and girls of a broad age group and that have a vital point of view. These hold all kinds and ages of children spellbound, no matter how diversified their interests and backgrounds may be. P.S. Such books are hard to find.

4. A BOOK MUST BE FEASIBLE AS FAR AS PRODUCTION GOES. I do not consider publishing books with complicated formats — for example, a story with illustrations of a house whose windows have to open and close. And I have to sheer away from picture books with very expensive color effects or trick bindings or those requiring very large page sizes. Some companies *can* publish these because they are set up to manufacture toys as well as books; but they probably have to print a first edition of 100,000 or more, because large quantities bring down costs.

5. A BOOK MUST HAVE POSSIBILITIES OF SELLING FOR AT LEAST FIVE YEARS. This factor is a real publishing safeguard. While the last point deals with the *width* of appeal, this one emphasizes *length* of appeal, which is quite different.

For instance, I came into the publishing field during the last year of World War II, and nothing was quite so dead as all the books on the army, the navy, and other wartime subjects. There is great interest in these now, but when publishing them you must remember that you run the risk of their being out-of-date soon after publication. Books on space are in this category.

On the other hand, no one working in a good bookstore or library could help but be impressed with the longevity of a sizable percentage of children's books. Some have old-fashioned-looking illustrations, but children don't seem to mind. Some are quite modern in style, and some are long-winded; but all the books that live any length of time have the basic qualities that make children love them. They want to read them over and over and to keep them. Often these books have the same appeal for the younger brothers and sisters and even the next generation. Examples can be seen in the wonderful Beatrix Potter picture books, *The Tale of Peter Rabbit, et al.* (Warne), and the immortal stories and verses of A. A. Milne (Dutton).

This intangible quality of immortality is one thing that makes juvenile publishing so satisfying. Modern novels are mostly read and tossed away as is much nonfiction. They die in a year or less. Not so with children's books. They live — if they are good and if they do not have too dated a subject, point of view, conversation, phrasing and the like.

6. A BOOK MUST HAVE A POTENTIAL SALE OF AT LEAST TEN THOUSAND COPIES IN TWO YEARS. That is an arbitrary figure that can vary up or down depending on the cost of production. A color picture book would need to sell more copies to pay for itself; a straight letterpress book with a few line illustrations would not require so many.

Publishing, you see, *is* a business, at has been explained before. Plates, printing, paper, binding, advances to author and artist — all these constitute a big investment before one copy is sold. This investment has to come back with a reasonable rate of interest for a firm to keep going, and it is definitely part of one's job as an editor to see that it does.

Whether or not a book sells depends largely on the six points just mentioned, but its potentialities must show costwise in a manuscript from the very start. To measure these qualifications requires vision, imagination and production knowhow.

Occasionally, books are published when actual sales seem of minor consideration. You feel that for some reason a certain book *must* be published. However, when you feel that strongly, the book usually sells. Or, if it does not, the author's next one is apt to. So, self-confidence and faith return to both the author and you.

These then form my set of publishing "standards," a grandiose word that I do not care for. Before leaving the subject, however, I would like to mention my "unpublished" books. To me those are almost as important as the published ones, and a good deal easier to define. Here are a few "don'ts" taken from my publishing primer:

1. A BOOK SHOULD NOT BE DULL. Many apparently worthwhile books I have declined because they were heavy and sagged with the weight of their message.

2. A BOOK SHOULD NOT BE POORLY WRITTEN. I'm old-fashioned in this, but I do believe that writers who claim authorship as their profession must take the time to learn the fundamentals of their trade — clarity, organization, grammar, punctuation and spelling. In other words, I do not believe in wholesale revision or rewriting by the editor.

3. A BOOK SHOULD NOT BE WRITTEN DOWN TO CHILDREN.

The age of "my dear little ones" and such phrases as "teeny-weeny" went out with World War I, and since then authors who know and love children write for them with respect. Author intrusion is unforgivable.

4. NO MORE THAN HALF THE BOOKS ON A LIST SHOULD ORIGINATE FROM THE PUBLISHER. MOST REALLY GOOD BOOKS COME DIRECT FROM THE AUTHORS. This origination of books by the publisher applies only to nonfiction, and if you will look at the many series now flooding the market and more springing up about us every month, you will see what I mean. Many of these books are ordered, or at least instigated, by the editor and/or others pushing in back of him. In nonfiction such as a biography, geography or science series, this is unavoidable. Often the procedure works satisfactorily where an author is approached with an idea or a project congenial to him and can throw himself heart and soul into making the book seem wholly his. Sometimes, however, the original seed of the idea, so carefully planted by the publisher, may show through the entire book like a lump, swallowed but not digested, and the result is "just another book" in that series. It follows the pattern of the others, it contains an appropriate amount of information, but it is not a good book.

5. ART WORK SHOULD NOT BE PUBLISHED FOR ITS OWN SAKE. During the past twenty years it has become obvious that children's books offer one of the few opportunities for displaying modern art. In many cases, especially where the artist can write as well as draw, this marriage of the two arts has produced some of our most beautiful and satisfying books. On the other hand, there have been books published that are nothing but a display of an artist's pictorial skill.

4 · Aspects of the Children's Book Field that Affect Editing

A. THE LARGE NUMBER OF NEW BOOKS

One important aspect is certainly the large numbers of children's books being published and the fact that the number grows larger almost every year.

In 1947 Frederic G. Melcher commented on page 853 of the August 30 issue of *Publishers Weekly*, in an editorial: "In the past 25 years the market for children's books has increased with great rapidity. The number of titles has become half again as great, while the total sales must have risen three times in that period."

In 1952 *Publishers Weekly* on page 1773 printed charts showing the increase in publishers' trade-book sales from 1947 to 1952. They commented on the increase of juvenile *nonfiction* even then:

The increase in the sales of children's nonfiction in the last several years seems to be following a trend which has been very marked in the adult book field for a number of years. Some booksellers say that non-fiction accounts for as much as between 35% and 50% of their sales of juveniles.

Some booksellers see in this trend an indication of a growth of the child's reading ability and of a widening of the child's interests. Others are alarmed at the over-emphasis on facts at the expense of the cultivation of imagination in children and, moreover, feel that, while one or two biographical series were welcome, the field is now being flooded and a real problem of overstock threatens. . . .

Doesn't that sound familiar? And that was fourteen years ago!

In 1955 on February 12, page 1019, *Publishers Weekly* reported under "News and Trends of the Week:"

Some fifty booksellers, replying to a recent PW questionnaire, say the sale of juveniles continues to increase and continues to spread through the whole year. As to the books which helped create this business for the stores, about half the booksellers mention the Landmark Series especially.

To show a more recent side to the picture, here are some paragraphs in an article in the *New York Herald-Tribune Book Week*, Fall children's issue of November 1, 1964, written by William Cole and entitled, "All Around the Moneybush."

Children's books, once regarded by publishers as pleasant sidelines, now account for almost one fourth of the book industry's revenue. Some 150 firms have special juvenile departments or are engaged exclusively in the field; last year they sold $127 million worth of children's books.

There are 3000 books a year, and the variety is staggering.

Name it, and they've got it; or name it in the presence of a children's book editor, and they soon *will* have it.

Series publishing is a trend that came to stay. Today's trends are harder to nail down. . . . The recent great to-do about "controlled vocabulary books," for example, seems to have abated. . . . There are many who feel that it is cruelty to children to so limit their vocabularies; and many authors *know* that it is cruelty to authors to limit them to a word list.

Paperbacks for children have been appearing with more frequency. . . . but [they] have never enjoyed anything like the boom that hit adult paperback publishing some ten years ago. And they probably never will. . . . [He may be proven wrong.]

The truly major trend in children's book publishing for the past 40 years has been the continuing growth of children's rooms in public libraries, and the increasing importance of the school library. . . . [And he is writing before the present burst of federal funds for school libraries!]

People are frequently surprised to hear — almost offended — to hear that some books are actually written *for* library sales. "You mean that books are committed in cold blood? With both eyes on the market?" Darn right, lady. Publishing is a business and businesses supply demands.

I don't know where Mr. Cole got his facts, but they hold true today, except for the remark about paperbacks, and he still may be right about that.

Jean Karl, children's book editor for Atheneum, writing in *Library Journal*, December 15, 1964, gives the editor's reasons for publishing so many books:

Because we do not know tomorrow, but must anticipate it, because we must cope with a divergence of information to be communicated, and most of all because we cannot give children a narrow look at what interests them or what they have come to need, because we do not dare to pour children into tight moulds, because we must encourage diversity, in authors and in minds of children, the avalanche [of new books] must exist.

I am not sure I agree with that, because it seems as if the older people living today, products of an age when there were few children's books and when information came from geographies, histories and encyclopedias, are much better informed in a usable, practical way than their children or grandchildren. Still you cannot generalize and come out with anything worthwhile. Hence the facts are that there *is* an avalanche of books, and we editors are hired to "supply the demand."

Publishers Weekly reports on page 159 in their issue of February 21, 1966:

> The total number of juvenile titles in 1964 and 1965 was about the same — not quite 2900 in 1965. What is perhaps significant is that the number of *new* books for children dropped from 2533 to 2473, while the number of new editions — which includes paperback reprints, reissues of classics, revised editions of factual books — rose from 275 to 422. This is roughly 20 per cent of the total output.

Interesting?

The Census of Manufactures report for the book industry for 1963 compared with data from 1958 showed that the copy sale of juveniles selling for over $1 increased from 34.3 million to 55 million, and receipts rose from $40 million to $72 million! (*Publishers Weekly* March 7, 1966; p. 36)

Quote those figures if anyone should ask you about the future (financial) of children's books.

So, last year three thousand or so new books were published for children. That number is large from anyone's point of view: that of the publishers, the authors, the artists, the booksellers, the librarians and the reviewers.

There are many reasons why I say this — the first and most obvious is that when you have this great number coming out year after year you are bound to get a lot of mediocre, even poor, books. There are not that many topnotch writers in this country or any country, although the number in the United States, in fact all over the world, has increased enormously. Each year some outstanding, distinguished volumes are brought out, and these are followed by a broad group of fairly good or utilitarian books. And finally, there emerges a group of barely adequate pieces of writing of which the style, technique or material just plainly lack distinction. These three groups exist in any literary stockpile and have to be tolerated — at least until they grow to such numbers that they get out of hand, thereby crashing this lovely profitable era down on our heads.

Sheer numbers of books might do this, I believe, because books have to be sold in order for publishers (and therefore authors and artists, too) to exist. Furthermore, at the present time, much larger editions of each title have to be sold to surmount the terrific price of manufacture. The spending of federal funds in such programs as the NDEA and ESEA has put off the day of reckoning but not forever. The market for science books for the elementary grades is glutted and full of repetitive material. There is such a thing as a saturation point. Original fiction and humor has been hit in this age of nonfiction, the retelling of folklore, and so on. The price spiral may tend to make publishers cut down their lists to those that sell at least 20,000 copies, and as in general no newcomer to the field has a chance at that figure, it would limit the author list to old established names. Such a move in itself would not be salutary, for no art can exist without continued infiltration of new blood. It would be particularly unwise in the children's book business because by its very nature it depends on freshness and new ideas.

Sufficient sales, therefore, are important — even vital — and the number of new titles, if it continues to grow larger, may make such sales extremely difficult to obtain. Suppose, for instance, you were a bookseller trying to cope with this literary "title wave." Even if you had a large children's book section, you would throw up your hands in defeat about November first because it is impossible to select intelligently from three thousand books. It is hard to display even a tenth of that number. I should think it would be impossible to keep track of their billing and storage.

Wholesalers face the same problem. Automation has helped stock control, but many cartons of books are returned unopened because sheer numbers prevent display and sale.

The theory is that the really good books come to the top regardless. That is partly true — and much of the credit for it should go to the librarians, who make an earnest effort to divide up the publications among themselves and read them all. Still, there is no way for a complete analysis of every book to be circulated. No magazine would have that much room for reviews or that large a staff to read them. Thus, when an avalanche like the inevitable November one hits an office, the reviewer's only choice is to pick as best he can.

Representation is poor, too. Authors and publishers are annoyed to find that their books are not present in every store and every library. But how many stores or libraries could afford to buy three thousand new titles a year? That they buy as many as they do is wonderful and awe-inspiring. And, as I have shown you, the sales of trade juveniles go up every year.

Let us summarize the reasons for this flood of children's books: *first, the market has expanded tremendously in the last ten years;* not the bookstore over-the-counter market, but the public and school library market. Hundreds of school libraries have been built and stocked with trade books. More and more trade books are used in actual class work. Federal money can now be obtained for library building and for buying books. In fact, at present writing, as one prominent jobber told me, there are more orders than wholesalers can handle or publishers fill. In other words, one could almost say the millennium is at hand!

This new market is responsible for the great increase in the number of books published for utilitarian (not literary) needs. "Curriculum-slanted" is the term.

For example, take the 6-to-9 age group. The "easy-reading" books, once so rare, are now abundantly provided. Controlled vocabulary books are selling at a great rate, because the demand for these books was and still is a real one. There is a much longer period when a child struggles through the periphery of reading skill than there used to be — probably because of the necessarily large classes — and so these books sell. And there is room for more books to help establish reading skills. (The Initial Teaching Alphabet books are an interesting example. They are explained later on in this chapter.) Whether the market can absorb *all* the books of this kind that are published is a question. Certainly, to my mind the actual literary standards for this age group could be raised much higher. This in itself will be necessary if beginning readers are to go on reading. Junket is nice, but not when you get out of the junket age.

A second reason for the great number of books is that *the market is now so varied.* There are whole new categories of books that sell — for instance, the simple science books for the primary grades, the nonfiction segments of history for the middle age group, the craft books, the folklore collections, the social-studies books about different lands, the biographies for the very young, and so on. These classifications may have always existed in that there were random volumes brought out in all of them, but now it seems that every publisher almost every year brings out one or more such books in each age group — the 2 to 5, 6 to 9, 9 to 12, 12 to 15 — and then books *in* the special subjects listed above. Many new series are starting. Old ones are expanding.

Lastly, *publishers who have never before brought out juveniles have been attracted to the field, because it has grown so lucrative.* They figure that children's books do not sell in the hundred thousands like adult best-sellers, but if a back list is built up, juveniles keep on selling year after year. They do not die practically at birth as do many adult novels nor go out-of-date as does some adult nonfiction. Consequently, it is partly these new companies that are flooding the market. At least ten new "lists" have been formed in this way in the last ten years, and hardly a publishing season goes by that does not see another addition.

But it is not only the new companies and new juvenile departments that are responsible for the growing piles of new titles. This spring I sat next to a fellow editor at a meeting of The Children's Book Council, and we discussed the length of our lists. She said, "Last year I published ten books in one season, and the salesmen did so well with them that they urged me to publish twice as many. So this year that is what I am doing." Not too long ago one of the most prominent publishers of juveniles announced that they were going to *double* their already large list!

And there are good reasons why we editors do not contemplate cutting our lists at present. For one thing, if an outstanding book comes in, one feels duty bound to publish it. Secondly, there are a number of authors whose present manuscripts may not be perfect, but who may produce a best-seller next year. Thirdly, the market for juveniles, as I have explained, has been greatly enhanced by the addition of federal funds given to institutions. Those, to my mind, are the important reasons for the size of the juvenile output. Not-too-sparkling books are published because the publisher thinks that there is a demand for that kind of book on that subject. And there are editors like myself who feel that talented beginners should be encouraged, and so we bring out their first rather risky offerings to give them a start, hoping that their second and third books will show we were right in having confidence in their ability.

B. THE SERIES OF SERIES IN CHILDREN'S BOOKS

DO SINGLE TITLES STILL SELL?

The present emphasis in juvenile publishing of the series idea merits some discussion. Almost 85 per cent of the publishers in the business have a series — sometimes two or three or four — that they are promoting as unified projects.

What *is* a series? Webster defines one as follows: "A number of things or events standing or succeeding in order and connected by a like relation."

Now as far as children's books are concerned, let us assume that a series consists of books conceived on the same general subject for the same general purpose. They may or may not be written by the same person and usually follow no particular order, but are "connected by a like relation" by their underlying intent and often by similarity of price, size, shape, length and general format. They almost always have the same contractual terms and are promoted and advertised as a unit.

Most of these series have some worthwhile purpose. They present certain aspects, however, that should be considered.

The first is that, like many other things, we may produce too many. It is a typical American trait to start something good; it is also typically American to overdo it. Series of all kinds are coming on the market. I have started three myself: two on conservation (different age groups) and one on vital United States industries.

What first began as a natural trend in authorship has grown into a merchandising scheme to take advantage of the huge market for juvenile literature of the factual or semifactual sort. (We as a nation want our children to *learn* things when they read.) There are now so many series that at the present rate of increase they may soon lose their identity and hence their value. Meanwhile, though, I will admit they offer added income and "spread" to authors and publishers — which, of course, is good. There are two sides to every coin.

The second difficulty with some of these series is the fluctuation of quality and value of the individual books. Consequently, the bookstore buyer or librarian finds himself confronted with the necessity of buying "the works" (i.e., the whole series) in order to get the ones he can sell or use. This means overstock on some titles and scarcity in others. No two titles in a series ever sell the same.

A third trouble very evident now is the duplication of material. Nature series, for instance, are so common that there must be twenty or more books for the elementary grades on shells, or trees, or birds. Dozens of biographical series contain books on historical figures, explorers, generals, scientists and so on ad infinitum. Which are the best? Do you buy a whole series even though the quality is not consistent, or do you pick a few from different series?

Perhaps the worst result of the growing numbers of series is the parallel neglect of the individual volume. Many booksellers and jobbers like the series idea, because it means more sales, less effort and hence more money to them. These people depend on institutional sales — schools and libraries — for their yearly bulk, and many of the institutions like the series idea. Librarians and teachers are always looking for books that cover loopholes in their collections, and that fill school demands for books on certain periods or certain subjects for certain age groups. They often take a book in a series because it fills a specific need and sometimes overlook an individual volume already published that might have served the purpose equally well.

Individual volumes still sell and, I believe, always will. But the sledding is difficult and becoming more so because of sheer competing numbers. Sales managers have generally agreed that a series is not a series unless at least twenty titles come out in it, and preferably twice that many. That adds up to a lot of books being issued and offers unparalleled opportunity to authors. But even if the national bookshelf extended across the whole continent, it would soon fill up under such treatment; and the books pushed off the other end will be the individual volumes.

Some say this loss of individually published books would be a good thing, because there are too many mediocre titles published every year. Maybe they are right. Only time will tell, but right now the ever-expanding series (most of them nonfiction) make up too large a percentage of books published. They are useful books and are making money for authors and publishers; but they are pushing more creative writing to the wall, and that should not be.

C. INTERNATIONAL PUBLISHING: EXPORTING AND IMPORTING BOOKS

As was mentioned in Part I, Chapter 4, there is an increased trend in selling books to and buying books from foreign lands and in copublishing books with foreign publishers. This is not new. Certain of our juveniles have become standard fare abroad: those by Louisa May Alcott and Samuel Clemens, for instance.

But just as more books are being published on foreign lands by U.S. firms — from picture books on Japan to teenage novels on life in Spain — so is there more buying of our books by foreign publishers and more importing or translation of their books by us. It is not uncommon for an American book to be published in French, German, Japanese, Arabic and so on. It has to be a book of universal interest to children — for instance, a pony story like Wesley Dennis's *Flip* (Viking) — and it must not contain too American a background, be too American in dialogue or concern itself with a segment of our history or economics that is of little interest in Europe or Asia.

257

There are other difficulties to be overcome in selling our products to foreign countries. *Publishers Weekly* of January 16, 1961, cites as one of these the shortage of American dollars in many foreign countries. The Informational Media Guaranty program, administered by the U.S. Information Agency apparently helps in the conversion of currency, but the easiest way is to establish relationship with several foreign publishing houses and import some of *their* books at the same time they are importing yours. This is not always possible and should be done with great caution, because you may find yourself with stock that does not sell well here for many reasons. For instance, we imported a series of semigeography books that were too romantic and diverse in focal point to satisfy the new American demand for direct, well-organized nonfiction. They would have sold well here twenty-five years ago.

Another imported title suffered an unfair fate because of type size. I had thoroughly enjoyed an historical novel for older boys and girls in manuscript form and had agreed to taking sheets from the English printing to be bound here. When a sample page arrived I protested immediately about the small type; but the English editor was out of the country, and her assistant informed me the type was quite all right. I should have cabled to hold up our printing, but it is difficult to do that. Anyway the book did not sell here, and even in England it was criticized for type like that "on the back of a bus ticket."

Perhaps English children can see better than ours. Anyway, the above difficulty is frequently encountered — also too little leading between lines — so that it is often preferable to set the type here and use their illustrations. However, discussion of type and leading beforehand with the foreign editor can often circumvent this difficulty and is well worth it because of the saving of a combined printing.

The difficulty of our selling American books abroad is our high prices. It is better to sell the foreign publisher film positives and have him print in his own country than for him to import our books. Then all or most of the money comes from royalties, which are small, because their retail prices are low, but they do mount up.

As to our importing foreign books in sheets or bound books, there is the translation problem unless they come from England, and it often exists with their books too because of their different spelling and unfamiliar words. However, translation is not hard to arrange, and I always insist on the privilege of changing the text a bit in case the translator comes out with an awkward phrase or two. Some of the foreign books are so beautiful they are well worth the trouble, but have your man on foreign rights guide your letters so that you know what you would be paying for sheets and what for rights.

It is often better to import sheets in spite of the customs complications, because foreign bindings are not like ours. Overseas publishers do not think books have to be bound for use as third base or by the next generation.

Copublishing is the answer to many problems, especially costs. In this case your edition and the foreign one are run right after the other with the English text stripped in place of the foreign one. You can work on the text with the foreign editor so that both of you are satisfied, and if it is printed abroad, you save a lot of time dealing with the author and artist and a good deal of production detail, too. Mostly you save money and get more exciting looking books. Helen Hoke Watts of Franklin Watts, Inc. has been a pioneer in the business of importing beautiful children's books.

Fabio Coen, editor of Pantheon juvenile books and Mr. Robert Baensch of the McGraw-Hill Book Company gave interesting talks last year before the Children's Book Council on this subject. Mr. Baensch mentioned the fact that several foreign countries are particularly interested in coproduction or copublishing: Yugoslavia, Germany and Mexico were mentioned. There are others.

Mr. Coen emphasized a fact that I have found to be very true: do not expect American efficiency in answering letters, making arrangements or printing and shipping the sheets. The pace is different over there. Plan your book for the publication list *after* the one for which you expect it to be ready.

A word of warning regarding agents and advances might not be amiss: if you want to import a book in a small quantity, be sure you do not pay more advance than the number of books imported could pay off if sold. This sounds fundamental, but one agent demanded that I pay a sum for an Indian story that was more than the book could earn if sold out. She said that this author always received this advance (for her adult books), and I could not make her see that in this case the amount was not logical.

On the other hand, agents can be a real help in obtaining good foreign books, although I have mostly dealt with editors or foreign rights experts. Actually, besides studying foreign catalogues it is important to visit foreign publishing houses if you can and to attend the annual Bologna and Frankfurt book fairs. There you can actually see the books, talk with the editors and — have fun doing so.

Watch out for duties on foreign books printed abroad and also on American books printed abroad. The duties vary according to whether a title has been previously imported and whether it has been previously printed here. Also the duty is different on unbound books and books on which a royalty is paid. There are complications on what you may include as cost of production. Also you may lose the copyright on an American book published abroad and imported here. Books printed behind the Iron Curtain are subject to higher duties than books printed in other nations.

All of which sounds complicated — and is — but with the help of your rights man and the U.S. customs inspector for the Port of New York or wherever you are, the situation can be handled. Just persist.

There is an International Board on Books for Young People, which hopes to support and unify all those forces that are in a position to influence young people through books. They also plan to spare publishers considerable work, as many of the tasks described heretofore will be taken on by this agency. They publish *Bookbird*, a quarterly on children's books, and give the Hans Christian Andersen Award every two years for the best children's book. The United States is one of the member nations participating in this worthwhile endeavor, and Virginia Haviland of the Library of Congress is our very able board member.

NEW METHODS OF LEARNING TO READ

Theoretically the fact that there are several new ways to learn to read should not affect the writer, the illustrator or the editor, but it does. Older books and some fairly modern ones are being "translated" into the symbols of these systems, thereby creating new markets for both writers and illustrators.

I.t.a. stands for Initial Teaching Alphabet, which is a teaching device to be replaced by the standard alphabet as

Initial Teaching Alphabet symbols (i.t.a.)

soon as the pupils gain a mastery of the reading system. It consists of forty-three symbols instead of the usual twenty-six, each of which represents only one sound. As you know, most of our vowels can be pronounced in several different ways depending on the words they are in. Getting to know these i.t.a. symbols is quite easy, and a child can depend on each one being the same each time. Hence five-year-old children of normal mentality can learn to read rather quickly, and mentally retarded children capable of differentiating between the symbols and the sounds can also learn to read. It is a special learning method and not a phonetic alphabet, but it seems to work well.

Here are lines from *Kuma Is a Maori Girl* by Dennis Hodgson and Pat Lawson (Methuen and Hastings), printed in i.t.a. and English.

i.t.a.

ᴎiss Collins is our teecher. tœdæ ∫hee tœld us about ∫he wield animals in africa. ᵴum ov ∫hem ɑr in ∫he zꝏ at auckland. on saturdæ ie am gœiᴎ tꝏ see ∫hem.

English: Miss Collins is our teacher. Today she told us about the wild animals in Africa. Some of them are in the zoo at Auckland. On Saturday I am going to see them.

According to the *New York Times* of January 30, 1966, i.t.a. is being used in schools in forty-six states and is very well known and popular in England, where it started. Sir Isaac Pitman, the inventor of Pitman shorthand worked on the idea from 1842, his son continued the work and his grandson, Sir James Pitman, is responsible for the present i.t.a. alphabet now in use.

One of the virtues of the system is the easy transition by a young pupil from i.t.a. to regular English. Also time is saved in the learning-to-read process, which had become so prolonged and so boring under the modern American educational system.

I.t.a. has not yet been universally accepted by educators and has several drawbacks, but experiments in this country and in England would indicate that a class taught reading by i.t.a. had caught up in two years to a class taught reading for three years by the conventional method. One school near my home started i.t.a. with their reluctant readers two years ago. It worked so well that now they are going to teach all pupils, beginning with those five years old, by that method.*

Another method is the Unifon one, consisting of an alphabet of forty letters, each of which stands for one sound, and which covers all sixteen vowel sounds in the English language. Another is the Diacritical Marking System, which uses traditional spelling but with certain letters marked to show the exact pronunciation of words.

A quantity of literature on these systems is available in educational media. It is quite fascinating, especially if you have had children of your own floundering through the usual learning-to-read procedure and been told "hands off" when you felt that you could do the job yourself faster and better.

The impact on the book world should be considerable. Not only is there demand for books in i.t.a. and other methods to supplement school texts, but it looks as if we might see the last of those sterile limited-vocabulary things called books that have consumed millions of dollars of publishers' money. These funds, I hope, can soon be turned into more creative channels. Also, we may live to see six- or seven-year-old children who can read all kinds of stories and books with ease. Then I won't be marking in the margin of manuscripts for this age "too adult" — at least, not because of the wording. There still will be a limit to what a child of this age can understand and enjoy.

---

* The Foundation headquarters is at 9 Southampton Place, London WC 2, England. It is the clearing house for i.t.a. information of all sorts and publishes the i.t.a. Journal. It handles transliteration of English into i.t.a., including the checking of proofs. In the United States the Foundation is at Hofstra University, Hempstead, Long Island, New York (Dr. Richard Black, Director).

BOOKS IN FOREIGN LANGUAGES

Of course, there have always been books for children in foreign languages, but they were mostly for the junior high school boys and girls who were pushed into learning the grammar and syntax of French, Italian or Spanish for the first time. Unless the teacher was unusually gifted, the result was a surface knowledge that time soon dissipated after school or college was over — hence the pitiful impression we Americans usually give when we try to speak foreign languages abroad.

There is more hope for the next generation. It has been proven that French or almost any language can be taught in the elementary school, and it often is. Also publishers now are translating some of their popular picture books into foreign languages and new ones are being written. For instance, Hastings House combined with an English firm in bringing out an English and German version of a German picture book with gay pictures and a simple text, *Joba and the Wild Boar (Joba und das Wildschwein)* by Gaby Baldner, with pictures by Gerhard Oberlander. Here is how the text looks side by side:

"O, you poor little things," cries Joba. "Are you lost? Come, stay with me, I will love you and look after you!"	"O du armes, Kleines Ding," ruft Joba. „Has do dich verirrt? Komm, bleib bei mir, ich will dich lieb-haben und fur dich sorgen!"

Printed in large type, this is a much less formidable introduction to German than a declension of a noun or a list of verb forms, but it was not intended as a substitute for them.

Other books contain simply foreign words and phrases like *This Is Paris,* one of M. Sasek's beautiful books on cities over the world (Macmillan).

Many other titles published by other companies are available in French and/or Spanish like *The Story of Ferdinand* by Munro Leaf (Viking).*

There is some possibility that Latin may be given up entirely in schools, which would be a shame in my opinion, but at least there are several generations of us who remember our Gallic Wars and the orations by eyeless Cicero enough to enjoy some of the translations of old favorites into Latin. A. A. Milne's *Winnie Ille Pu* is a lot of fun, and I cannot wait to see *Fabular de Jemima Anata-Agnatica,* which is Beatrix Potter's immortal *The Tale of Jemima Puddle Duck** as translated by Jonathan Musgrave (Warne) — and what a good time he must have had doing it!

POSTQUAM ad summum collem pervenit, silvam quamdam remotam aspexit quam existimavit locum tutum ac tranquillum esse videri.

* Some language teachers are not enthusiastic about these books, and publishers usually do not urge their use as basal texts; but as extra curricular reading for young language students or for classes of mixed language backgrounds they can be enjoyable aids.

5 · Children's Book Awards

There are many book awards, but two sets of children's book prizes that American authors, artists and publishers especially like to win are: the Newbery and the Caldecott Medals, given each year by the Children's Services Division of the American Library Association, and the *New York Herald-Tribune* Spring Book Festival prizes, also awarded annually.

Let us consider the Newbery-Caldecott awards. Here are the rules laid down by the American Library Association:

1. The publication date must lie between January 1 of the year to be considered and December 31 of the same year.

2. The Newbery Medal is to be awarded annually to the author of the most distinguished contribution to American literature for children, written during the year just elapsed, by an author who is a citizen or resident of the United States. There are no limitations as to the character of the book except that it be an original work, or if traditional in origin, new to children's literature as the result of individual research, the retelling and reinterpretation being the author's

own. The unanimous vote of the Newbery Committee is no longer necessary if the work of a previous recipient of the medal is being considered.

3. The Caldecott Medal is awarded for the most distinguished American picture book for children chosen from those published in the United States during the previous year.

The artist must be a citizen or resident of the United States. Only by unanimous vote of the judges can the medal be awarded twice to the same person. The Caldecott Medal can be given to two artists who work together.

The book must be "the creation of an artist, the product of his initiative and imagination."

The text need not be written by the artist, but should be worthy of the book. The judges are asked to distinguish between "a picture book" and an "illustrated book." The story should not be as important as the pictures. There are no limitations on the character of the illustrations or on the age level of the book, but naturally most picture books are intended for young children.

The Newbery-Caldecott Committee is made up of twenty-two members: the officers and committee chairmen of the Children's Services Division, the president and four members of the American Association of School Librarians and three elected members at large.

Soon after the first of the year each member of the committee casts a ballot of first, second and third choices for nominations of books to be considered. These nominations are tabulated and redistributed for further examination before another ballot is cast. The votes from the general membership of both C.L.A. and A.A.S.L. come in, are tabulated and distributed to committee membership as an indication of general interest before a second voting. A second ballot is cast with first, second and third choices for both awards. Points are assigned, and the winner must receive a certain number of points and be so many points ahead of the next title. If no title emerges that far ahead, a third and possibly a fourth ballot must be cast.

Ruth Hewitt, committee chairman for the 1949-1950 awards, wrote:

> I found it a fairly rugged experience (as I suppose all chairmen do). But it seems this year more than some others one needs to look at the whole group of runners-up to be aware of some of the problems and how interesting but sharp are the differences of opinion. . . . The committee represent a complete cross section of types of work with children as well as wide geographic representation. The whole procedure is set up as democratically as they can make it.

Reports from other chairmen since would indicate that it must, indeed, be a "rugged" experience. (See the following list of articles.) So much hangs on those prizes that feelings run high.

Actually, the choice itself cannot help but be very difficult. There are so many books published that some very good ones are lost in the shuffle for one reason or another. Books of high quality are often closely alike in virtue, making it difficult to decide which is "the most distinguished."

Everyone should realize that as long as human nature remains fascinatingly varied, these awards are not marks of divine choice, nor do they make the books any better, nor should the committee be criticized because their choice seems peculiar to those outside who do not have a library degree or even on occasion, to those inside who do. Also it is especially important to realize that you can be a very superior and successful author, artist or editor and never have won this kind of recognition.

Let us look at the awards and see what they are. I should like to suggest that editors, illustrators and authors-to-be read many of these books. They show the literary qualities most prized by librarians — who, after all, have studied the children's book field and have done more to support it than any other group of people. Also they buy more books than anyone else.

There have been some interesting articles on the subject of the Newbery-Caldecott medals, three of them in the January 1966 *Top of the News*. Here they are along with others that I would recommend:

Batchelder, Mildred L. "Newbery-Caldecott Awards. Authorization and Terms — 1966." *TOTN* Jan. 1966.

Broderick, Dorothy M. "The Newbery Committee that Never Was." *TOTN* March, 1964.

Hodges, Margaret. "They Also Serve. The Newbery-Caldecott Runners-Up." *TOTN* Jan. 1966.

Izard, Anne. "Behind Doors With the Newbery-Caldecott Committee." *TOTN* Jan. 1966.

Rue, Eloise with Evrard, Connie. "Student Evaluations of Newbery Award Books." *Elementary English* Nov. 1963.

Sattley, Helen R. "Voting Procedures for the Newbery-Caldecott Awards." *TOTN* Oct. 1963.

Viguers, Ruth. "Beyond Prejudice." *The Horn Book*. Apr. 1966.

And there are many more.

Here are the awards:

THE JOHN NEWBERY MEDAL AWARDS

1922   *The Story of Mankind* — Hendrik Van Loon

1923   *The Voyages of Doctor Dolittle* — Hugh Lofting

1923   *The Dark Frigate* — Charles B. Hawes

1925 *Tales from Silver Lands* — Charles Finger
1926 *Shen of the Sea* — Arthur B. Chrisman
1927 *Smoky, the Cowhorse* — Will James
1928 *Gay Neck* — D. G. Mukerji
1929 *Trumpeter of Krakow* — Eric P. Kelly
1930 *Hitty, Her First Hundred Years* — Rachel Field
1931 *The Cat Who Went to Heaven* — Elizabeth Coatsworth
1932 *Waterless Mountain* — Laura A. Armer
1933 *Young Fu of the Upper Yangtze* — Elizabeth F. Lewis
1934 *Invincible Louisa* — Cornelia Meigs
1935 *Dobry* — Monica Shannon
1936 *Caddy Woodlawn* — Carol Brink
1937 *Roller Skates* — Ruth Sawyer
1938 *The White Stag* — Kate Seredy
1939 *Thimble Summer* — Elizabeth Enright
1940 *Daniel Boone* — James Daugherty
1941 *Call It Courage* — Armstrong Sperry
1942 *The Matchlock Gun* — Walter Edmonds
1943 *Adam of the Road* — Elizabeth Janet Gray
1944 *Johnny Tremain* — Esther Forbes
1945 *Rabbit Hill* — Robert Lawson
1946 *Strawberry Girl* — Lois Lenski
1947 *Miss Hickory* — Carolyn Sherwin Bailey
1948 *Twenty-One Balloons* — William Pène du Bois
1949 *King of the Wind* — Marguerite Henry
1950 *The Door in the Wall* — Marguerite de Angeli
1951 *Amos Fortune, Free Man* — Elizabeth Yates
1952 *Ginger Pye* — Eleanor Estes
1953 *Secret of the Andes* — Ann Nolan Clark
1954 *And Now Miguel* — Joseph Krumgold
1955 *The Wheel on the School* — Meindert De Jong
1956 *Carry On, Mr. Bowditch* — Jean Lee Latham
1957 *Miracles on Maple Hill* — Virginia Sorensen

1958 *Rifles for Watie* — Harold Keith
1959 *Witch of Blackbird Pond* — Elizabeth George Speare
1960 *Onion John* — Joseph Krumgold
1961 *Island of the Blue Dolphins* — Scott O'Dell
1962 *The Bronze Bow* — Elizabeth George Speare
1963 *A Wrinkle in Time* — Madeleine L'Engle
1964 *It's Like This, Cat* — Emily Neville
1965 *Shadow of a Bull* — Maia Wojciechowska
1966 *I, Juan de Pareja* — Elizabeth Borton De Trevino

THE CALDECOTT MEDAL AWARDS

The author's name — or the source — where different from the artist's, is given in parentheses.

1938 *Animals of the Bible* — Dorothy Lathrop — (*The Holy Bible,* King James Version)
1939 *Mei Li* — Thomas Handforth
1940 *Abraham Lincoln* — Ingri and Edgar Parin d'Aulaire
1941 *They Were Strong and Good* — Robert Lawson
1942 *Make Way for Ducklings* — Robert McCloskey
1943 *The Little House* — Virginia Lee Burton
1944 *Many Moons* — Louis Slobodkin (James Thurber)
1945 *Prayer for a Child* — Elizabeth Orton Jones (Rachel Field)
1946 *The Rooster Crows* — Maud and Miska Petersham
1947 *The Little Island* — Leonard Weisgard (Golden Mac-Donald)
1948 *White Snow, Bright Snow* — Roger Duvoisin (Alvin Tresselt)
1949 *The Big Snow* — Berta and Elmer Hader
1950 *Song of the Swallows* — Leo Politi
1951 *The Egg Tree* — Katherine Milhous
1952 *Finders Keepers* — Nicolas Mordvinoff (William Lipkind)

1953 *The Biggest Bear* — Lynd Ward

1954 *Madeline's Rescue* — Ludwig Bemelmans

1955 *Cinderella, or The Little Glass Slipper* — Marcia Brown

1956 *Frog Went A-Courtin'* — Feodor Rojankovsky (traditional)

1957 *A Tree Is Nice* — Marc Simont (James Udry)

1958 *Time of Wonder* — Robert McCloskey

1959 *Chanticleer and the Fox* — Barbara Cooney (Geoffrey Chaucer)

1960 *Nine Days to Christmas* — Marie Hall Ets (traditional)

1961 *Baboushka and the Three Kings* — Nicolas Sidjakov (Ruth Robbins)

1962 *Once a Mouse* — Marcia Brown (traditional)

1963 *The Snowy Day* — Ezra Jack Keats

1964 *Where the Wild Things Are* — Maurice Sendak

1965 *May I Bring a Friend?* — Beni Montresor (Beatrice de Regnier)

1966 *Always Room for One More* — Nonny Hogrogian (Sorche Nic Leodhas)

After examination of the above lists, what would appear to be some of the determining factors besides a general excellence of idea and style?

I would vote format for one. There are some titles that might not have received either prize unless they had been "dressed up." This shows how important design, paper and binding are, for anyone, young or old, likes a book better when it is handsome.

Another factor in giving the awards used to be related to an author's past performance, but that has certainly changed in the last few years. Some of the Newbery winners are quite new to the field and there is a definite foreign flavor, which is good — at least, if it is not a determining factor.

Of course, there have been "notable" omissions that have been pointed out by others, explained and reexplained, such as all the Laura Ingalls Wilder books — she finally received a prize named after her and before she died, too. Then there are such outstanding candidates as *The Courage of Sarah Noble* by Alice Dalgliesh (Scribners), *Charlotte's Web* by E. B. White (Harper), *Seabird* by Holling Clancy Holling (Houghton), *George Washington's World* by Genevieve Foster (Scribners) or any of that marvelous series. Well, so it goes.

Let us not dwell on that subject but instead consider another fine group of prizes, the Spring Book Festival Awards, given by the *New York Herald-Tribune*. The following information was kindly provided by them:

In 1937 the *New York Herald-Tribune*, New York, New York, started the Children's Spring Book Festival Awards to encourage the publication and sale of children's books in the spring by offering a stimulus that children's books had hitherto received only in the fall and at Christmas-time. Any new book for children published from January through the end of May each year is eligible. Books are judged in three age groups: picture-book age (4-8), middle-aged children (8-12), older or teen-age youth (12 and up). Awards are decided by six judges, two for each age group, chosen each year from among those prominent and qualified in this field. Annually, in May, three cash prizes of $200 each are given to the winning authors of the best books in the three age groups, at the special award presentation held in the reception room of the *New York Herald-Tribune*. In addition, four honor books in each age group are named. A special issue of the *Herald-Tribune Book Week*, devoted to the festival, with reviews of winners and honor books, opens the Festival Week.

Each year a famous artist has donated a poster, which is given national distribution. Also a package of two posters, lists of prize books and other promotion material such as gay stickers to put on the prize and honor books is available at low cost. It is indeed a boost to spring publishing and to authors, artists and publishers — in fact, everyone connected with the children's world.

Unfortunately word has just come of the demise of the *New York Herald-Tribune*. The Awards will probably be discontinued.

PRIZE WINNERS

The Honor Books are omitted from the following list because of lack of space.

1937	Younger:	*Seven Simeons*	Boris Artzybasheff
	Older:	*The Smuggler's Sloop*	Robb White, III
1938	Younger:	*The Hobbit*	J. R. R. Tolkien
	Older:	*The Iron Duke*	John R. Tunis
1939	Younger:	*The Story of Horace*	Alice M. Coats
	Older:	*The Hired Man's Elephant*	Phil Stong
1940	Younger:	*That Mario*	Lucy C. Crockett
	Older:	*Cap'n Ezra, Privateer*	James D. Adams
1941	Younger:	*In My Mother's House*	Ann Nolan Clark
	Middle Aged:	*Pete*	Tom Robinson
	Older:	*Clara Barton*	Mildred Mastin Pace
1942	Younger:	*Mr. Tootwhistle's Invention*	Peter Wells
	Middle Aged:	*I Have Just Begun to Fight*	Commander Edward Ellsberg
	Older:	*None But the Brave*	Rosamond Marshall
1943	Younger:	*Five Golden Wrens*	Hugh Troy
	Middle Aged:	*These Happy Golden Years*	Laura Ingalls Wilder
	Older:	*Patterns on the Wall*	Elizabeth Yates

1944	Younger:	*A Ring and a Riddle*	M. Ilin & E. Segal
	Middle Aged:	*They Put Out to Sea*	Roger Duvoisin
	Older:	*Storm Canvas*	Armstrong Sperry
1945	Younger:	*Little People in a Big Country*	Norma Cohn
	Middle Aged:	*The Gulf Stream*	Ruth Brindge
	Older:	*Sandy*	Elizabeth Janet Gray
1946	Younger:	*Farm Stories*	K. & B. Jackson
	Middle Aged:	*The Thirteenth Stone*	Jean Bothwell
	Older:	*The Quest of the Golden Condor*	Clayton Knight
1947	Younger:	*Oley: The Sea Monster*	Marie Hall Ets
	Middle Aged:	*Pancakes-Paris*	Claire Huchet Bishop
	Older:	*Twenty-One Balloons*	William Pène du Bois
1948	Younger:	*My Father's Dragon*	Ruth Stiles Gannett
	Middle Aged:	*Daughter of the Mountains*	Louise Rankin
	Older:	*Crimson Anchor: A Sea Mystery*	Felix Riesenberg, Jr.
1949	Younger:	*Bonnie Bess: The Weathervane Horse*	Alvin Tresselt
	Middle Aged:	*Bush Holiday*	Stephen Fennimore
	Older:	*Start of the Trail*	Louise Dickinson Rich
1950	Younger:	*Sunshine: A Story about the City of New York*	Ludwig Bemelmans
	Middle Aged:	*Windfall Fiddle*	Carl Carmer
	Older:	*Amos Fortune: Free Man*	Elizabeth Yates
1951	Younger:	*Jeanne-Marie Counts Her Sheep*	Françoise
	Middle Aged:	*Ginger Pye*	Eleanor Estes
	Older:	*Americans before Columbus*	Elizabeth Chesley Baity
1952	Younger:	*Looking for Something*	Ann Nolan Clark and Leo Politi
	Middle Aged:	*The Talking Cat*	Natalie S. Carlson
	Older:	*Big Mutt*	John Reese
1953	Younger:	*Pet of the Met*	Lydia and Don Freeman
	Middle Aged:	*Captain Ramsay's Daughter*	Elizabeth Fraser Torjesen
	Older:	*The Ark*	Margot Benary-Isbert
1954	Younger:	*Alphonse, That Bearded One*	Natalie Savage Carlson
	Middle Aged:	*Winter Danger*	William O. Steele
	Older:	*Engineers' Dreams*	Willy Ley

1955	Younger:	*Frog Went A-Courtin'*	Feodor Rojankovsky and John Langstaff
	Middle Aged:	*Crystal Mountain*	Belle Dorman Rugh
	Older:	*The Buffalo Trace*	Virginia S. Eifert
1956	Younger:	*Lion*	William Pène du Bois
	Middle Aged:	*Beaver Water*	Rutherford G. Montgomery
	Older:	*Cold Hazard*	Richard Armstrong
1957	Younger:	*Madeline and the Bad Hat*	Ludwig Bemelmans
	Middle Aged:	*Gone-Away Lake*	Elizabeth Enright
	Older:	*Because of Madeline*	Mary Stolz
1958	Younger:	*Crictor*	Tomi Ungerer
	Middle Aged:	*Chucaro, Wild Pony of the Pampas*	Francis Kalnary
	Older:	*Sons of the Steppe*	Hans Baumann
1959	Younger:	*Sia Lives on Kilimanjaro*	Astrid Lindgren and Anna Riwkin-Brick
	Middle Aged:	*The Long-Nosed Princess*	Priscilla Hallowell
	Older:	*An Edge of the Forest*	Agnes Smith
1960	Younger:	*The Secret Hiding Place*	Rainey Bennett
	Middle Aged:	*The Trouble With Jenny's Ear*	Oliver Butterworth
	Older:	*The Walls of Windy Troy*	Marjorie Braymer
1961	Younger:	*Gwendolyn the Miracle Hen*	Nancy Sherman
	Middle Aged:	*Norwegian Folk Tales*, from the collection of Peter Christen Asbjornsen and Jorgen Moe	
	Older:	*Adventures in the Desert* Herbert Kaufmann	
1962	Younger:	*Adam's Book of Odd Creatures*	Joseph Low
	Middle Aged:	*The Orphans of Simitra*	Paul-Jacques Bonzon
	Older:	*Dawn Wind*	Rosemary Sutcliff
1963	Younger:	*The Seven Ravens*	the Brothers Grimm
	Middle Aged:	*A Dog So Small*	Philippa Pearce
	Older:	*The Cossacks*	B. Bartos-Hoppner
1964	Younger:	*The Coconut Thieves*, adapted by Catherine Fournier, ill. by Muriel Batherman	
	Middle Aged:	*The Family Conspiracy*	Joan Phipson
	Older:	*The Story of Design*	Marion Downer
1965	Younger:	*Salt: A Russian Tale*, adapted by Harvey Zemach, illus. by Margot Zemach	
	Middle Aged:	*Dorp Dead*	Julia Cunningham
	Older:	*Jazz Country*	Nat Hentoff

These awards are interesting to review because on the one hand so many of the titles have been forgotten and on the

277

other so many have gone on to win the Newbery or Caldecott medals or some other award. The important thing to remember is that the *New York Herald-Tribune* by this Spring Festival has kept up interest in children's books all year long. Their children's book editor, Margaret Sherwood Libby, has also helped the cause along by her intelligent and searching weekly reviews of children's books in the Sunday book section. Ruth Viguers, editor of *The Horn Book*,* Polly Goodwin of the *Chicago Tribune* and Zena Sutherland of the University of Chicago Center of Children's Books have added their very considerable knowledge and enthusiasm to making the business of children's books a year-round affair. There are many other reviewers who also deserve special mention. Unfortunately there is not room here to list them all.

There are many other awards given in the children's book field, several of which originated quite recently. Some of the most interesting of these are:

THE JANE ADDAMS CHILDREN'S BOOK AWARD offered annually by the Women's International League for Peace and Freedom for the best special-interest book for children.

THE HANS CHRISTIAN ANDERSEN PRIZE offered biennially by the International Board on Books for Young People and given at their International Congress to an author for his complete list of books.

THE AURIANNE AWARD given annually by the Children's Services Division of the American Library Association to the best children's book on animal life that develops a humane attitude. (This award may be discontinued as of 1966.)

---

* I recommend Mrs. Viguers' *Margin For Surprise* (Little, Brown) as required reading for all those interested in children's books. Here is a creative and deeply perceptive mind at work.

The Canadian Books of the Year for Children Awards, given by the Canadian Library Association for outstanding children's books, one English, one French, written by Canadian citizens.

THE BOYS CLUBS OF AMERICA JUNIOR BOOK AWARDS awarded every spring for favorite books of Boys Clubs members.

THE CHILD STUDY ASSOCIATION AWARDS given annually for a children's book dealing with contemporary problems.

THE THOMAS ALVA EDISON FOUNDATION AWARDS given annually for the best children's science book, the best science book for youth, for special excellence in portraying America's past and for special excellence in contributing to the character development of children.

Juvenile books are eligible to be considered for the American Institute of Graphic Arts' "Fifty Books of the Year Exhibition." These are selected for excellence of design and manufacture. The display of these award-winning books is well worth seeing. I find the details specified for each of these books quite fascinating.

THE REGINA MEDAL AWARD given by the Catholic Library Association at their annual convention Easter week to the most distinguished contribution to children's literature.

THE LAURA INGALLS WILDER AWARD given every five years by the Children's Services Division of the American Library Association to an author or illustrator the body of whose work published in the United States over a period of years has made a substantial contribution to literature for children. The first award was given in 1955 to Mrs. Wilder; since then it has been given twice: 1960 and 1965.

Besides these there are numerous state and regional awards, such as the *William Allen White Children's Book*

Award given by the White Library of the Kansas State Teachers College for a superior children's book chosen by Kansas schoolchildren, grades 4-9.

As you can see, there are many, many awards, and often authors think their books should certainly win one or more of them. Sometimes it *does* seem as if certain titles should have made at least the honor roll that in some cases lists the runners-up. I would be guilty of an understatement if I said there have been some odd choices and extraordinary omissions.

Perhaps when you consider the whole question of awards and who *is* great in the children's book field, you come to a fundamental conclusion. This is the fact that, as in all literature, there is one judge who is not appointed or chosen, but who is the greatest and most conclusive medal-giver of all: *time*. Great books live. Rarely is there a let-up of sales even though they go unadvertised and unpromoted. The books that are *supposed* to be good for children but are not soon die out. The artistic creations that are striking but lack fundamental appeal for children end up on the shelves of libraries and stay there. Time tells the story in this field as it does in many others.

As Alice Dalgliesh said in the January 22, 1966, issue of *Saturday Review:* "In the end, while medals have a remarkable effect on sales, it is, as I've said before, children's hands reaching for the books on the shelves that give the final verdict and keep the volumes in print."

6 · The Children's Book Council

No volume on children's books would be complete without mention of the history and contributions of the Children's Book Council. Literature on its start and growth and also its many promotional materials are available at the offices, 175 Fifth Avenue, New York, New York 10010. The Council is the headquarters for Children's Book Week, and it also maintains a library at that address of books for children published during the last three years by the Council members. There is a permanent collection of books of prize-winning titles, the latest book lists as well as encyclopedias and other subscription sets for children. The library subscribes to the chief reviewing media and has the latest publishers' catalogues. It is open to the public week days from nine to five, and on Saturdays by appointment.

Public and school librarians, teachers, authors, illustrators, students — everyone is welcome — and if you really want a good glimpse of what is being published today for children, this is the place to go.

The Council itself has changed a good deal. It is necessary to start back in the early 1900's to understand how it has grown along with the whole business of children's books.

At that time only a few hundred trade books for children were published, and most of those were editions of the classics printed in tiny type, and cheap fiction series like the Horatio Alger books.

In 1913 a publisher, one E. W. Mumford, delivered an unusual speech entitled "Juvenile Books as an Asset" at the annual American Booksellers convention. The *New York Times* reprinted it, and it came to the attention of Franklin Mathiews, librarian of the Boy Scouts of America. He printed a list of good books for boys and persuaded several bookstores to devote a week in November to the promotion of better children's books. An enthusiastic newcomer to the bandwagon was Frederic G. Melcher of the R. R. Bowker Company, who, after World War I was over, proposed a resolution at the Booksellers convention in 1919 to organize a campaign for a Children's Book Week in November. Later that year at the first Children's Librarians session of the American Library Association's annual conference, Book Week was given the official support of the A.L.A.

Anne Carroll Moore at the New York Public Library and Alice Jordan at the Boston Public Library both helped to further the good work, and the next year, the new National Association of Book Publishers became the headquarters for Book Week. When they discontinued their organization in 1934, the Bowker Company took over the office responsibilities, and a committee of children's book editors ran the program.

In 1938 the Association of Children's Book Editors was formed, and in 1945 this became the Children's Book Council. It was incorporated in 1957 as a year-round nonprofit organization.

From 1938 to 1961 it was composed entirely of editors, but in 1961 it was voted to include one person from each publishing house who was in charge of the promotion of children's books. Since that has always been the basic work of the Council, the move seemed logical, although it changed the character of the meetings drastically from a small, well-acquainted group to a large, impersonal one. However, by that time the children's book business had changed similarly, so it was appropriate.

Today the Council's office is Book Week headquarters, where a Book Week Committee labors almost year long. By July orders are pouring in for the free and priced materials they offer, including a poster, book mark, streamers and sometimes a gay mobile. The deadline for orders is October 1.

The Council sponsored eight large book fairs in centrally located cities over the United States. The publishers donated the books, and these fairs were such a success that most of them are now on their own — out from under Council guidance and control — and eager to keep up the good work. Now, new fairs in different locations are planned by the Council and will be operated by them and cooperating organizations (a public library is always one of the sponsors) until they too can go it alone.

Besides the book fairs, Book Week and Vacation Reading program materials, the Council cooperates with many national organizations that work with children and books. The Girl Scouts, the U.S.I.A. and the Library of Congress Division for the Blind are examples of such organizations.

The Council keeps its members informed on the pressing problems in the field of publishing and sends representatives to groups that meet to discuss these problems. For instance, when the subject of bindings was so acute (not that it is not still) they informed us on the general requirements of so-called library bindings. As a member (I have been a member since 1946) I received "A Preliminary Survey of Questions Regarding the Binding of Children's Books," dated January 29, 1962. A list of binding terms was also supplied. So many requests were received on how to enter the juvenile field that they issued in 1962 a directive entitled "Some Suggestions for Those Who Are Considering a Career in Children's Book Publishing," from which I have quoted in my last chapter. (This directive is no longer available, but may be revamped at a later date.) Another helpful article is entitled "When You Submit a Manuscript," which is free to authors on receipt of a stamped, addressed envelope.

The Council issues a "Calendar," which is a quarterly publication giving news about children's books, special events and awards. Teachers and librarians may send for this at no charge.

The meetings are not as frequent now as they used to be but are often very interesting panel discussions on current issues. Prominent librarians, booksellers and reviewers give their viewpoints and criticisms so that we may learn how the children's book business looks from their side of the fence. It is all very enlightening, and when you think that it all started from scratch not too long ago, it is remarkable and commendable, too.

7 · Advice to Editors

This section is not the usual one on editing procedure. Almost everyone in any kind of a job has to make a mistake in order to find out why it is wrong. With children, warnings are so useless that often the best way to use them is backward: in other words, if you want a child to do something, imply that he should not.

However, because some of the mistakes I have made prey on my mind, I shall put them down in a general manner with a vague hope that their recital will be helpful to others.

1. *Trust your own judgment.* Of course, it is wise to consult your company's executives, your fellow workers, your friends, any authority on the subject you can find, but in the end, *make up your own mind* and get on with the task.

2. By the same token, if you have made a mistake, *let it be your own mistake and admit it.* Don't blame it on some underling or on anyone but yourself.

An example of this occurred in some flap copy I wrote about a book that took place in colonial days in western

Massachusetts. In this section many of the towns' names end in "field": Springfield, Westfield, Byfield, and so on. I wanted to put down the birthplace of a prominent gentleman in the story and, thinking the author would change it for me, I facetiously wrote that he was born in "*What*field." When I type fast, the upper case or capital letters do not fall down in line with the others, and so only the bare bottom of the *W* showed. The author never did see the copy, because she had left to live in Europe earlier than I expected. The copy was simply returned to my office where my secretary, thinking it had been okayed, sent it to the production department to be set. The typesetter dropped the *W* completely; I do not read the flap copy after it is set, so it came out on the final bound volume that the gentleman was born in *Hatfield*. (There is such a place.) A storm of protest ensued to the point that we had to reprint the jacket, and it was all my gay little mind's fault. . . . I have made many other worse mistakes than that, but this will give you the idea.

3. Be cautious with well-known authors whose *scripts have been turned down elsewhere*. But keep an open mind too! Some of my most successful scripts were rejected by other editors, and I know of at least two Newbery winners that had to travel a bit before landing in the final triumphant hands.

Yet it is also true that these scripts may have been turned down because they did not deserve publishing. Then you have to make up your mind as to whether it is worthwhile to publish this poor one in the hope of getting better scripts later on. A good deal of this sort of thing is done. I would say let your conscience be your guide, but my real advice is that if a book isn't worth publishing, it isn't, that's all.

Margaret Horner, children's consultant of the Onondaga

Library System in New York State says in the June 1965 issue of *The Bookmark*: "Authority and accuracy are not synonymous. It has been too long assumed that a writer qualified by training and experience has acquired some sort of immunity from error. Critical reviewers have pointed out the fallacy in such assumption."

4. *Sometimes authors of adult fiction and nonfiction take a flyer in the children's book world.* Often they are tremendously successful — take E. B. White, for instance. Certainly their wares deserve instant and careful consideration. Often their mastery of the English language is so impressive and different from the usual run of juvenile rejections that an editor is sorely tempted. And on occasion there is an editor from the adult department pushing a bit. Still, hold to your guns. If it is worth publishing for children, take it. If it isn't, don't.

Eudora Welty, for instance, is one of my favorite stylists in adult literature. She wrote a fantasy for children a few years ago that some reviewers raved about, so I went to the library and read it. I was disappointed. I had the feeling that without her name it might not have been mentioned, but I may have been entirely wrong. That is the trouble with publishing. Being an editor is a lonely business. In the end it is your judgment that counts, and sometimes you wish you had stayed with your first impression.

5. *Edit a manuscript as little as you can.* This point scarcely needs mentioning, because all of us editors would love to have the perfect story or piece of nonfiction land on our desks. I have actually had it happen three times. Once it was the author who wanted to change it, not I.

The script in question was a volume of folk tales whose yellow edges showed that it had been in and out of many other publishers' offices. However, the more I read in it, the more I liked it, so I took it home that night to read to my children. They really enjoyed it.

The next day I decided to call the author to tell him we would publish it, but unfortunately the address given was in the West Indies. So I had to write him instead.

His answer started out with a recipe for Planter's Punch, which ended with the line, "Then you ask the neighbors in and read them Mrs. Colby's letter."

A contract was signed, and I prepared the manuscript for production when a series of cables began to arrive suggesting that Story Two be cut, Story Three be changed as to ending, and so on. Finally I wired him, "Am publishing manuscript as is. Save your money for rum."

Some scripts do have to be edited, though, but changes must always be made by the author or with the author's approval. That is *very* important. Perhaps the height of editorial diplomacy was reached in the following letter dated January 2, 1903, to B. L. Farjeon from Mary Mapes Dodge, editor of *St. Nicholas Magazine:**

... However, I am happy to say that all your changes and substitutions have been made with admirable discretion, and a most sympathetic discernment of our good Saint's peculiar crotchets. And so we owe you most complete and hearty thanks for all that you have done and for the way in which you have done it.

Believe me, we fully understand what a wrench to an author's feelings some of the changes and omissions involved, and all the more deeply do we appreciate, therefore, the favor

* *The Horn Book,* August 1965.

you have shown us in making the sacrifice. Our one consolation is our firm conviction that the story has thereby gained both in force and popularity as a narrative for *young* folk. Indeed we feel sure that it cannot fail to delight all our boy and girl readers, and afterwards, in book form, a far wider circle.

Newcomers to the field are especially apt to overedit, and for them I would like to quote from B. W. Huebsch's article in *Publishers Weekly* of December 7, 1959, page 20:

> Arrogant editing can do things to manuscripts that would not be tolerated in the other arts. The laws of perspective have been outraged in many canvases that are sacrosanct to the connoisseur; sculptors have flouted Nature in chiselling the human form even to the extent of making great holes in it; there are painters to whom objects are two-dimensional. Editors who are guided by what they think the public wants would hold a tight rein on such experiments. They would make the Lord order Abraham to sacrifice a chicken instead of Isaac. They would probably restore the leaning tower of Pisa to the perpendicular, and would virtuously have returned the manuscripts of some of Beethoven's later works with a suggestion or two for simplification.
>
> All honor, then, to the editor as the coadjuter of creative imagination, who restricts his corrective surgery to the limits of the author's conception.

6. *Check with the author all illustrations, maps and flap copy.* I know that many editors do not do this, but I do for two reasons: 1) I want illustrations and flap copy to be right; 2) I want them to be the way the author wants them.

It is the author's book, and many times he alone can spot errors in the illustrations. For instance, the art director and I passed a whole batch of drawings in a sports story on baseball. When the author saw the art work, he was enthusiastic about the artist's style, but he pointed out quietly that the pitcher mentioned was a left-hander and the artist had portrayed him as right-handed! Of course, I, the editor, should have caught this.

The same sort of thing happened in a book about eastern Indians. The drawings were dramatic and nicely detailed. They certainly looked as if the artist had spent weeks on research. The author, however, pointed out to me that the men wore the garb of western Plains Indians; the women had on dresses of a much later era and the feathers in the braves' caps resembled the headdress of the Greek god Mercury more than anything any American Indian ever fashioned or wore.

From the above you will suspect that I use the research and the brains of my authors to keep me from making mistakes. That is true. I think it shows a certain amount of sense on my own part, but anyway, it works.

Now about the flap copy, I send it to authors because again they can help me out. After I have written descriptions of a dozen books for catalogues and for flaps, I have run dry, and the copy shows it. Again and again authors have helped me to revive it. And, of course, they should see what is being said in any copy that is biographical. Certainly I would have appreciated the opportunity to rewrite some of the flap copy on my own books even though I am sure it was written with the best intentions — and the world will never know how much better I could have made it!

7. *Be not distracted by criticism of your list* that it is too full of creative material and that it is not curriculum-based. For the last ten years there has been a great deal written and

said about the neglect of the creative and the original. I go along with that criticism. But it is hard to sell the creative and original unless it is by a well-known author. I have published such books as *Tom and the Red Coats* by Barnett Spratt, *Blanche of the Blueberry Barrens* by Anne Molloy, *The Desperate Dragons* by Norris Lloyd — beautifully real in their originality, engaging in their artistry and well reviewed; but they have not sold as well as inferior titles on the same list that are "curriculum oriented."

Dan Lacy, managing director of the American Book Publishers Council, gave testimony last year before a special subcommittee of the Senate Committee on Labor and Public Affairs in support of legislation to establish national foundations for the arts and humanities. I quote from a condensation printed in *Publishers Weekly* of March 29, 1965:

> Far more than any other single factor in American life, the resources and purchasing policies of libraries determine the rewards of creative writing. What libraries can and will buy will prosper; what they cannot or will not buy will not prosper and indeed may not be published at all. It has been my experience that libraries are deeply and profoundly committed to research and scholarship; to teaching; to adult education; to self-help; to reference service, in ways that make them one of our finest and most indispensable institutions. But it has also been my experience that, with a few notable exceptions, they feel no such commitment to the processes of creative literature. To be concrete, libraries buy copiously in children's informative nonfiction works; in history, and foreign affairs; in books on how to cook, play golf or bridge, or repair homes; and in dozens of similar fields. In all of these fields, it is now possible to publish several times as many titles as could be brought out 25 years ago. But . . .

Yes, "but —" It is true that in the children's field, you had better watch your step in straying from the beaten path. Most of us editors have long solved the problem by publishing both kinds of books. Writers who are truly creative are and always have been hard to find. Let it be known that we editors publish all we *can* find. We also publish the scientific, social science, world-minded nonfiction that is demanded by public librarians, school librarians and teachers for their educational purposes.

8. In connection with the above goal, *make it a point to publish one or more new authors a year*, if you can find ones with promise. It is an obligation of every editor to encourage new writers. The first book may not pay, but the next one probably will. Then you will have the satisfaction of establishing a sound author and giving him a hand when he needed (and deserved) it.

It has been my privilege to publish the first books of such authors as Olivia Coolidge, Edward Eager, Joan Balfour Payne, Leonard Wibberley, and many others who have not achieved the fame of those named but who have contributed their share to the wealth of children's literature.

9. *Watch out for titles.* They are very important. A poor title — and some authors like me hang on to them with determination — can ruin a book. For instance, my own book *Tear Down to Build Up* is really the history of building wrecking, its methods and its present importance, which is considerable. The purpose of the title was to show that most demolition is vital for the future. It has the subtitle, "The Story of Building Wrecking," but who reads subtitles? As far as I know, it is the only book on the subject, and Joshua Tolford's drawings are graphic, dramatic and accurate; but the title is wrong. It is not descriptive enough. Another poor

title on my list is *Tea Meeting Winner* by Edith Palmer. This is an enchanting picture story of Nova Scotia, where tea meetings take place, but the title does not give any idea of the humor and moral point that it has. The author came up with some variants, and we thought of several; but none seemed better than this one. We should have kept trying.

Men on the adult editorial staff and some of our salesmen have helped me with titles. Usually a book comes equipped with the right one but if not, wait for a good one.

Lavinia Russ of *Publishers Weekly* spoke on this subject at a meeting of the Children's Book Council. She cited some good titles from the classics: *Treasure Island*, for instance. I can think of others — titles that draw children toward and into the books: *Mike Mulligan and His Steam Shovel* by Virginia Lee Burton (Houghton), *Mr. T. W. Anthony Woo* by Marie Hall Ets (Viking) and *The Little Woman Wanted Noise* by Val Teal (Rand McNally).

10. *Watch out that nothing in any of the books you publish* resembles in text or pictures anything in any other book, modern or classic. *Publishers Weekly* of February 21, 1966, points out two examples of poaching, probably unintentional. Whether they were or not, the editor should have known enough about children's literature to recognize them and ask for their change or removal.

11. *Be sure you keep up with present-day developments in the adult world as well as the juvenile.* Along with the vast amount of trade literature pertaining to juveniles, published in the Sunday literary supplements of large newspapers like the *New York Times,* the *New York Herald-Tribune** and the *Chicago Tribune* and in such fine publications as *Publishers*

---

* Now The World Journal Tribune.

Weekly, Library Journal, The Horn Book, Top Of the News, Elementary English, The Saturday Review, the *Bulletin of the Center of Children's Books,* the *Bookbird* and literally dozens of other periodicals, it is vital to read other newspapers, magazines and books that have nothing to do with the children's field at all. For instance, to me the daily *New York Times* is a must, the *Christian Science Monitor* has excellent world coverage, the *Wall Street Journal* is a lot more varied and vital than it sounds and is very well written. The *Atlantic* is a magnificently adult magazine — and, oh well, who am I to tell you what to read in your spare time, if you have any. I simply hate to see authors, artists and editors enter the "small, low door" (I forget who said that and I remember resenting it bitterly but later decided that there was some truth in the phrase) of children's books and shut it behind them.

Most editors, what with having to read books on nuclear weapons, space exploration, wonder drugs, the new math and so on have to be up-to-date anyway. For instance, who besides a juvenile editor and those in a photographic laboratory, would have to learn about holography. This happens to be — as you probably know — the science of photographing objects by the light of a laser. The use of laser light, which is a single-color light not ordinarily obtainable from other light sources, enables scientists to capture on film special patterns of light reflected from an object. It may lead to such things as television and movies in true three dimension, to cheaper data processing and faster transmission of pictures from outer space. By the time this book comes out, it may affect the publishing business.

Incidentally, I am as backward as any editor in the world.

I lifted the above information from the March 7, 1966, *Wall Street Journal* and can take no credit for it.

12. *Realize that there is such a thing as censorship,* and then use your own common sense and good taste to avoid trouble. If you are au courant with world and national events, you will not offend religious or racial groups. In fact, you will try to aid the progress that has been made in the thinking of children toward such vital movements as world peace and antisegregation. Your books will try to present the wide scope of life in the United States and abroad. They will be broad-minded and liberal but not militant. They will be varied and contain food for the spirit as well as the brain.

MINOR ERRORS THAT EDITORS HAVE TO LOOK FOR

To give a light touch to this somber volume, I am listing some sentences that had to be changed because of poor grammar, lack of common sense, scientific inaccuracy or what-will-you. At the bottom of the page are given the reasons — which probably are not needed — for changing them. They all occurred in manuscripts by experienced authors, thereby proving that an editor has to be careful, even with a proven writer.

1. "A pleasantly warm April wind lazily blew across freshly seeded lawns and gardens, which were beginning to burst into color."

2. "She cast a spell on the Ojibways which made them forget their fields and the worship of their gods."

3. "About a year later the company put up fresh haddock in frozen packages."

4. "In any country or part of a country where the way

people earn their living changes, their daily lives and that of their children may become very different."

5. "Franklin proposed a method as how to determine if thunder clouds are electrified. This method was read before the Society. . . ."

6. "She was a smaller but exact image of her mother."

7. "Sally and Bill sat on the front steps and waited for their grandmother a seemingly endless time for she did not return at once."

8. "A soft wandering breeze brought him the sweet whiff of a clear, blue pond."

Faults in the sentences above are:

1. A freshly seeded garden is not going to begin to burst into bloom for weeks. Flowers grow slowly.

2. This sentence should read: "She cast a spell on the Ojibways *that* . . ." Also, the Ojibways were not a farming nation.

3. Putting fresh haddock in "frozen packages" would be hard to do!

4. This sentence had to be completely rewritten. Try it.

5. ". . . as" should be changed to "on" and the words *A description of* inserted before "This method" because you cannot "read a method."

6. If she was smaller than her mother, she could not be an *exact* image of her.

7. This sentence is redundant and should either stop after "time" or the last phrase should be changed to "before she returned."

8. A breeze can carry lots of whiffs but not that of clarity or a color.

8 · Requirements of a Children's Book Editor

This section is written by request. It is, in part, a repeat of previous information and should not be necessary, because by the time you have read this far you should know what are the requirements of an editor. However, for those many eager young people who knock on the doors of editors' offices seeking to learn the basic necessities of the job of editing, I am going to put down a few of them.

I will start with an advertisement for a children's book editor run recently in *Publishers Weekly*, which should convey a message to an aspirant:

> Originate ideas for books. Read manuscripts, rewrite and clarify manuscripts, consult with authors, copy edit and see that a book is prepared to specifications. Will be consulted about book design, illustrations, jackets, advertising and promotion. Must have proven experience in carrying a book through from inception to completion. . . . Do not reply unless you have had experience in children's books.

In 1962 the Children's Book Council brought out a preliminary draft to be used for job applicants entitled: "Some

Suggestions for Those Who Are Considering a Career in Children's Book Publishing." It pointed out that there are three areas of work: a) editorial, b) production and design, and c) publicity and promotion.

I will skip b) and c), because they have been discussed and do not concern us at this time. There are many courses on them, especially production and design. There are also courses on editing, some of them carrying through the academic year and some only in the summer months. These vary in worth depending on the teacher or teachers. Many of them change from year to year, so it would be unwise to list them; but there is one that deserves special mention because it is so good, and it has been held every summer since 1947 with a very fine roster of teachers, all of whom are experts in their particular branch of publishing. It is the Radcliffe Publishing Procedures Course (address: Radcliffe College, Cambridge, Massachusetts). It covers a, b and c, and its graduates find publishing jobs all over the country.

To continue with the Children's Book Council advice, they suggest *a thorough knowledge of children's literature past and present*. I would add to this: *a thorough knowledge of adult literature*. You cannot judge children's books by themselves. World literature is one big whole, and you should know a great deal about it before you can judge children's books or any books.

This presupposes a college education with a major in literature or at least two courses, more if possible.

With the present variety in the children's book output, you also should have had courses in science and economics and one or more languages. In other words, to put it simply: *you must be educated.*

Another must is, and I quote from the CBC suggestions: *"A sensitivity for correct English usage,* spelling and grammar, and an appreciation of the high value of accuracy." I would add to this a good solid background of source themes so you yourself know the handling of other people's material and the necessity for organization and clarity.

An ability to write "clearly and concisely yourself with some flair." You will be doing it constantly.

A willingness to help out in other departments in a pinch. I have done billing, worked in the production department, wrapped packages and stuffed envelopes when illness or some other disaster has cut the work force in half. Possibly my contribution was not too much, but an editor should not put himself on a pedestal and imply that he is above any other person in the organization . . . because he is not. His job of contacting authors and obtaining manuscripts is a key one, to be sure, but so is everyone else's. The transit strike in New York showed this to be true in a lovely way. The secretaries, the accountants and the shippers were put up in hotels for the duration by the smart companies. It did not matter so much whether the executives came in or not.

A definite familiarity with mathematics and the ability to do casual figuring in your head and on paper. At Houghton Mifflin I used a slide rule when there were a lot of estimates to worry over; now office computers do a better job. However, you still have to be able to understand the figures that are thrown at you when the costs of a book are discussed.

I have worked for four different publishing companies, and the costing procedure has differed widely in each. However, in only one was I treated as the lady editor and never consulted on estimates or asked to change or modify the specifications I had turned in on a book's production. In the others I have worked hard with the production managers and other executives to bring down the expenses of individual books. To me this is part of the editor's job, because he cannot visualize a book at the beginning unless he knows that each detail is feasible cost-wise. Actually I enjoy thinking out the problems as they come along. Sometimes I have spent hours trying to "bring in" a book at the right cost, trying small changes here and there such as cutting the book to even forms, putting the endpapers on the sheet, using a different cloth for binding, and so on.

Once at Houghton Mifflin we were really stuck on the costs of a title. It looked as if we would have to raise the price fifty cents, which would price it out of competition. At that moment the stock inventory of the bindery happened to arrive at my desk, and I saw a memo stating that the Riverside Press would like to use up some remnants of buckram that were too short for textbook or dictionary runs (buckram is too expensive for trade books). A telephone call to the production department, which prompted a call from them to the bindery, showed that there was a real possibility of a saving there — *if* we did not mind our title being bound in several different colors!

The idea appealed to me, because buckram is the best cloth you can buy — no juveniles had ever been bound in it — and the colors were really beautiful. I thought I had better call the author, though, to get her permission, which I did. She was a good sport and said yes, so the book came out, bound in five different colors of buckram (not on one book!), each one more handsome than the last, and with a price agreeable to publisher and customer alike.

This happened only once and is not a procedure I recommend but it is an example of the fact that, if you are working with intelligent, interested men,* you can sometimes find a solution to the terrible costs of the publishing business without raising the price or cheapening the article you are manufacturing. I will admit, though, that today's cost spiral would defeat Houdini if he were in publishing right now.

It is obvious that a certain dedication to the job is necessary, which means on occasion you pay no attention to time. If something has to be done, you do it until it is finished even if you have to work nights and week ends. You can always take time off later when things quiet down.

Remember that there is a great deal to be learned about publishing and you never know it all.

Of course, to be a really great editor, you have to have been in business long enough so that your books speak for you. They are the proof that cannot be denied. Naturally, it helps for a new editor to inherit a strong back list and a roster of established authors. To start a new list takes time, a bit of courage, foolhardiness and a lot of persistence. I ought to know. I have done it twice.

However, the editors who really deserve a hand are those like Alice Dalgliesh and May Massee, whose books stood for excellence in every way year after year. They deserve some kind of medal, but perhaps it would be superfluous. Their books have already received many, and they have had the tremendous satisfaction of helping others to creative success. That is the one thing that really counts in this whole business.

To end all this, I would like to tell you about a boy who lived down the hall in the same dormitory with my son Peter when he was a student at a boy's school in Milton, Massa-

* I owe a special thank-you to Ben Tilghman, production manager of Houghton Mifflin, surely one of the most able and astute men in the business.

chusetts. As I sat in the car of a Friday afternoon waiting to take Pete home for the week end, I used to enjoy watching the boys come pelting out of the dormitory, climb into the waiting cars of other parents or head off across the campus with skates, a tennis racket, baseball bat or whatever it happened to be. I especially liked to watch Jake. He walked with a little spring in his step, his body alive with a hidden vigor, his face carefully masked to conceal the intent of the moment and his eyes casting from one side to another, not missing the smallest thing in his view. To me he was future mischief incarnate, the very essence of youth.

Pete used to bring home stories of his pranks — each one a marvel of ingenuity — because he knew I liked to hear them. One particular one, however, he phoned about and said he could not describe it; I had to *see* it. So that week end, instead of waiting in the car, I went inside, where Pete and several other boys who were also admirers of Jake took me up to his room. (Jake had been "campused," it seems, and was at that moment incarcerated in study hall.) Anyway, into his room we went, and straightway I began to laugh. It seems that Jake had a baby sister, whose cast-off shoes he had appropriated and taken to school. Outside the dormitory all that week had been a pail of fresh black tar that workmen were using on a wall nearby. What I saw in Jake's room was simply a path of tiny-sized footprints that started over his bed, went up the wall, across the ceiling, down the other side and out the window!

I have treated this subject of children's books in just such a way: I have written beside, above, and around it, never completely solving the problems of writer, illustrator or editor, leaving only tracks leading to an inglorious but definite exit.

BIBLIOGRAPHY

BOOKS ABOUT BOOKS FOR CHILDREN

Arbuthnot, May Hill. *Children and Books*. Chicago: Scott Forsman, 1957.
———. *Children's Books Too Good to Miss*. Cleveland: Press of Western Reserve University, 1963.
Becker, May Lamberton. *First Adventures in Reading*. Philadelphia: Stokes, 1936.
Blanck, Jacob N. *Peter Parley to Penrod*. A bibliographical description of best-loved American juvenile books. New York: R. R. Bowker, 1956.
Bodger, Joan. *How the Heather Looks*. New York: Viking, 1965.
Chase, Mary Ellen. *Recipe for a Magic Childhood*. New York: Macmillan, 1951.
Duff, Annis. *Bequest of Wings*. New York: Viking, 1944.
Eakin, Mary K. *Good Books for Children*. Chicago: University of Chicago Press, 1962.
Eaton, Annie Thaxter. *Reading with Children*. New York: Viking, 1940.
Fenner, Phyllis K. *The Proof of the Pudding: What Children Read*. New York: John Day, 1957.
Fisher, Margery. *Intent upon Reading*. New York: Watts, 1965.
Frank, Josette. *Your Child's Reading Today*. Garden City, New York: Doubleday, 1960.
Fryatt, N. R. (ed.). *A Horn Book Sampler*. Boston: *Horn Book*, 1962.
Hazard, Paul. *Books, Children and Men*. Boston: *Horn Book*, 1947.
Huck, C. S. and Young, D. A. *Children's Literature in the Elementary School*. New York: Holt, 1961.
Kingman, Lee (ed.). *Newbery and Caldecott Medal Books 1956-1965 with Acceptance Papers*. Boston: *Horn Book*, 1965.
Kunitz, S. J. (ed). *The Junior Book of Authors*. New York: Wilson, 1951.
Lane, Margaret. *The Tale of Beatrix Potter*. New York: Warne, 1946.
Larrick, Nancy. *A Parent's Guide to Children's Reading*. Garden City, New York: Doubleday, 1960.
———. *A Teacher's Guide to Children's Books*. Columbus, O.: Merrill, 1960.
Meigs, Cornelia L. *A Critical History of Children's Literature*. New York: Macmillan, 1953
Potter, Beatrix. *The Journal of Beatrix Potter*, New York: Warne, 1966.
Sayers, F. C. *Summoned by Books*. New York: Viking, 1965.
Smith, Lillian H. *The Unreluctant Years*. Chicago: American Library Association, 1953.
Viguers, Ruth Hill. *Margin for Surprise*. Boston: Little Brown, 1964.
West, D. H. and Shor, R. *Children's Catalog* (10th ed.). New York, Wilson, 1961.

BOOKS ON WRITING AND EDITING. ALSO BOOKS SUGGESTED AS EDITORIAL EQUIPMENT.

A Manual of Style. Chicago: Chicago University Press, 1949.
Bartlett, J. (comp.). *Famous Quotations*. Boston: Little Brown, 1955.

BIBLIOGRAPHY

Bernstein, T. M. *The Careful Writer*. New York: Atheneum, 1965.
————. *Watch Your Language*. New York: Atheneum, 1965.
Berry, E. and Best, H. *Writing for Children*. New York: Viking, 1947.
Bowen, C. D. *The Writing of Biography*. Boston: *Writer*, 1950-1951.
Burack, A. S. (ed.). *The Writer's Handbook*. Boston: *Writer*, 1965.
Burlingame, Roger. *Of Making Many Books*. New York: Scribner, 1956.
Campbell, W. S. *Writing Non-Fiction Books*. Boston: *Writer,* 1961.
Columbia Encyclopedia (3rd ed.). New York: Columbia University Press, 1963.
Gross, Gerald. *Editors on Editing*. New York: Grosset & Dunlap, 1962.
Harrison, Maurice. *The Story of the Initial Teaching Alphabet*. New York: Pitman, 1965.
Kierzik, John M. *The Macmillan Handbook of English*. New York: Macmillan, 1960.
Lee, Marshall. *Bookmaking*. New York: R. R. Bowker, 1966.
Lewis, N. (ed.). *Roget's Thesauraus of the English Language*. Garden City, N.Y.: Garden City Books, 1961.
Literary Market Place. New York: R. R. Bowker, yearly.
MacCampbell, Donald. *Writing for Publication*. Cleveland: World, 1966.
Robinson, Mabel L. *Writing for Young People*. New York: Nelson, 1950.
Turner, M. C. *The Bookman's Glossary*. New York: R. R. Bowker, 1961.
Webster's Biographical Dictionary. Springfield, Mass.: Merriam, 1953.
Webster's Geographical Dictionary. Springfield, Mass.: Merriam, 1957.
Webster's New Collegiate Dictionary (7th ed.). Springfield, Mass.: Merriam, 1963. (For desk use).
Webster's New International Dictionary (3rd ed.). Springfield, Mass.: Merriam, 1961 (For office use).
Weeks, Edward. *This Trade of Writing*. Boston: Little Brown, 1935.
————. *Breaking into Print*. Boston: *Writer*, 1962 (rev. ed. 1966).
Whitney, Phyllis. *Writing Juvenile Fiction*. Boston: *Writer*, 1960.

BOOKS ON ILLUSTRATION AND BOOK DESIGN

Bland, David. *The Illustration of Books*. London: Faber & Faber,
————. *A History of Book Illustration*. Cleveland: World, 1958.
Brunner, Felix. *A Handbook of Graphic Reproduction Processes*. New York: Hastings House, 1965.
Ellis, Richard W. *Book Illustration*. Kingsport, Tenn.: Kingsport Press, 1952.
Gamble, C. W. *Modern Illustration Processes*. London: Pitman, 1950.
Herdeg, Walter (ed.). *Graphic Annual*. New York: Hastings House, yearly.
Hudson, Derek. *Arthur Rackham, His Life and Work*. New York: Scribner, 1961.
Hutchings, R. S. *A Manual of Script Typefaces*. New York: Hastings House, 1965.
————. *A Manual of Decorated Typefaces*. New York: Hastings House, 1965.
————. *A Manual of Sans Serif Typefaces*. New York: Hastings House, 1965.

Kingman, Lee. *The Newbery and Caldecott Medal Books: 1956-1965*. Boston: *Horn Book*, 1966.

Latimer, Louise P. *Illustrators*. Washington, D.C.: The Public Library, 1927.

Lee, Marshall. *Bookmaking*. New York: R. R. Bowker, 1965.

Lewis, John. *Type and Illustration*. London: Faber & Faber.

Mahoney, B. E., Latimer, L. P. and Folmsbee, B. (comps.). *Illustrators of Children's Books 1744-1945*. Boston: *Horn Book*, 1947.

Miller, B. G., Viguers, R. H., and Dalphin, M. (comps.). *Illustrators of Children's Books 1946-1956*. Boston: *Horn Book*, 1958.

Moore, Anne Carol. *The Art of Beatrix Potter*. London: Warne, 1958.

Morris, C. H. *The Illustrators of Children's Books*. London: Library Association, 1957.

Peak, Robert (ed.). *Illustrators' 19--*. New York: Hastings House, yearly.

Pitz, Henry C. *Illustrating Children's Books*. New York: Watson-Guptill, 1963.

————. *The Practice of Illustration*. New York: Watson-Guptill, 1947.

————. *A Treasury of American Book Illustration*. New York: Studio, 1947.

Smith, Janet A. *Children's Illustrated Books*. London: Collins, 1948.

Spencer, Herbert (ed.). *The Penrose Annual*. New York: Hastings House, yearly.

Stone, Bernard and Eckstein, Arthur. *Preparing Art for Printing*. New York: Reinhold, 1965.

Wirth, Kurt. *Drawing: When — How*. New York: Hastings House, 1965.

TRADE AND REVIEWING MAGAZINES AND NEWSPAPERS

For the convenience of the reader, the name of the magazine is listed first, then the publisher and his address. Unfortunately, there was not room for many of the excellent magazines, newspapers, booklets and other media published by school and public library systems and state boards of education.

ALA Booklist. American Library Association. 50 E. Huron St., Chicago, Ill. 60611

American Artist. Billboard Publishing Co. 165 W. 46 St., New York, N. Y. 10036

Book Production Magazine. 404 Park Ave. S., New York, N. Y. 10016

Book Review Digest. H. W. Wilson Co. 950 University Ave., Bronx, N. Y. 10452

Bookbird. Verlag für Jugend und Volk, Tiefer Graben 7-9, Vienna I.

Bookmark. N. Y. State Library, State Education Dept., Albany, N. Y. 12224

Books Today. *Chicago Tribune*, Tribune Tower, Chicago, Ill. 60611

Bookseller. 13 Bedford Square, London, W.C. 1, England

Bulletin of the Center for Children's Books. University of Chicago Press, 5750 Ellis Ave., Chicago, Ill. 60637

BIBLIOGRAPHY

Elementary English. National Council of Teachers of English, 508 S. Sixth St., Champaign, Ill. 61822

English Journal. National Council of Teachers of English, 508 S. Sixth St., Champaign, Ill. 61822

Famous Artists Magazine. Famous Artists School, Westport, Conn.

Horn Book. 585 Boylston St., Boston, Mass. 02116

Instructor. Dansville, N. Y. 14437

Kansas Teacher. 715 W. Tenth St., Topeka, Kans. 66612

Library Journal. R. R. Bowker Co., 1180 Ave. of the Americas, New York, N. Y. 10036

London Times Literary Supplement, London, England

New York Times Book Review. 229 W. 43 St., New York, N. Y. 10006

Publishers' Weekly. R. R. Bowker Co., 1180 Ave. of the Americas, New York, N. Y. 10036

Quill & Quire. Seccombe House, 443 Mt. Pleasant Rd., Toronto 7, Ontario, Canada

Saturday Review. 380 Madison Ave., New York, N. Y. 10017

Scholastic Magazines. Scholastic Magazines, Inc., 50 W. 44 St., New York, N. Y. 10036

School Library Journal. R. R. Bowker Co., 1180 Ave. of the Americas, New York, N. Y. 10036

School Libraries. American Association of School Librarians, 50 E. Huron St., Chicago, Ill. 60611

Top of the News. Children's Services Division and the Young Adult Services Division of the American Library Association, 2901 Byrdhill Rd., Richmond, Va. 23205

Virginia Kirkus' Service, Inc. 317 W. 4 St., New York, N. Y. 10014

Wilson Library Bulletin. H. W. Wilson Co., 950 University Ave., Bronx, N. Y. 10452

Writer. 8 Arlington St., Boston, Mass.

Writer's Digest. 22 E. 12 St., Cincinnati, O. 45210

Young Children. National Association for the Education of Young Children, 3700 Massachusetts Ave., N.W., Washington, D.C. 20016

Young Readers Review. Box 100, Greenfield Park, N. Y. 12435

LISTS TO HELP WITH BOOK SELECTION:

Aids to Choosing Books for Your Children. Compiled by Alice Dalgliesh and Annis Duff for the Children's Book Council, 175 Fifth Ave., New York, N. Y. 10010. No charge.

Book Selection Aids for Children and Teachers in Elementary and Secondary Schools. Prepared for the United States Office of Education, Washington, D.C. by Milbrey L. Jones, Specialist, School Library Resources. Superintendent of Documents, U. S. Government Printing Office, Washington, D.C. 20402. 15 cents each.

Problems in Book Selection for Children. Prepared by Rachel De Angelo and Carolyn Field for the *Drexel Library Quarterly*. Drexel Institute of Technology, Philadelphia, Pa. 19104. $3.

INDEX

Abbey, Edwin, 93, 150
Abraham Lincoln (d'Aulaire), 272
Abraham Lincoln's World (Foster), 87
Academy of Graphic Art, 96
Adam of the Road (Gray), 71
Adam's Book of Odd Creatures (Low), 277
Adams, Adrienne, 120
Adams, James D., 275
Adler, Irving, 17
Adler, Ruth, 17
Advances on royalties, 72
Advertising department, costs of, 223; duties of, 222
Adventures in the Desert (Kaufmann), 277
Adventures of Huckleberry Finn, The (Twain), 63
Adventures of Tom Sawyer, The (Twain), 8, 63
Adventure stories, 6
Advice to editors, 285-293
Age groupings, arbitrariness of, 22; baby age, 23, 97, 161; beginning-to-read, 29, 100, 161; first real book age, 26, 98, 161; "middle" age, 33, 101, 164; teenage, 18, 19, 35, 37, 104, 164
Agents, misbeliefs about, 77; value of, 77, 260
Agnew, Seth, 168
Albrecht, Lillie V., 35
Alcott, Louisa May, 93, 257
Aldrich, Thomas Bailey, 93
Alger, Horatio, 127, 282
Alice in Wonderland (Carroll), 14
All Around the Money Bush (Cole), 247
All Around You (Bendick), 105
Alphonse, That Bearded One (Carlson), 276
Always Room for One More (Leodhas), 273
Amazing Seeds, The (Hutchins), 105
America's biographical series, 201
America's Robert E. Lee (Commager), 201
American Association of School Librarians, 268
American Book Publishers Council, 75, 291
American Booksellers Convention, 282

American Institute of Graphic Arts (AIGA), 9, 95, 151, 168, 193, 241, 279
American Library Association, 13, 67, 267, 278, 282
Americans Before Columbus (Baity), 45, 104, 276
Amos Fortune, Free Man (Yates), 271
And Now Miguel (Krumgold), 271
Andersen, Hans Christian, 14
Animals of the Bible (Lathrop), 272
Anthropomorphism, 17
Apple and the Arrow, The (Buff), 100, 202
Ardizzone, Edward, 99
Ark, The (Benary-Isbert), 276
Armer, Laura A., 271
Armstrong, Richard, 277
Arrow Book Club, 31
Art portfolio, contents of, 129
Art work, 112; acetate method of color separations, 115-121; blueprint method, 121; color reproduction, difficulty of, 143; "complete and satisfactory art work," 124; fees for, 124; relation to text, 245; required knowledge of printing methods, 173, 186; schedule of, 231; selling of, 127
Artzybasheff, Boris, 94, 275
Arundel, Jocelyn, 7, 168, 169, 195
Asbjornsen, Christen, 277
Association of Children's Book Editors, 282
Atlantic Monthly, The, 5, 294
Atlantic Monthly Press, 238
Attention span, children's, 24
Augustus Caesar's World (Foster), 43
Aurianne award, 278
Authors, advice to, 52-54; additions to manuscripts, 75; responsibilities of, 73
Authors League, 61
Authorship, benefits from, 54; cash returns, 56

Babcock, Janet E., 220
Babe Ruth: Baseball Boy (Van Riper), 32
Babushka and the Three Kings (Robbins), 273

INDEX

Baby age books, 23; cloth, 25; durability of, 25
Baensch, Robert, 260
Bailey, Carolyn Sherwin, 271
Baity, Elizabeth, 45, 104, 276
Baldner, Gaby, 265
Bare, Arnold, 60
Bartos-Hoppner, B., 277
Baskerville, John, 157
Batchelder, Mildred L., 270
Bathermann, Muriel, 277
Baumann, Hans, 277
Bayley, Verna Hills, 33
Beacon Press, 33
Bears (Krauss), 6
Beaver Water (Montgomery), 277
Because of Madeline (Stolz), 277
Beginning-to-read group, requirements for, 29
"Behind Doors with the Newbery-Caldecott Committee" (Izard), 270
Beim, Jerrold, 33
Bell, Margaret, 6
Belloc, Hilaire, 14
Bemelmans, Ludwig, 9, 28, 273, 276, 277
Benary-Isbert, Margot, 78, 276
Bendick, Jeanne, 105
Benjamin Franklin (d'Aulaire), 100
Betsy-Tacy (Lovelace), 48
"Beyond Prejudice" (Viguers), 270
Bibliography, 303
Big Book of Wild Animals (Green), 103
Biggest Bear, The (Ward), 273
Big Matt (Reese), 276
Big Snow, The (Hader), 272
Big Susan (Jones), 4
Big Tiger and Christian (Muhlenberg), 104
Billings, Henry, 105
Billy Jo and the Rangers (Harris), 32
Binding, equipment for, 187; process of, 188-192
Bindings, durability of, 30; foreign, 259; special library, 59, 195
Biography, 10, 15
Birch, Reginald, 93, 150
Bishop, Claire Huchet, 12, 276
Black, Dr. Richard, 264
Blake, Eunice, 53
Blanche of the Blueberry Barrens (Molly), 291
Blueberries for Sal (McCloskey), 48, 99
Bonnie Bess: The Weathervane Horse (Tresselt), 276
Bonzon, Paul-Jacques, 277
Book clubs, 63
Book design, a practical art, 150; aspects of, 151; importance of, 273; layouts, 153, 175
Book fairs, 70, 260, 283
Book of Nursery and Mother Goose Rhymes (de Angeli), 25
Book of the Year, A (Peters), 105
Book production, 220
Book Production (magazine), 57
Bookbird, The (magazine), 261, 294
"Bookmaking" (Publishers Weekly), 75
Bookmaking, The Illustrated Guide to Design and Production (Lee), 159, 173
Bookmark, The (magazine), 16, 20, 287
Borrowers, The (Norton), 14, 46
Boston Museum of Fine Arts, 151
Boston Public Library, 282
Bothwell, Jean, 276
Boy Scouts of America, 282
Boys Clubs of America Junior Book Awards, 279
Braymer, Marjorie, 277
Bread Loaf Writer' Conference, 53
Brenner, Barbara, 97
Bright April (de Angeli), 46
Brindge, Ruth, 276
Brink, Carol, 271
British Broadcasting Co., (BBC), 67
Broderick, Dorothy, 3, 270
Bronze Bow, The (Speare), 272
Brooks, Robert, 69
Brown, Marcia, 12, 96, 107, 273
Brown, Margaret Wise, 44, 98, 161
Buck, Florence, 6
Buff, Conrad and Mary, 100, 202
Buffalo Trace, The (Eifert), 277
Bulletin of the Center of Children's Books, 294
Bundle Book, The (Krauss), 26
Burnett, Frances Hodgson, 93
Burton, Virginia Lee, 4, 46, 100, 181, 272, 293
Bush Holiday (Fennimore), 276
Busoni, Rafaello, 104
Butterworth, Oliver, 277

Caddy Woodlawn (Brink), 271
Caesar, Julius, 88
Caldecott Medal Award, 11, 68, 95, 107, 108, 110, 241, 267, 272

INDEX

Dalgliesh, Alice, 33, 274, 280, 301
Dalphin, Marcia, 91
Daniel Boone (Averill), 100
Daniel Boone (Daugherty), 271
Dark Frigate, The (Hawes), 270
Dash and Dart (Buff), 100
Dated material, 48
Daugherty, James, 96, 104, 271
Daughter of the Mountains (Rankin), 102, 276
d'Aulaire, Edgar Parin, 94, 100, 272
d'Aulaire, Ingri, 94, 100, 272
David Livingstone (Eaton), 48
Davy's Day (Lenski), 26
Dawn Wind (Sutcliffe), 277
de Angeli, Marguerite, 25, 46, 271
de Brunhoff, Jean, 8, 28, 99
De Jong, Meindert, 271
de la Mare, Walter, 14
Dennen, William, 6
Dennis, Wesley, 103, 168, 169, 170, 195, 257
de Regnier, Beatrice, 110, 273
Desperate Dragons, The (Lloyd), 291
De Trevino, Elizabeth Borton, 272
Diacritical Marking System, 264
"Dimensions in Time" (Horovitz), 14
Dobry (Shannon), 271
Dodge, Mary Mapes, 288
Dog So Small, A (Pearce), 277
Door in the Wall, The (de Angeli), 46, 271
Dorne, Albert, 127
Dorp Dead (Cunningham), 277
du Bois, William Pène, 102, 271, 276, 277
Duff, Annis, 28, 38
Dummy, artist's, 129; 135; printer's, 142
Duncan, Prof. C. J., 75
Durant, John, 11, 49
Duvoisin, Roger, 69, 96, 108, 272

Eager, Edward, 292
Eagle of the Ninth, The (Sutcliffe), 104
"Early Pressures in Child Development" (Hartrup), 23
Easy reading books, 31, 252
Eaton, Jeanette, 48
Eckstein, Arthur, 112
Edge of the Forest, An (Smith), 277
Editing, advice on, 285-296; authors, consultation with, 298; authors, establishing new, 292; book list, depth and variety in, 295; discrepancies,

guarding against, 295; need for moderation in, 287; personal decision, importance of, 285
Editorial criticism, 41, 53
Editorial department, 214, 231
Edmonds, Walter, 6, 271
Egg Tree, The (Milhous), 272
Eichenberg, Fritz, 108
Eifert, Virginia S., 277
Elementary English (magazine), 23, 270, 294
Elementary School Paperback Project (Newman), 63
Ellen Tebbits (Cleary), 8
Ellsburg, Commander Edward, 275
Engineers' Dreams (Ley), 276
Enoch Pratt Free Library, 20, 92
Enright, Elizabeth, 7, 271, 277
Estes, Eleanor, 7, 35, 271, 276
Ets, Marie Hall, 28, 98, 273, 276, 293
Evans, Maurice, 69
Evers, Alf, 48
Evers, Helen, 48
Everybody Eats (Green), 97
Evrard, Connie, 270
Executive committee, duties of, 229; membership of, 228

Fabular de Jemima Anata-Agnatica (Potter, Musgrave), 266
Falls, C. B., 104
Family Conspiracy, The (Phipson), 277
Famous Artists Magazine, The, 127
Famous Artists School, 127
Fantasy, examples of, 46; requirements of, 13
Farjeon, B. L., 288
Farjeon, Eleanor, 14
Farm Stories (Jackson), 276
Federal Trade Commission, 80
Fennimore, Stephen, 276
Fiction, historical, 6, 14, 16; exact backgrounds of, 10; for young adults, 20; honesty in, 19; teenage, 18
Field, Eugene, 46
Field, Rachel, 271, 272
"Fifty Books of the Year, The" (AIGA), 95, 279
Finders Keepers (Lipkind, Mordvinoff), 272
Finger, Charles, 271
First Book series, 10
First real book age, 16; needs of, 27
Fisher, Leonard Everett, 104

INDEX

INDEX

Remington, Frederic, 93
Rey, H. A., 8
Rich, Louise Dickinson, 276
Ridington family (reviewers), 85
Riesenberg, Felix, Jr., 276
Rifles for Watie (Keith), 272
Ring and a Riddle, A (Ilin and Segal), 276
Riverside Press, 181
Riwkin-Brick, Anna, 277
Robinson, Tom, 275
Rojankovsky, Feodor, 94, 100, 273, 277
Roller Skates (Sawyer), 271
Rooster Crows, The (Petersham), 272
Royalties, 57-64; advances on, 72; artist's share, 59, 126
Rue, Eloise, 270
Rugh, Belle Dorman, 277
Runaway Bunny, The (Brown), 98
Russ, Lavinia, 293

St. Nicholas (magazine), 287
Sales conferences, 198, 206, 218-231
Sales department, importance of, 218; keeping books in print, 76, 221; manager, duties of, 217; members of, 217; schedule of, 231
Salt: A Russian Tale (adapted by Zemach), 277
Sandy (Gray), 276
Sasek, Miroslav, 103, 265
Sattley, Helen R., 270
Saturday Evening Post, 127
Saturday Review, 280, 294
Sawyer, Ruth, 271
Schindel, Morton, 69
Scholastic Book Clubs, 64
Science, 16, 38
Scoggin, Margaret, 19, 67
"Scratchboard Illustration" (Cooney), 112
Scribner Classic series, 150
Sea Around Us, The (Carson), 7
Seabird (Holling), 102, 274
Seaweed Hat, The (Slobodkin), 46
Secret Hiding Place, The (Bennett), 277
Secret of the Andes (Clark), 271
Segal, E., 276
"Selection Policies for Young Adult Books" (Pratt Free Library), 21
Sendak, Maurice, 12, 68, 96, 98, 103, 108, 273
Seredy, Kate, 35, 96, 102, 271
Series publishing, pitfalls of, 245,

255-257
Seuss, Dr., 4, 28, 31, 99
Seven Ravens, The (Grimm), 277
Shadow of a Bull (Wojciechowska), 272
Shakespeare's Theatre (Hodges), 105
Shannon, Monica, 271
"Shape of Music, The" (Sendak), 108
Shaun and the Boat (Molloy), 190, 195
Shen of the Sea (Chrisman), 271
Shepard, Ernest, 93
Sherman, Nancy, 277
Shinn, Everett, 150
Shippen, Katherine, 38, 105
Shipping department, duties of, 226; time element in, 226
Sia Lives on Kilimanjaro (Lindgren and Riwkin-Brick), 277
Sidjakov, Nicolas, 273
Silas Marner (Eliot), 63
Silver Pennies (Thompson), 28
Simont, Marc, 273
Slobodkin, Louis, 32, 46, 101
Slobodkina, Esphyr, 28
Smith, Agnes, 277
Smith, Jessie Wilcox, 93
Smith, John, 88
Smoky, the Cowhorse (James), 271
Smugglers' Sloop, The (White), 275
Snow White (fairy tale), 25
Snowy Day, The (Keats), 273
"Some Suggestions for Those Who Are Considering a Career in Children's Book Publishing" (Children's Book Council), 284
Song of Robin Hood, The (Malcolmson), 181
Song of the Swallows (Politi), 272
Sons of the Steppe (Baumann), 277
Sorcerer's Apprentice, The (film), 69
Sorensen, Virginia, 271
Speare, Elizabeth George, 272
Sperry, Armstrong, 271, 276
Spier, Peter, 69
Sports of Our Presidents (Durant), 49
Spratt, Barnett, 159, 160, 291
Start of the Trail (Rich), 276
Stevenson, Robert Louis, 92
Stobbs, William, 129
Stolz, Mary, 277
Stone, Barnard, 112
Stone, Helen, 26
Stone Soup (Brown), 12
Stong, Phil, 275
Storm Canvas (Sperry), 276

316